LEO STRAUSS ON PLATO'S *EUTHYPHRO*

# Leo Strauss on Plato's *Euthyphro*

## The 1948 Notebook, with Lectures and Critical Writings

EDITED BY HANNES KERBER AND SVETOZAR Y. MINKOV

The Pennsylvania State University Press
University Park, Pennsylvania

Library of Congress Cataloging-in-Publication Data

Names: Strauss, Leo, author. | Kerber, Hannes, 1987– editor. | Minkov, Svetozar, 1975– editor.
Title: Leo Strauss on Plato's Euthyphro : the 1948 notebook, with lectures and critical writings / edited by Hannes Kerber and Svetozar Y. Minkov.
Description: University Park, Pennsylvania : The Pennsylvania State University Press, [2023] | Includes the text of Plato's Euthyphro in Greek with English translation. | Includes bibliographical references and index.
Summary: "An examination of Leo Strauss's 1948 notebook and other writings on the Euthyphro, Plato's dialogue on piety, using close analysis and line-by-line commentary"—Provided by publisher.
Identifiers: LCCN 2022060791 | ISBN 9780271095318 (hardback) | ISBN 9780271095325 (paper)
Subjects: LCSH: Plato. Euthyphro. | Piety.
Classification: LCC B370 .S77 2023 | DDC 184—dc23/eng/20230211
LC record available at https://lccn.loc.gov/2022060791


Printed in the United States of America
Published by The Pennsylvania State University Press,
University Park, PA 16802–1003

The Pennsylvania State University Press is a member of the Association of University Presses.

It is the policy of The Pennsylvania State University Press to use acid-free paper. Publications on uncoated stock satisfy the minimum requirements of American National Standard for Information Sciences—Permanence of Paper for Printed Library Material, ANSI Z39.48–1992.

# CONTENTS

# ACKNOWLEDGMENTS

We would like to thank Jenny Strauss Clay and Nathan Tarcov for their permission to publish the Strauss materials; Ethan Benardete for permission to publish Benardete's translation of the *Euthyphro*; John Gibbons and the Leo Strauss Foundation for their support; Gayle McKeen for making available the *Jerusalem and Athens* manuscript; Timothy Burns, editor-in-chief of *Interpretation*, and David Bolotin, Christopher Bruell, and Thomas Pangle, the editors of the 1952 *Euthyphro* lecture, for their permission to reprint it here; Jenny Strauss Clay for making available to us Strauss's marginalia to his copy of Burnet's edition of the *Euthyphro*; Robert Bartlett, Heinrich Meier, and Stuart D. Warner for their comments; Wiebke Meier for her many helpful corrections; Brian Beer, Josie DiNovo, Archna Patel, and Ryan Peterson of Pennsylvania State University Press for their continued assistance; and Susan Tarcov for copyediting the texts.

# Introduction

## *The Significance of Strauss's Notebook on Plato's* Euthyphro

HANNES KERBER AND SVETOZAR Y. MINKOV

### THE CURIOUS ABSENCE OF THE *EUTHYPHRO*

Among the philosophers of the twentieth century, Leo Strauss (1899–1973) stands out because he turned his most serious attention to the relationship between "Athens" and "Jerusalem." Directly or indirectly, the tension between Socratic philosophy and revealed religion is at issue in all of Strauss's writings. As he himself noted, "the theologico-political problem" remained "*the* theme" of all of his "investigations."[1] Plato's *Euthyphro*—*the* Platonic dialogue on piety—is, therefore, most relevant to Strauss's theme. What is more, that dialogue played a central role in Strauss's understanding of "what philosophy is or what the philosopher is": the *Theaetetus-Sophist-Statesman* trilogy of dialogues articulated one pole or charm that philosophy was to resist while the *Euthyphro* represented the other.[2] The study of the dialogue also enhanced Strauss's understanding of certain modern tendencies and in particular assisted him in his critical examination of a new, religious kind of political science.[3]

It is striking then that a discussion of the *Euthyphro* is almost completely absent from writings published by Strauss. While in his work from the early 1930s he refers occasionally to a specific passage in the dialogue (7b–d) to highlight the nature and subject of all fundamental disagreements, references to the dialogue are rare even in places where one would expect them, such as *The City and Man* and *Studies in Platonic Political Philosophy*.[4] In his courses and seminars, too, he rarely discusses the *Euthyphro*.[5] While Strauss lectured twice on the *Euthyphro* (about which more below), he taught the dialogue only once, in the spring semester of 1948 at the New School for Social Research in New York.[6] Unfortunately, this course took place before there were common class recordings and transcriptions.[7] As far as we know, no one alive today attended that course, and no written record by any students is to be found.

## STRAUSS'S *EUTHYPHRO* NOTEBOOK

And yet we have something even better: Strauss's own notebook containing a detailed commentary on the dialogue. On thirty-two pages, most of which are accompanied by additional commentary on the verso pages, of a spiral "Pen-Tab" notebook, Strauss gives a line-by-line interpretation of the *Euthyphro*. The running commentary on the text is frequently interspersed with long summaries of the argument and the action of the dialogue. In all likelihood, these summaries served as Strauss's introductions to the individual sessions of the seminar he taught in 1948. This course had the heading "Readings in Philosophy: An Introduction to Philosophy, Especially Political Philosophy" and the following description: "The primary aim of this course is to show students how to read a philosophical classic. Interpretation of two of the smaller Platonic dialogues."[8] Judging by the contents of the notebook, including the sheets and notes inserted in it,[9] the course may have included, in addition to a thorough consideration of the *Euthyphro*, a brief discussion of the problem of piety in the first book of Xenophon's *Memorabilia*, an examination of Plato's *Apology of Socrates*, and a close reading of Plato's *Crito* (a line-by-line commentary on the *Crito* immediately follows the *Euthyphro* commentary in the notebook).

On two sheets included in the archival folder containing the *Euthyphro* notebook, Strauss discusses the history of ideas in a way that leads up to the question of Socrates's piety. The history of ideas is "the account, in chronological order, of the changes in human thought concerning the whole of human life or concerning the whole *tout court*." Such history deserves "methodical priority" over the sociology of ideas or any other explanation of ideas because "one <u>cannot</u> explain a thing before one <u>knows</u> what the thing to be explained is." "<u>Interpretation</u> has to precede <u>explanation</u>." But if the history of ideas is "centered around history of philosophy," "what is the relation of history of philosophy to philosophy itself?" Philosophy is "the attempt to replace opinions about the whole by science, or evident knowledge, of the whole," which means that "philosophy itself is a-historical." But the fundamental difference between history and philosophy is no longer recognized: "today we are confronted with a fusion of philosophy and history"; "today, it seems impossible to carry through the distinction between philosophy and history." In trying to understand this fact, "one is eventually driven to assume a fundamental difference between modern thought and pre-modern thought." In delineating the peculiarity of premodern thought, Strauss takes up Socrates, "a turning point" in the history of political thought. Socrates "turned from the universe, from the divine things to the human things." He did this, according to this account by Strauss, "for reason of piety: he was the founder of an emphatically pious, 'religious' tradition." "Yet, Socrates was indicted and condemned and executed for his impiety. Should there be a connection between the emphatically pious presentation of his teaching and the fact of his condemnation? The question is usually not even raised: the prevalent teaching is to minimize the importance of the impiety charge and to assume that Socrates was persecuted for reasons of no fundamental nature." Strauss notes that Plato's *Apology of Socrates* shows that Socrates "did not believe in the gods worshipped by the city of Athens," though this is "somewhat disguised by the story of the oracle in Delphi." This "does not mean that Socrates was an atheist, of course—but it certainly means that he was not a martyr for his convictions, a religious zealot. His relation to the public was totally different from that of a religious zealot." It is through such considerations that Strauss would have presented to his students the need for an interpretation of the *Euthyphro*.[10]

## STRAUSS'S "SHIPWRECK"

Apart from this historiographic motive, Strauss had his own interest—as a philosopher, not only as a historian of ideas—in an interpretation of the *Euthyphro*. To explain the nature of Strauss's interest in the dialogue, it might help to go back two years. The summer of 1946 was a period of rethinking for Strauss, a period in which he experienced what he himself calls a "shipwreck," "a radical dissatisfaction" with himself.[11] The rethinking was spurred or facilitated by Strauss's confrontation with Kierkegaard and Pascal, who made him realize he needed to reexamine the basis of the philosophical life.[12] The reconsideration would eventually lead to the conclusion, indicated in a lecture in 1946, that a "philosophy which believes that it can refute the possibility of revelation—and a philosophy which does not believe that: this is the real meaning of *la querelle des anciens et des modernes*." Strauss implies that it may have been the ancients who believed that such a radical refutation was possible.[13] It is hard to imagine a better way to explore this provocative possibility than by studying closely Strauss's commentary on the *Euthyphro*.

While Strauss's 1948 "Reason and Revelation" lecture is likely the best expression of his rethinking and his overcoming of the "shipwreck," his notebook on Plato's *Euthyphro*—dating from the same year—is a remarkable testament to his endeavor to unfold the meaning of both philosophy and revelation. In a note from August 11, 1946, Strauss wrote that "the topic 'Socrates' and 'Introduction to pol[itical] philos[ophy]'" had become much less important than "*Philosophy and The Law* or (perhaps) *Philosophy or The divine guidance*."[14] The *Euthyphro* notebook, however, shows that these themes belong together. The question of Socrates's piety and his stance on orthodoxy is closely related to the question of whether any traditional doctrine can be absolutely binding. While the *Euthyphro* notebook refers to monotheism or the Bible only occasionally (as does the posthumously published *Euthyphro* lecture in which Strauss warns against seeing philosophy "through Biblical glasses," though he also allows himself to refer to "our Saviour" by way of a quotation from Thomas More, see p. 94), Strauss writes, and underlines, the following sentence at the top of a sheet (inserted in the notebook) with the heading, "Plan of exposition of idea of *Euthyphron*": "Restate the whole argument with a view to monotheism."[15]

It seems to have been during this period of 1946–48 that Strauss thought through the questionableness, and established the solidity, of the natural certainty of things, as well as grappled intensively with the problem of intelligibility and ideas: "there must be necessity at the bottom of arbitrariness: there must be ideas determining even the will of God" (p. 39). Both the *Euthyphro* notebook and the posthumously published *Euthyphro* lecture deal directly with the question of intelligibility and the permanence (or lack thereof) of the class character of things.[16] This question is related to but not the same as the questions that arise from the first definition of piety in the dialogue (to be pious is to imitate the gods): What is a god? What is the most perfect being?

## THE CORE ISSUES OF THE NOTEBOOK

The notebook raises these questions and treats them within the framework of the "problem of justice" and the "problem of piety"; these two problems are present as headings throughout the notebook (along with that of "Socrates's crime"). The relation between these two problems, in turn, accounts for Plato's art of writing or the second, subordinate pair that structures Strauss's notebook: the argument and the action of the dialogue in their interrelation. But perhaps the most significant feature of the notebook is its treatment of the relation of philosophy to justice. In the notebook, after remarking that "the only possible premise" is that the gods give all good things to men "out of pure kindness" (rather than because the gods need men's services), Strauss emphasizes that what "ultimately counts" is "justice proper": the gods demand men's gratitude to them in order to train men to be grateful to their fellow human beings. If we take this as a provisional indication of the relation of justice to piety, we can now highlight a related remark on the relation between philosophy and justice: "While in itself philosophy is primary, πρὸς ἡμᾶς [for us] justice is primary."[17] What is this "primacy of justice"? Strauss explains, "philosophy requires a certain preparation, a moral preparation, in fact, a conversion of the whole soul → all Socratic dialogues present this preparation (various stages) or rather they assist us in our preparation: how we can acquire a philosophic attitude—what obstacles we have to overcome in order to become philosophers—from what claims we have to liberate ourselves if we want to become philosophers." The meaning of the primacy of justice is that the philosophical life requires and presupposes the overcoming of "the prejudices nourished by the passions, by our self-assertiveness," prejudices that lead to misconceptions concerning the (in)justice of divine worship and of divine punishment.[18]

The posthumously published lecture, for which the notebook is a kind of matrix, covers much of the same ground as the notebook with regard to these core issues. The notebook, however, is more emphatic and clearer about the greater and more evident need for philosophizing than for justice or piety; the notebook all but begins with the radical question "why philosophy?" and later raises explicitly the questions "why piety?" and "why justice?" whereas the lecture does not do so. In the notebook, Strauss underscores that "the one thing needful is to philosophize," while in the lecture he never mentions the evident need for philosophy and rarely even speaks of philosophy (though he does so very conspicuously when he raises the question of the piety of the philosopher). Finally, the notebook is more explicit about the implication of the ignorance and injustice of the gods, and hence it explains the arguments about making an angry being worse by appeasing that being, about the absurdity of the high serving the low, and about the questionable wisdom of administering (divine) punishment by inflicting misfortunes on human beings. Only in the notebook does Strauss underscore, having gone through these arguments, that "the pious has no other reason than the inscrutable will of the gods" (making this point three times).[19]

## THE HISTORY OF STRAUSS'S *EUTHYPHRO* LECTURES

Having provided these initial suggestions as to the philosophic significance of the notebook (see part II, chapter 1 below), we now turn to the historical background of the postumously published lecture that grew out of the 1948 notebook.[20] In February 1952, Strauss delivered a lecture, "Plato's *Euthyphron*," at St. John's College, Annapolis.[21] Various typescripts based on a now lost recording circulated widely among students and friends beginning in the mid-1950s.[22] It appears, however, that the 1952 lecture was not the first occasion on which Strauss spoke publicly about the *Euthyphro*. In a letter to a fellow student from August 13, 1951, Leo Weinstein—one of Strauss's closest students at the time—mentions an article Strauss planned to write on Plato's *Euthyphro* "based on a lecture he delivered last fall" (placing it in the fall of 1950). While nothing more is currently known about this first lecture, a set of handwritten notes among Strauss's papers bears the heading "Ad lecture on *Euthyphron*."[23] It is likely that these notes form the basis of the earlier of the two lectures. Even though the draft for the first lecture resembles in some important features the second lecture (from 1952), Strauss here follows the notebook more closely both in language and in substance. The earlier lecture therefore marks an important intermediate step in the development of Strauss's presentation of the *Euthyphro*. As a kind of summary, the 1950 lecture compiles many of the results of Strauss's 1948 notebook. At the same time, it does not make any use of what may be the rhetorical hallmark of the 1952 lecture: the concept of an "irritating half-truth."[24] In light of Strauss's outlines for the lecture,[25] it becomes clear that the second lecture comes closer than the first to what Strauss might have seen as the right way of understanding the argument and the action of Plato's *Euthyphro*. One might object that the fact that Strauss never published an essay on the *Euthyphro* indicates that he was not satisfied with his reading of the dialogue. This is, however, only part of the story.

Strauss considered publishing an essay on Plato's *Euthyphro* on at least three occasions and in at least three different books.[26] He first raised the possibility of making his interpretation public in the early 1950s. In the aforementioned letter from August 1951, Leo Weinstein reports that Strauss was entertaining the idea of including in the planned *Persecution and the Art of Writing* "articles on Maimonides, Spinoza, Persecution, classical political philosophy," and "perhaps a new one on P.'s *Euthyphro* based on a lecture he delivered last fall."[27] Had Strauss followed through with this plan, the essay on the *Euthyphro* would have been his first published piece devoted to an interpretation of a Platonic dialogue.[28] Moreover, *Persecution and the Art of Writing* would have been a book of a very different character than the one Strauss ultimately published under the same title: including "On Classical Political Philosophy" (1945) and the lecture on the *Euthyphro* would have broadened visibly the historical scope of the book and the argument it unfolds. It is also likely that the article on the *Euthyphro* Strauss had in mind for *Persecution and the Art of Writing* would have been somewhat closer in character to the first (1950) than to the second lecture (1952): while the early lecture contains an explicit discussion of the hermeneutical challenges of Plato's dialogues as well as of the political and moral reasons for the indirect way of teaching and writing employed by Plato, the later lecture is almost completely silent about these topics.[29]

In 1956, Strauss's interest in publishing an essay on Plato's *Euthyphro* reemerged.[30] Fred D. Wieck,[31] a fellow émigré from Berlin and one of the major figures in US academic publishing after the Second World War, had approached Strauss with the idea of publishing Strauss's 1950 lecture series "Jerusalem and Athens"[32] as a book with the University of Michigan Press, where he served as the director.[33] Strauss not only immediately responded favorably to Wieck's plan but in March 1957 even signed an advance contract for the project that was approved by the executive board of the press.[34] According to Strauss's plan, the projected volume, titled *Jerusalem and Athens*, was to include the eponymous lecture series that had drawn Wieck's interest as well as the then-unpublished lecture "On the Interpretation of Genesis"[35] and, finally, the lecture "On Plato's *Euthyphron*."[36] This combination of the three different lectures indicates the central role Strauss assigned to the *Euthyphro* for his articulation of the proper relation of revealed religion and philosophy. The first chapter of *Jerusalem and Athens* would have presented the issue in question from both sides, as it were; the second chapter would have treated the Bible on its own terms; and the third chapter undoubtedly would have attempted to understand, as Strauss puts it at the end of his 1952 lecture, "philosophy as it is," that is, it would have attempted to avoid seeing philosophy "from the outset through Biblical glasses."[37] Strauss's intention to present the duality of "Jerusalem" and "Athens" in this tripartite manner—as opposed to a monographic treatment of the issue—was so firm that he consented to the abandonment of the entire project when Wieck demanded a "single treatment of the single theme." The three lectures seem to belong so closely together that Strauss even refused Wieck's generous offer to publish the lecture series "Jerusalem and Athens" on its own as an exceptionally short book.[38]

Almost a decade after the failed project with the University of Michigan Press, Strauss again considered publishing his lecture on Plato's *Euthyphro*. In a letter to Allan Bloom from July 21, 1967, Strauss writes, "I just thought of my lecture on the *Euthyphro*. Is there any chance of it being published? Or should I consider publishing it as a part of *Liberalism Ancient and Modern*?"[39] It is unclear why the idea to publish "On Plato's *Euthyphron*" on its own or in the context of the planned collection of essays came to nothing yet again. Unlike *Persecution and the Art of Writing*, *Liberalism Ancient and Modern* would not have dramatically changed in character by the inclusion of an essay on the *Euthyphro*, since Plato is already represented in that book by a chapter on the *Minos* (with its treatment of piety) as well as by a discussion of the *Protagoras*.

It is possible that Strauss hesitated about publishing the lecture because it is too radical or far-reaching on the question of reason and revelation, though it is less so than the notebook. As Strauss puts it in the lecture, "the *Euthyphron* is an unusually radical dialogue" and it "suggests the most uncompromising formulation of the problem of piety,"[40] though in the lecture itself Strauss is relatively reserved about identifying and spelling out the problem. In the notebook Strauss repeatedly refers to the problem (six times), but it is only in the additional private notes (perhaps not delivered in class) that Strauss states the problem directly and comprehensively: "Problem of piety: Piety = right attitude to the gods—but anthropomorphic gods are essentially hostile to each other → they are unjust → piety and justice are incompatible. But what about non-anthropomorphic gods? No piety possible or required. Above all: They would be just by participating of justice—hence be less just than αὐτό τὸ δίκαιον [the just itself]."[41]

## THE PRESENT VOLUME

In addition to the 1948 notebook (together with a selection from Strauss's separate notes on the *Euthyphro*), this volume includes the draft of the first lecture on the *Euthyphro* (1950), outlines for the second lecture (1952), and the text of the second lecture itself. We also make available Strauss's marginalia to the *Euthyphro* in his copy of the Burnet edition of Plato. The marginalia almost certainly date from the period of the composition of the notebook (see Strauss's reference in the notebook to a note in his own copy of the *Euthyphro*). Strauss's editorial decisions in his annotations (e.g., salvaging ὀρθῶς [correctly] at 4b1 and εἴρηται γάρ [for that is what I said] at 7b1) conform with the translation by Seth Benardete, also featured (with minor revisions) in the present volume.[42] The volume also includes a commentary on the *Euthyphro* part of the notebook by Hannes Kerber, comments by Svetozar Minkov on Strauss's *Crito* notes, and an essay by Wayne Ambler on Strauss's interpretation of the *Euthyphro* in the second lecture.

### Notes

1. Preface to the American edition of *The Political Philosophy of Hobbes: Its Basis and Its Genesis* (Chicago: University of Chicago Press, 1952), paragraph 3. See the letter to Gershom Scholem (November 17, 1972): "I am glad that you received my two books on Xenophon's Socrates. They are not the last thing I have written, but I believe they are the best and part of it may be of interest to you. They develop at some length, if not *eo nomine*, what I indicated in *The City and Man* p. 61 regarding the difference between Socrates and The Bible" (Leo Strauss, *Gesammelte Schriften* [*GS*], 3rd edition, ed. Heinrich Meier [Hamburg: Felix Meiner, 2022–], 3:764–65).

2. *What Is Political Philosophy? and Other Studies* (Glencoe, IL: Free Press, 1959), 39–40. In a letter to Seth Benardete from October 25, 1954 (which also mentions that Strauss and Benardete had studied the *Euthyphro* together; see nn. 19 and 42 below), Strauss writes that the

> two dialogues [*Sophist* and *Statesman*] together are of course the φιλόσοφος

> [philosopher]. It seems to be that the Platonic notion of "philosophy" is nowhere as clearly indicated as in the 2 dialogues taken together. Philosophy is striving for knowledge of the whole; but the whole consists of parts; we have only knowledge of some parts, and hence imperfect knowledge of these very parts. . . . We may call, not the τέχναι [arts], but the thought charmed by the τέχναι [arts], σοφιστική [sophistry]. At the other pole, we find another charm: the charm caused by the awareness of the whole which is divined from awareness of the parts—"mysticism," the εὐσέβεια [piety] of the *Euthyphro*. Something is sensed in εὐσέβεια [piety], but it is falsely articulated. Philosophy is the right mean between cocksure (ἀνδρεία [courage]) sophistry and fearing and trembling (σώφρων [moderate] εὐσέβεια [piety]).

See also, in Strauss's posthumously published lecture (1952) on the *Euthyphro*:

> When speaking of the nature of the philosopher, i.e., on the most exalted level of the discussion of morality in the *Republic*, Socrates does not even mention piety. In spite or because of this, there is no Platonic dialogue devoted to wisdom. Yet wisdom is a kind of science, and there is a dialogue devoted to science, the *Theaetetus*. Now the *Euthyphron* and the *Theaetetus* belong together, not merely because they deal with particular virtues, but also because they are contemporaneous: the two conversations take place about the same time, after the accusation and before the condemnation. (See I.2, p. 81 below)

The *Euthyphro* and the *Theaetetus* take place on the same day; the *Sophist* and the *Statesman* take place on the next day.

3. In considering Eric Voegelin's 1952 *New Science of Politics*, Strauss notes, "Voegelin's contention: political things can be understood ultimately only as representing transcendent reality—i.e. not as attempts of human beings to order their affairs in regard to the happiness = the end of man as knowable to man → absorption of political things by religions—just as in other modern theories, political things lose their identity by being absorbed by sociology or psychology or psychoanalysis. Also: absorption of philosophy or science by religion or theology (→ classical philosophy is the explication of the religious experience). The only basis for that: kinship between experience and *noêsis*—but: *noêsis*, *logismos* ≠ the division of 'experience' from *logismos* in Voegelin = return to position of Euthyphro" ("Leo Strauss' Anmerkungen zu Eric Voegelins *The New Science of Politics*," presented by Emmanuel Patard in *Glaube und Wissen: Der Briefwechsel zwischen Eric Voegelin und Leo Strauss von 1934 bis 1964*, ed. Peter Opitz, with the collaboration of E. Patard [Munich: Wilhelm Fink, 2010], 145). Strauss devoted a considerable part of his "Basic Principles of Classical Political Philosophy" Autumn 1961 course to a consideration of Voegelin's position.

4. "Notes on Carl Schmitt, *The Concept of the Political*," in Heinrich Meier's *Carl Schmitt and Leo Strauss: The Hidden Dialogue*, trans. J. Harvey Lomax (Chicago: University of Chicago Press, 1995), 114, and *The Political Philosophy of Hobbes: Its Basis and Its Genesis*, 141, 143. *The Argument and the Action of Plato's "Laws"* has an important remark on the synonymous use of εὐσέβεια and ὁσιότης in *Euthyphro* 5c9–d7, but it contains no elaboration. One would expect that *On Tyranny*, which has a chapter entitled "Piety and Law," would have a reference to the *Euthyphro*, especially since *On Tyranny* contains references to at least fourteen Platonic dialogues, but that is not the case.

5. In lecture 12 of the 1962 "Natural Right" course Strauss stresses the lasting historical significance of the *Euthyphro* in referring to Francisco Suarez: "He [Suarez] fights against two fronts, as far as the natural law teaching is concerned. One front, one school which he fights, says that nothing is good and bad intrinsically but only qua commanded or forbidden by God. This is a very old question—the Platonic dialogue called *Euthyphro* where this question is discussed in this form: do the gods love the just because it is intrinsically just or is the just just because the gods established it as just? This is fundamentally the same question.

The other wing against which he fights says the realization that something is intrinsically good or bad is the natural law. In other words, the natural law is the same as natural reason, a view to which you find an allusion, incidentally, in Locke's *Civil Government*, somewhere. So no extrinsic cause outside of man's natural reason is required for making it a natural law." See, for further references, http://leostrausstranscripts.uchicago.edu/query?report=concordance&method=proxy&q=euthyphro (in one of which instances Strauss compares Euthyphro to Tartuffe).

6. *New School Bulletin* 4, no. 37 (May 12, 1947): 38. Cf. also *New School Bulletin* 5, no. 1 (September 1, 1947): 49. It is possible that there was a previous lecture course on the *Euthyphro* as Strauss's student David Lowenthal wrote in an email to the editors on May 29, 2017: "My first course with Strauss in 1945 [*sic*] was on the combination of *Apology* and *Crito* with *Euthyphro*. It was a lecture course, not a seminar."

7. Strauss's students began to record and transcribe his courses not much earlier than the winter quarter of 1954; it appears that before that students only typed up their notes. The collection of those audio files and transcripts is substantial: of the thirty-nine courses Strauss taught at the University of Chicago, 34 were recorded and transcribed; after Strauss left Chicago, courses taught at Claremont Men's College and St. John's College were also recorded, a practice that continued until his death in 1973. Starting in 2014, the existing audio files were made available on the Leo Strauss Center's website (http://leostrausscenter.uchicago.edu/courses).

8. *New School Bulletin* 4, no. 37 (May 12, 1947): 38.

9. Leo Strauss Papers, box 18, folder 15, Hanna Holborn Gray Special Collections Research Center, University of Chicago Library. See below, appendix 1, for a sample of some of the more striking passages in the additional notes.

10. For a full transcription of Strauss's considerations, see appendix 1 below (note 16), pp. 107–9.

11. Strauss to Karl Löwith, August 15, 1946 (*GS*, 3:660).

12. "Impressed by Kierkegaard and recalling my earlier doubts, I must raise the question once again and as sharply as possible whether the right and the necessity of philosophy are completely evident" (archival note from August 11, 1946; Heinrich Meier, *Leo Strauss and the Theologico-Political Problem* [Cambridge: University of Cambridge Press, 2006], 29). In the fall of 1947, Strauss taught a New School seminar on "Philosophy and Revelation" that had Pascal and Kierkegaard, among others, on the syllabus. Some of Strauss's notes on Pascal are found in Leo Strauss Papers (box 20, folder 10).

13. "Notes on Philosophy and Revelation," in Meier, *Leo Strauss and the Theologico-Political Problem*, 177. The implication is made clear in a note related to Strauss's study of Spinoza in connection with the 1946 "Jerusalem and Athens" lecture. Strauss explains:

> 1) Modern philosophy has to admit the limitation of philosophy, it cannot maintain the possibility of refuting revelation, whereas classical philosophy does not admit this limitation of philosophy and it does maintain the possibility of refuting revelation. Why? 2) Classical philosophy implies natural theology—it does not suspend judgment on God, as the "critical" or "positive" philosophy of modern times must. It is true, modern philosophy prior to Kant had natural theology and attacked sometimes, on the basis of that natural theology, revelation. But: the classical concept of natural theology differs from the traditional and modern one as follows—it consists of two parts: a) elaboration of what "God" means—antedates philosophy proper, is practically identical with fundamental reflection of philosophy; b) demonstration of existence of God—as the culmination of philosophy. a) question of right life—σοφία [wisdom]—idea of σοφός [wise one]: the σοφός' [wise one's] pity for the μωροί [fools], no strict demands on them, indifference to them—connection between love and need → God ens perfectissimus [most perfect being] = sapientissimus [most wise]

> cannot be the God of the Bible. God of the Bible presupposes cosmic significance of man's conduct—a fantastic, if intelligible, presupposition. b) since rejection of revelation precedes philosophy, it does not determine the structure and task of philosophy—it does not compel philosophy to be dogmatic—modern philosophy wants to exclude a priori the possibility that there is place left for revelation → system: identity of φύσει πρώτα [first things by nature] with πρώτα πρὸς ἡμᾶς [first things for us] (idea Dei [idea of God] = origins and foundations totius naturæ sunt notissimæ [of the whole nature are most knowable]). For classical philosophy, the argument against revelation was the actual life of investigation, not any specific arguments which could always be questioned. (Leo Strauss Papers, box 16, folder 11)

14. Meier, *Leo Strauss and the Theologico-Political Problem*, 29n1 (the note has been transcribed and translated by Heinrich Meier). The 1948 lecture is found on 141–67 of the same volume.

15. One might mention that Strauss's interpretation of Xenophon's *Hiero*, which appeared in the summer of 1948 as *On Tyranny* and has as its final chapter the subject of "Piety and Law," also confirms this connection among the themes of "Socrates," "Political Philosophy," and "Philosophy or the Divine Guidance."

16. The Leo Strauss archive at the University of Chicago Library contains a number of notes by Strauss on Husserl, Heidegger, sense perception, the religious question, and the ideas. For example:

> The reflection leading to realization of fundamental character of αἰσθητά [perceptibles] disposes of the religious problem. This reflection is prephilosophic, in so far as in it and through it the constitution of philosophy takes place. More precisely: it excludes the possibility of asserting theism on any but theoretical grounds, i.e. on any grounds other than the teleological character of the φύσει ὄντα [beings by nature]. By its analysis of the ἀνθρώπινα [human things], it excludes the moral and the "existential" grounds. The fundamental (and hidden) reflection of the classics is something like a critique of practical reason as in any way justifying "postulates."

Leo Strauss Papers, box 18, folder 2. Strauss's reflections on Husserl and Heidegger seem to have been an integral part in Strauss's survival of the "shipwreck."

17. See appendix 2 below, p. 112.

18. See appendix 2 below, p. 112. The use of the dialogue form is related to this movement and the "essential limitation of teaching" as Plato's teaching "cannot be understood without a previous conversion of the whole soul."

19. I, 1 below, pp. 55, 57, 58. One should not forget, of course, the notebook's literary character. Strauss was not ready to include even the finished 1952 lecture on the *Euthyphro* in either *Liberalism Ancient and Modern* or *Studies in Platonic Political Philosophy*, though he considered doing so in both cases. In a letter to Joseph Cropsey from March 24, 1971, Strauss writes, in response to Cropsey's "conceit that I should bring together my Platonic studies," that "I cannot reprint the Plato-chapter of the *History* [*of Political Philosophy*], for the section on the *Republic* in a revised and enlarged form forms already part of *The City and Man*. Also what I wrote on the *Euthyphro* is a lecture, not an interpretation, and I overlooked a very important point of which I became aware only lately. But I would include an essay on the *Euthydemus* which requires only a slight revision. And I might write an interpretation of the *Euthyphro*." The "very important point" is mentioned a few months later (September 25, 1971) in a letter to Benardete: "If I should succeed in completing my essay on the *Laws*, I would like to re-study the *Euthyphro* (I have not been attentive to the difference between ὁσιότης [holiness] and εὐσέβεια [piety]. Do you know of any recent commentary or study at which I might have a look?" In the Benardete translation of the *Euthyphro* we have included in this volume, we have preserved the difference, which Strauss himself does not preserve in his notebook commentary; he himself never uses the English "holy" or "holiness" in the notebook, though he refers to

ὅσιον as "hallowed" on the first page. As for the significance of that difference, see n. 2 above and this comment, again in a letter to Benardete (January 15, 1972): "I just came across the passage in Nietzsche about the non-holiness of the Greek gods (≠ Biblical God): *Morgenröthe* aph. 68. Jenny [Strauss Clay] drew my attention to Nägelsbach's *Die Homerische Theologie* who makes the same point with much greater detail but with much less incisiveness." See also session 9 (April 19, 1972) of Strauss's course on Nietzsche at St. John's College. (It may be worth considering why Strauss, in the 1940s or the 1950s, would have omitted stressing the difference between the pious and the holy. He wrote a review of Rudolf Otto's *The Holy* as early as April of 1923 [*GS*, 2:307–10]. Otto does not refer to the *Euthyphro*, but only to the *Timaeus* and the *Republic*.)

20. The lecture was first published in a more heavily edited form and on the basis of one single typescript in *The Rebirth of Classical Political Rationalism*, ed. Thomas Pangle (Chicago: University of Chicago Press, 1989) 187–206. A critical edition based on two different typescripts was published in *Interpretation* 26, no. 1 (Fall 1996), ed. David Bolotin, Christopher Bruell, and Thomas Pangle, 5–23. The lecture, rather than being untitled, was called "On Plato's *Euthyphron*," as appears from one of the typescripts and, more important, from an unpublished preface (see below, n. 36).

21. The date of the lecture appears from a preface by Joseph Cropsey to a planned collection of Strauss's essays on the relation of philosophy and theology (see below, n. 36). It can be corroborated by the report on Strauss's lecture by Edward Bauer in the *St. John's Collegian* (May 1952): 22–23, as well as the catalogue issue of the *Bulletin of St. John's College in Annapolis* (March 1952): 29.

22. In a letter to Leo Weinstein, Robert Horwitz mentions "an hour and a half lecture on the Euthyphro" (June 15, 1954). About a month later, he reports, "Kennington did the Euthyphro, which is being mimeographed by [Robert] Goldwin now" (July 12, 1954). (These letters are found in the Leo Weinstein archive which is in the possession of Stuart D. Warner. We thank Professor Warner for making these letters available to us.) The transcript was circulated widely. For example, Alexandre Kojève received a transcript of Strauss's St. John's lecture on the *Euthyphro* from Robert G. Hazo in early April 1957. In his letter to Strauss from April 11, 1957, Kojève writes, "Although I had not reread the *Euthyphro* for a long time, I remember the text quite well. I had the impression that your interpretation is entirely correct" (*On Tyranny: Including the Strauss-Kojève Correspondence*, ed. Victor Gourevitch and Michael S. Roth [Chicago: University of Chicago Press, 2013], 265). On February 28, 1956, Strauss writes to Joseph Cropsey, "Mr. George Tovey is willing to lend you a copy of my lecture on the *Euthyphron*. Perhaps you will take up the question soon after having read my lecture" (see also letter of April 20, 1956); the letters are housed in the Strauss archive, though they have not yet been catalogued.

23. See below, appendix 2, pp. 111–18.

24. Compare I.2 with II.3 below.

25. See appendix 3 below.

26. See also n. 19 above.

27. "On Classical Political Philosophy" first appeared in February 1945 in *Social Research* 12, no. 1 (1945): 98–117. It was eventually included in *What Is Political Philosophy?* (1959).

28. Strikingly, the first time Strauss published extensive interpretations of Platonic dialogues was in the Plato chapter in *History of Political Philosophy*, ed. Joseph Cropsey and Leo Strauss (Chicago: Rand McNally, 1963). Cf. "Farabi's *Plato*," *Louis Ginzberg Jubilee Volume* (New York: American Academy for Jewish Research, 1945), 357–93; "On a New Interpretation of Plato's Political Philosophy," *Social Research* 13, no. 3 (1946): 326–67; and "How Fārābī Read Plato's *Laws*," in *Mélanges Louis Massignon* (Damascus: Institut Français de Damas, 1957), 319–44—the only other Strauss texts published before 1963 that have Plato's name in their title.

29. One might add that the whole premise, or ploy, of the later lecture—to speak, for example, of the "irritating half-truth" that "piety is superfluous" (or exaggerated)—may have been a theme of *Persecution and the Art of Writing*. The equivalent in "The Literary Character of the *Guide for the Perplexed*," in *Persecution and the Art of Writing* (Glencoe:

Free Press, 1952) is "an excellent justification of ascetic morality—for what Maimonides would call 'exaggeration'—and in particular for an ascetic attitude toward sexuality" (76); in Strauss's own marginalium to this passage he cites *Euthyphro* 12c3–d4.

30. For what follows, see Hannes Kerber, "'Jerusalem and Athens' in America: On the Historical and Biographical Background of Leo Strauss's Four Eponymous Lectures from 1946, 1950, and 1967, and an Abandoned Book Project from 1956/1957," *Journal of the History of Modern Theology/Zeitschrift für Neuere Theologiegeschichte* 29, no. 1 (2022): 90–132.

31. Friedrich Otto Kent Wieck (1910–73) was born in Berlin as the second son of the writer Luise Wieck-Dernburg. He graduated from the University of Berlin Law School in 1932 and emigrated to New York in 1935. After leaving the US Army in 1946, he became the social sciences and humanities editor at the University of Chicago Press. From 1954 to 1961 he served as the director of the University of Michigan Press. He then became a senior editor with Harcourt, Brace & World and held a similar position with Harper & Row from 1962 to 1967. Having served for two years as the director of the National Translation Center at Austin, Texas, he became the director of the University of Pennsylvania Press in 1969, where he remained until his death in November 1973. He is also the translator of Carl Friedrich von Weizsäcker's *The History of Nature* (1949) and cotranslator of Heidegger's *What Is Called Thinking?* (1968).

32. On October 25, November 1, and November 8, 1950, Strauss delivered a series of lectures on the topic "Jerusalem and Athens" at the Hillel Foundation at the University of Chicago. Cf. "Leo Strauss's *Jerusalem and Athens* (1950): Three Lectures at Hillel House, Chicago," *Journal for the History of Modern Theology / Zeitschrift für Neuere Theologiegeschichte* 29, no. 1 (2022): 132–73. Strauss returned to the same topic at the same place for a series of lectures called "Progress or Return?" on November 5, 12, and 19, 1952 (transcripts of the three "Progress or Return?" lectures have been published by Kenneth Hart Green in *Jewish Philosophy and the Crisis of Modernity* [Albany: SUNY Press, 1995], 87–136). As far as we know, the first time Strauss spoke publicly on "Jerusalem and Athens" was on November 13, 1946, in the General Seminar at the New School for Social Research. The surviving typescripts of the 1946 and of the 1950 "Jerusalem and Athens" lectures differ in crucial respects from the one published under the same title in 1967 (which in turn is based on two lectures delivered at the City College of New York on March 13 and 15, 1967). See Meier, *Leo Strauss and the Theologico-Political Problem*, xvi.

33. In his letter of October 24, 1956, Wieck writes, "Herbert Paper of Michigan, whom you know, I believe, told me about the series of lectures you delivered at the Hillel Foundation some time ago, under the title 'Athens and Jerusalem.' I believe they are on tape recordings at the Foundation, and I have written to Rabbi [Maurice] Pekarsky asking him whether we could borrow the tapes for transcription. I am hoping all the while that you would be agreeable to prepare them for publication if we could put a transcript in your hands." Leo Strauss Papers, box 3, folder 18. Unfortunately, Strauss's letters to Wieck have not been found. The University of Michigan Press does not have an author file labeled "Strauss, Leo" or "Leo Strauss."

34. In a letter of February 21, 1957, Wieck writes, "I am now prepared to offer you an advance contract for *Jerusalem and Athens*, the manuscript to be delivered when you specify it and as long as you specify, with a royalty of 10% of the listed price on all copies sold, and with an advance against these royalties in the amount of $1,500, payable when the agreement is complete." As appears from Wieck's letter of November 4, 1957, Strauss eventually agreed to reduce the originally contemplated sum to $750 because of the shortness of the manuscript. Still, this was a staggering sum in a period in which paperback books often cost in the range of $0.35, and cloth books might cost as much as $2.00. According to Dr. Ellen Bauerle, the current executive editor of the University of Michigan Press, an equivalent amount now would be in the tens of thousands of dollars, unusual for a university press, to say the least.

35. Strauss gave his lecture on the Book of Genesis on January 25, 1957, in the Works of the Mind Lecture Series at the University of

Chicago. It was published posthumously for the first time in the January–March 1981 issue of *L'Homme: Revue française d'anthropologie.*

36. The book's contents appear from the preface for *Jerusalem and Athens,* written by Joseph Cropsey, which can be found in the University of Chicago's Leo Strauss Center (Foster 303) in a folder with the label "Jerusalem & Athens—Projected book," containing what must have been a draft version of the manuscript sent to the University of Michigan Press. The preface reads:

> The contents of this volume consist of adaptations of lectures delivered by Professor Leo Strauss under various circumstances during the last decade. The chapter "Jerusalem and Athens" has been prepared by taking under consideration a lecture on that subject given in November, 1946 at the Graduate Faculty, New School for Social Research, New York, and two series of lectures given at the Hillel Foundation's Jewish Student Center, University of Chicago, in October–November, 1950, and November 1952. "On the Interpretation of Genesis" is taken from a lecture in the "Works of the Mind" series given at University College, The University of Chicago, January 25, 1957. "On Plato's *Euthyphron*" is based upon a lecture given at St. John's College, Annapolis, in February 1952. The appearance in print of matter that was composed and solely intended for utterance in the public lecture hall represents an accession by Professor Strauss to repeated requests that he allow some of his statements on the relation of theology and philosophy to be formalized and collected in one place. For the form of the immediate manuscript of this volume as it went to the press, I am entirely responsible. The indispensable assistance of the Rockefeller Foundation to the preparation of this book is gratefully acknowledged. Joseph Cropsey.

37. "On Plato's *Euthyphron,*" p. 94 below.

38. After Strauss pulled back the manuscript at the beginning of November 1957, Wieck writes in a letter of November 6, 1957:

> What went wrong, I believe, is simply that we were thinking of one kind of manuscript, you of another. I certainly was thinking not of a volume of essays, however closely related, but of a single treatment of the single theme on which you delivered the lectures at the Hillel Foundation in Chicago. . . . I still think it a great pity that you did not expand these three lectures in themselves to normal booklength. Even as it stands, the essay "Jerusalem and Athens" would, I believe, make a very solid although very short book. Which, to be sure, does not solve the problem of the publication of the other two essays. But be that as it may, I don't see right now any other choice but letting you have your manuscript back. I am sending it separately. It goes with my sincere regrets.

That Wieck had taken an extraordinary interest in the project is evident from his letter on March 21, 1957, after Strauss had signed the contract: "I have done everything I could, and yet there is not a single book in my past or in my future as far as I can see it now, which could match in importance your *Jerusalem and Athens*. All the books I recall and now hope for lack ultimate conviction because they make only one-half of the case, avoid the tension, beg the true question. They provide fighting equipment at best, but none of them provide sustenance. Your book does."

39. In private possession.

40. Part I, chapter 2, p. 92 below.

41. Appendix 1, n. 6, p. 100 below. See pp. 11n13, 86–87, and 124.

42. The translation was originally meant for the Agora Series at Cornell University Press. Benardete recalls that Strauss's 1952 lecture on the *Euthyphro* grew out of a tutorial he had with Strauss (see *Encounters and Reflections: Conversations with Seth Benardete*, ed. Ronna Burger [Chicago: University of Chicago Press, 2002], 41). Benardete and Strauss had a long-standing discussion of the *Euthyphro*. See, e.g., Strauss's letter of October 1, 1961: "I almost finished reading *Civitas Dei* I–VIII—very little in it—except a confirmation of the point which occurred to us in *Euthyphro*—viz. that

S[ocrates] unhesitatingly attacks the poetic theology but is very cautious re: civil theology, although the latter teaches in substance the same as the poetic one (V 5–6, 8–9—cf. also V 1)." Or September 23, 1953: "the section [of Machiavelli's *Discourses on Livy*] beginning with 'uomini' [men] (I 46–59) deals in fact with religion: an emphatically human virtue, as we know from the *Euthyphron*." See also the mention of the *Euthyphro* in the context of a letter on Plato's *Symposium* (November 14, 1959): "The *Symposium* is the only dialogue explicitly devoted to a god; the *Epinomis* is devoted to the cosmic gods. The *Symp*. abstracts from the cosmic gods; it leads therefore just as the *Euthyphron* to an atheistic conclusion (Soc.'s hybris)."

# PART I

# Leo Strauss on Plato's *Euthyphro*

CHAPTER 1

# Strauss's Notebook on Plato's *Euthyphro* and *Crito*

[**p. 1**] *Euthyphron.* Spring 1948.

In the *Euthyphron*, piety is discussed in the form of a conversation between two individuals that takes place in a specific setting.

a) why 'piety'? b) why is piety treated conversationally? c) why this specific setting?

a) why 'piety'? Let us replace "piety" for a moment by its modern equivalent "religion" = human attitude to super-human beings. Obvious relevance of the question as to what is the proper attitude to super-human beings. The previous question: are there super-human beings? and are they "persons"?

The Greek terms: εὐσέβεια reverence toward gods or parents, piety or filial respect. "reverence"

ὁσιότης disposition to observe divine law and piety. "piety."

(ὅσιον—hallowed—opp. δίκαιος [just]: sanctioned by divine law (≠ human law)

opp. ἱερόν: permitted or not forbidden by divine law, profane

Comments in square brackets [ ] are editorial insertions; those in angular brackets < > are notes crossed out by Strauss; those surrounded by superscript V's have been inserted by Strauss on a verso page; those surrounded by superscript P's have been inserted by Strauss in pencil; and those marked by a superscript R have been underlined by Strauss with red pencil.

ἱερὰ καὶ ὅσια: things sacred and profane
of persons: pious, devout, religious.

<[V]The theme: one ἀρετή [virtue]—the 3 other ἀρεταί [virtues] that are subjects of dialogues:

ἀνδρεία [courage]—*Laches*
σωφροσ[ύνη] [moderation]—*Charmides*
δικαιοσ[ύνη] [justice]—*Republic.*

no dialogue on φρόνησις [practical wisdom] or σοφία [wisdom]—its place taken by ὁσιότης [piety]
(for the relation of ὁσιότης [piety] and σοφία [wisdom], cf. *Legg.* [*Laws*] 679b–c.)[V]>

b) why conversational treatment? A special kind of conversation: a conversation that serves the purpose of clarifying an issue and, if possible, reaching an agreement: a discussion. Why?

α) insufficiency of private thought—true thought is thought in which all men can agree—agreement a criterion of truth—but: not all agreement is agreement in truth—1) common bias; 2) one fools the other: persuasion ≠ conviction.—agreement between unbiased and intelligent people → question of the character of the interlocutors. This will decide on the value of the result of the discussion.

β) a wise man who knows the truth and wishes to teach the truth—teaching → conviction = agreement of teacher and pupil.
Conversational treatment may mean: α) common seeking of truth, β) teaching of truth by one who has found the truth. Are these possibilities exhaustive? The answer will depend on the circumstances of the discussion. The discussion of piety is preceded by a conversation that does not yet have the character of a discussion. This preliminary conversation (–5c3) will throw light on the character of the discussion: is its purpose to discover the truth? or to teach the truth already discovered? or something else?
But there is another reason why the discussion is preceded by a preliminary conversation. Raising questions such as "what is piety?" means to [**p. 2**] philosophize. Philosophizing is not a matter of course. It requires a justification, an understanding of the necessity of philosophizing—answer to question "why philosophy?" It must be understood why and how philosophy arises out of life. This will probably explain why philosophizing means to engage in conversation.

c) why this setting? Let us assume that philosophic treatment of piety = conversational treatment of piety. Conversation = exchange of speeches between two or more people. Absolute minimum: two. In the *Euthyphron*: two. If there were more than two, we would need a further reason: we do not need one here.

Which two? Socrates: the best philosopher = conversationalist known to Plato.

Euthyphron: expert on piety—S. is presented as discussing piety with E. because E. could have been S.'s teacher in piety (5a3–4). But were there not other experts on piety? Moreover: [V]S.'s crime[R].[V] S. asks E. about piety—when? in his old age, shortly before his death, when he is accused of impiety. [V]—and the result: he did not learn anything about piety.[V] Is it not a proof of his impiety that he never took the trouble of learning about piety?

Besides: does S. seek to learn from E.? does he attempt to meet E.?

2a1–4: It is E. who starts the conversation. There are various reasons why a man may start a conversation: he who wants something from the other, he who is less shy, he who is less patient . . . What is the reason in the case of E.? They meet by accident, by chance—they meet around the Hall of the King, S.'s regular haunt is a particular Gymnasium—E. is surprised to meet S. there, whereas S. is not surprised to meet E. there. Chance > rarity ([Aristotle,] *Physics* B). This is the reason why E. starts.

2a1: νέος (of events): new, unexpected, strange, untoward, evil.

νεώτερον (of events): newer, more recent, later, worse, calamity . . .

New = bad > old = good, and: E. divines evil: the μάντις [seer] E. believes in the identity of ἀγαθόν [good] and ἀρχαῖον [ancient/old][R]. Yet: the seer has not anticipated S.'s coming.

[V]2a2—repeated διατριβή [pastime] → S. seems to have changed his whole βίος [(way of) life].

E.'s motive for addressing S.:

a) surprise, curiosity → θαυμάζειν [to wonder]

b) desire to talk about his father → ἀλαζονεία [boastfulness][V]

2a4: ἄρχων βασιλεύς [king magistrate]: "he succeeded to the religious functions of the old kings"; his judicial competence "extends to all cases involving the state religion." [John Burnet, *Plato's Euthyphro, Apology of Socrates and Crito* (Oxford: Clarendon Press 1924), 2.]

2a3–4: E. unwittingly admits that S. is δίκαιος[R] [just]—not πολυπράγμων [busybody]—the King's Hall is on the ἀγορά [market-place]—S. is rarely on the ἀγορά [market-place]. [P]*Rep.* 405b6ff.[P] **[p. 3]**

2a5–6 δίκαι—ἴδιαι [private lawsuits]—prosecutor seeks reparation for injuries done to himself

δίκαι—δημόσιαι [public lawsuits] = γραφαί [indictments]—prosecutor demands punishment for injury done to city

In all cases, the prosecutor is, not the city, but any citizen.

S. is accused: he goes to the Hall under compulsion, whereas he goes to the Lyceum gladly (beginning of *Charmides* [153a1–3]). This compulsion is a condition of the conversation: without compulsion, the dialogue would never have taken place.

Cf. the different situations in *Rep.*, *Laches* and *Charmides*: discussion of piety the least voluntary discussion, discussion of σωφροσύνη [moderation] the most voluntary one[R].

2a5–6: Allusion to the arbitrariness of language; also:

δίκη [lawsuit] → δικαιοσύνη [justice]

γραφή [indictment] → νόμοι [laws]

= problem of justice. S. is not anxious to talk, to tell his story. (the solution: ad 2c2–3a5).—

2b1–2: E. again unwittingly recognizes S.'s justice[R] (or his πρᾳότης [mildness])—(καταγιγνώσκω: remark, observe, especially something to one's prejudice).

<[V]2b3—that someone should γράφειν [indict] S. is almost as impossible as that S. should γράφειν [indict] someone else.[V]>

2b3–6: S. is not anxious to tell his story—why? is he ashamed of it? or is he unwilling to accuse the accuser? or is he not interested in, or concerned with, his private affairs? S.'s justice[R]—[P]he does not want to be an accuser.[P] Consider the fact that the *Theaetetus* is "contemporary" [cf. *Theaetetus* 210d.]

2b7–11: The accuser is an unknown man—S. is not sure of his name even—he does know his political association (δῆμος [district], but not the father)—he knows how he looks—long straight hair (opp. to curly), somewhat hooknosed, not well-bearded. M[eletus] is inconspicuous: extremely normal—but certain things (ἐπίγρυπος [with a hooked nose]—character of the noble horse in *Phaedrus* 253d5, βασιλικόν

[kingly]: *Rep.* 474d7) remind possibly of a generous youth. [P]Cf. 2c2: οὐκ ἀγεννῆ [not ignoble].[P]
S. is less sure of the ὄνομα [name] than of the εἶδος [form/idea]: of what he has heard than of what he has seen. [V]S. despises Meletus—but: the emphasis on the contempt (cf. b9 ὡς ἐγῷμαι [as I believe] and yet he knows the name)—he does not despise him completely (an element of provocation (ὕβρις [arrogance]) in S.'s attitude toward Meletus).[V]

2c2–3a5: S. does not answer question as to what the charge is clearly (see especially the beginning: the quality of the charge rather than what it is about). Furthermore, he speaks exclusively of the διαφθορά-charge [corruption charge]. cf. ad 2a5–6 and b3–6: S. not anxious to talk. Cf. ad 3a1 [P]and 4a1.[P]
S.'s crime[R]

2c2: ἀγεννῆ [ignoble]—allusion to εὐγένειον [without a full beard] in 2b11 (reminding of εὐγένεια [noble descent]).
M. is young (2b8) **[p. 4]**

2c3–8: S.'s justice[R]. To accuse someone, one must know what the crime in question is—one must be σοφός [wise]—but S. is not σοφός [wise]—hence he cannot accuse anyone: his justice is due to his ἀμαθία [ignorance]. Meletus however thinks that S.'s ἀμαθία [ignorance] is the reason for his ἁμάρτημα [fault]: in this, he is wise—but he is unwise by accusing S.: for whatever is done ignorantly, deserves pity or pardon (*Ap.* 26a1–3)—M. should teach S.—instead he behaves like a child (runs to the mother).

2c8–d1: S. is not sure whether M. starts right—but he is sure that it is right to start from the young.

2d2–4: Special significance of γεωργία [farming]—teaching: the small seed and its complete transformation. [V]γεωργική [skill of farming] takes care first of the seeds: The young would grow φύσει [by nature] to be good men but for S.'s διαφθείρειν [corrupting]. cf. 3c2. M. forgets education (cf. the εἰκός [likely] (≠ ὀρθῶς [correctly]) in d3).[V]

3a1: ἡμᾶς [us]: S. is not the only corruptor—or the evasive character of his answer to E.'s question—or: S. suggests that his cause and that of E. are identical (cf. 3c3–4). [V]The "We" not necessarily S. and E., as is shown clearly by 6b1–3. "We" also possibly the ordinary men: cf. 6c1. Cf. ad 12e3–4. Cf. ad 3b5–c5 and d1–2.[V]

3a1–2: S. is accused of corrupting, not the young, but the sprouts (or the growth) of the young.

[V]3a1—"the sprouts of the young"—the promising part of the young—
a) the promising young individuals (Alcibiades etc.)
b) the promising element in each young men.
—not "corrupting the young" = debauching the young—[V]

3a2–5: Meletus's job is a youthful job: the big job will come later (to take care of the old ones)—S. never attempts "the big job." The problem of S.'s justice[R].

3a6–8: S. is the hearth of the city—Meletus's injustice, S.'s justice[R].
Ἑστία [Hestia] alone remains at home (*Phaedrus* 247a1)—does S. remain at home?

3a8–9: E. assumes that S. must do, or make something (≠ λέγειν [to speak])—this explains the θαυμάσιε [wondrous] in b1.

3b1–4: S.'s crime[R]: it consists radically in ἀσέβεια [impiety] and in denial of ἀγαθόν [good] (ἀληθές [true]) = ἀρχαῖον [ancient/old].
"on a first hearing," the charge is absurd.—[V]S.'s gods are made gods—actually: the old gods are made gods.[V]

[V]3b1—θαυμάσιε [wondrous]—E. divines that S. is accused of ποιεῖν τι [making something].[V]

3b5–c5: S.'s piety[R]. S.'s crime[R]. E. vouches for S.'s piety, as he has vouched for S.'s justice. He sees only one thing that could give umbrage to Meletus's attack: S. speaks of his δαιμόνιον [daimonion], but there is nothing newfangled about such-like things (even if the δαιμόνιον [daimonion] itself should never have happened to anyone but Socrates). E. declares that his cause and S.'s cause are identical. If they are, S. is innocent; if they are not, he may be guilty. E.'s declaration would be decisive if his competence were certain.

Common to E. and S.: μαντική [divinatory art] (and δαιμόνιον [daimonion]) and seeming μανία [madness], hence unpopularity. The popular notion: good = old = usual = normal—the old practice of soothsaying is abnormal—is it then true or untrue? E. explains the contradiction by tracing it to envy.

3c6: S. accepts the alliance: ὦ φίλε [oh dear]. **[p. 5]**

3c6–d2: S.'s crime[R]. The difference between E. and S.: E. is ridiculed, but S. is hated. Why? Not the δαιμόνιον [daimonion], but the fact that S. teaches and wants to make others δεινός [terrible, clever] like himself (he never claimed to make others capable of the δαιμόνιον [daimonion]). S. is unjust because he is thought to be a teacher [P]—because he is converting others to his βίος [(way of) life].[P] [V]Based on the premise that S.'s δεινότης [terribleness, cleverness] is of the same kind as that of E.—therefore, one must explain why S. is accused whereas E. is only ridiculed—the explanation is doubtful because the premise is doubtful

cf. also: οἴωνται [they believe/suppose] c6, 7 δοκῶ [seem] d7.[V]

3d1–2: S. is not satisfied with E.'s[1] explanation of the popular self-contradiction (respect for religion and ridicule of μάντις [seer])—cf. contradiction between Sancho Panza's belief and his peasant-distrust → the people get disturbed if someone draws the consequences from their native scepticism.

3d3–6: E. is not hated, because he keeps his wisdom to himself. [P]cf. 6a5–6, 11b1–2. E. is afraid of being known to teach his wisdom.[P]

3d6–9: S. is unpopular because he is thought to be a popular or public teacher—he is hated because of his φιλανθρωπία [philanthropy] (= justice). → S. is accused of impiety because of his justice. E. on the other hand is pious, but unjust (lacks φιλανθρωπία [philanthropy]). Far from having the same cause, they stand at opposite poles. Yet: E. is unaware of it; therefore, he is friendly to Socrates.

3e3: Setting[R]: E. is chosen because he is a fellow-μάντις [seer] (S.'s δαιμόνιον [daimonion]).

[P]3e5–6: E. is responsible for bringing up both cases. Compulsion[R].[P]

3e8: E. could διώκειν [prosecute] (cf. 2b1–2): he is not manifestly just.

4a1 / [P]4a1 > 3c2[P]:—cf. 2b6–3a5—whereas S. has hesitated in answering the question of the crime, and not hesitated in answering the question of the person (of the accuser), E. hesitates in answering the question of the person (accused) and does not hesitate in answering the question of the crime. Because, in the case of E., there is a difficulty only on account of the person (his father), whereas in the case of S. the difficulty concerns rather the crime.

4a7: βέλτιστε [best, most excellent]—E. questions the root of ἀγαθόν [good] = πάτριον [ancestral].

[V]Summary of last meeting (up to 4a10).

S. discusses what piety is with an expert in piety. The discussion, the speech, is related to actual facts: the alleged actual impiety of S. and the possible actual impiety of E.: S. and the expert in piety seem to be in the same boat (fellow-μάντεις [seers]). The expert in piety vouches for S.'s piety (as well as for his justice). Thus, the problem of S.'s piety does not seem to exist: S. is manifestly pious.

But <the expert proves to be a fool: his testimony is worthless: S.'s piety remains an open question. Furthermore,> S.'s case is only apparently identical with that of E.: S. is hated and E. is ridiculed (S. is considered dangerous and E. is considered harmless). S. is accused and E. accuses. E. accuses an old man of impiety, just as Meletus accuses old S. of impiety: the expert belongs rather to the accusers of S. (2c3–8, 4e4–5b7, 6a9–b3). Yet he is friendly to S.—why? There is no reason to suppose that he is in any way superior to the accusers (cf. the characterization of Meletus in 2b7–11). The only reason suggested is that E. knows S. personally, whereas Meletus does not. No—E. disregards public sentiment regarding piety, whereas M. does not.

Decisive: the expert proves to be a fool [P](he does not know what piety is; and: it is doubtful whether he himself is pious)[P]: his testimony is worthless: S.'s piety remains an open question.

While his piety remains an open question, his justice is proved by facts: his unwillingness to accuse or to prosecute.

Continue: 4a11.[V]

4a11: Ἡράκλεις [Heracles]: a beneficent, if slightly comical, ἥρως [hero].

4a11–b2: S. does not consider it altogether impossible to accuse one's father of murder.

4b3: The first oath—by Zeus (cf. 5e6)—E. is obviously a fool.

Setting[R]. S. discusses what piety is with a fool who claims to be an expert regarding piety—what can be the significance of such a discussion?

S. cannot possibly learn from E., nor can he possibly teach that conceited idiot—what can Plato wish to teach us by presenting S.'s discussion with that fool? **[p. 6]**

The general situation in all dialogues: talking of a superior to an inferior. Dialogue

4b4–6: According to law, "the right to institute φονικαὶ δίκαι [homicide/murder trials] was confined to near relatives (or, in the case of slaves, to masters)." [Burnet, *Plato's Euthyphro*, 22.] S. adopts the legal view. More precisely (since there is no reference to the law and E. directly attacks the view in question)—S. adopts a popular view: he adapts himself to the popular view. Is he under the spell of it? No—cf. 6a6ff.—he adapts himself to the popular view because he talks to Euthyphron, to an inferior. [P]S.'s injustice[R].[P] The purpose of the dialogue is to show the wise in his intercourse with the unwise, an intercourse that precludes the possibility of his communicating his views—for: 3c7–d9—for the multitude resents being taught—[P]cf. 15d7–8.[P]

4b7–c3: E.'s principle: it is at least plausible—if murder as murder is a heinous sin, that requires expiation, it does not make a difference whether the victim[2] is one's kin or not—what is important is rather whether the murderer is one's kin.[3] [V]The decisive thing is whether one may indict one's parents or not (5d8–e1).[V]

4c2: 2nd pers. sing.—applies to S. → S. would be ἀνόσιος [unholy].

4c3–d5: The circumstances of the case—in the first place, the murdered was E.'s own (ἐμός [mine]—4c4)—but: the victim was himself a murderer—the father was possibly correct: a complicated case, a case in which a sensible man would be hesitant to act.

4d5–e1: especially since it is considered to be ἀνόσιον [unholy] that a son prosecutes his father (for murder) (cf. Andocides—quoted by me at the beginning of my copy of *Euthyphron* [see in this volume appendix 4, p. 133]).

4e1–3: E.'s chief point is that he knows definitely that the principle referred to is wrong.

4e4–8: S. merely raises the question of whether E. may not be impious considering the difficulty of knowing τὰ θεῖα [the divine things] and τὰ ὅσια [the holy things]. But may not the others be impious for the same reason? The prejudice against E. is justified because he is such a great fool—but this does not give any guarantee that the accepted view is any truer. Why then does S. favor the latter? Plato deliberately chooses a special case where it is much more sensible to follow custom than to revolt against it—but what about the problem in general? [P]S.'s piety remains an open question[R].[P] [V]Cf. 4e6: the ambiguity of the case.[V]

[V]4e5: S. replaces τὸ θεῖον [the divine] by τὰ θεῖα [the divine things]: he denies implicitly to E. any knowledge of "God" ≠ what are considered the divine things—τὸ θεῖον [the divine] is one, τὰ θεῖα [the divine things] are many.[V]

[V]4e8: emphasis on πράττειν [to do]: S. prevents the πρᾶξις [doing] of E.[V]

Setting[R]. Socrates' crime[R]. The parallelism between E. and S.: E. has vouched for S.'s justice and piety—but is E. himself just and pious? does he know what piety is? [**p. 7**]

E. accuses his old father (4a3–4), just as M. accuses old Socrates—
E., far from belonging with S., belongs with Meletus.

S.'s crime[R]. The difference between M. and E.: E., who disregards public sentiment regarding piety, is friendly to S.; M., who follows public sentiment regarding piety, accuses S.[R]—but is it not the right thing to follow public sentiment regarding piety? Thus the question merely would be: did S. follow public sentiment or not? [P]cf. ad 5b8–c3.[P]
S. is accused of impiety—the philosopher is accused of impiety→ the problem of the relation of philosophy to piety.
S.'s piety remains an open question: it is vouched for by a fool who, in addition, disregards public sentiment regarding piety.
S. dismisses in the name of piety a foolish rebellion against τὸ πάτριον [the ancestral] that is attempted by a recognized leader in piety in the name of piety: is S.'s motive his piety (his acceptance of the principle that it is impious for a son to accuse his father) or his commonsense (in doubtful cases stick to the custom) → S.'s piety remains an open question.

5a3–b7: S.'s impiety[R]. S. wants to become a pupil of E., a student of piety: in his old age, when he is accused of impiety, [V]but E. is himself καινοτομῶν [innovating][V]—Ὀψιμαθής [late learner], in order to escape the accusation. We hear something about S.'s teachers. (*Menexenus*, e.g.), but nothing about his teachers in piety [P](but: Diotima!)[P]

[V]5a6: περὶ πολλοῦ [(make) much of] ≠ περὶ πλείστου [(make) most] (*Ap. Soc.* 32e4).[V]

[V]<5b8–c5: E. refuses to become the teacher of S.>[V]

5b8–c3: Setting: E.'s character[R]. E. is no danger—he could become dangerous to Meletus himself—he definitely belongs to "the accusers." Cf. 3e2–3.

5c4–8: S.'s injustice[R]. S. wants to become the pupil of E. because this will make him invisible: S. is easily visible. cf. 3d5–9: E. hides his wisdom, whereas S. is reputed to exhibit it to everyone. (Actually, E. reveals his wisdom, not only by boasting of it, but also by attacking custom by deed. S. does not attack custom by deed. In case he should question custom in thought,[4] he would be the one who hides his wisdom.)

5c8–d5: Ideas[R]. What kind of thing is the pious and the impious? In all pious actions the pious is the same, identical with itself, being one and the same shape or look, the opposite to everything impious.
All understanding means understanding something as something else.
If I say "this is this," I do not understand; I do understand if I say "this

is a match." To understand a "this" means to recognize it as a universal. The πρᾶξις [doing] is always this or that πρᾶξις [doing], but ὅσιόν [holy] or ἀνόσιον [unholy] is in all cases one and the same thing. [**p. 8**] Cherniss, p. m.[5] 5: "for every phenomenal multiplicity to which a common name is applied one (idea) exists as a real correlate." [P]*Rep.* 596a[P]

a) the common name has one and the same meaning.

b) that meaning is not arbitrary: what we mean by "pious" has not been arbitrarily posited by us—our very failures to grasp what we mean when we say "pious" shows that it is not dependent on us.

c) "the pious" is—

d) it is not in the ἕκαστα [particulars], for there is an infinite number of ἕκαστα [particulars], but only one ὅσιόν [holy].

The ideas: the fundamental necessity, the fundamental reason for everything.

The difficulty: from the above notion, it follows that there is an idea of "impiety." That there is such an idea, is here not only admitted, but emphatically asserted. Cf. *Phaedo* 104c7 (and context): ἐναντία εἴδη [opposite ideas].

But: there are ἄπειρα [infinite] kinds of κακία [evils] and only one of ἀρετή [virtue] (*Rep.* 445c5–7). The highest idea is the idea of the good (no idea of the bad).

Indicated here (5d1, 3): ὅσιόν [holy]—ταὐτόν [the same], ἀνόσιον [unholy]—ὅμοιον [similar]. Health is one, diseases are many. The idea is model or norm. This would be unintelligible if "common name" were the access to "idea." (When speaking to Euthyphron, who considers ὀνόματα φύσει [names by nature]—cf. *Cratylus* [e.g., 396d]—, S. not only admits, but emphasizes, the idea of impiety.) 6d11–e1: through one idea the impious things are impious and the pious things are pious. Also 6e3–6.

5d6: E.'s emphatic assent. cf. ad 5e2–5.

5d8–e2: Obvious misunderstanding of the meaning of S.'s <speech> question: particular instance instead of universal. What is 'bird'? A goose is a bird.

5e2–5: Ideas[R]. E.'s answer is meant to apply to ὁσιότης [piety] only, not to ἀνοσιότης [impiety]? Above all, what he has in mind, is not the οὐσία [being], but the νόμος [law] (ὄνομα [name]), because he is exclusively concerned with his action. [P](cf. 5d2)[P]

5e5–6a5: Setting: E.'s character[R]. E.'s proof of the piety of his action: it corresponds to Zeus' action; he imitates Zeus, the justest of the gods, the model of justice.

Ideas[R]. Socrates seeks the idea of justice as his model, E. seeks the justest god as his model.
The ideas replace the gods. [V]The new gods are the ideas.[V] S.'s impiety[R]. E. imitates Zeus who did not spare his own father—S. makes new gods and thus does not spare the old gods: he, too, imitates Zeus. [**p. 9**]
S.'s impiety[R]. The justification of S.'s impiety: even E. notices the self-contradiction ("it is unjust to harm one's father" "the justest of gods harmed his father")—except if the gods are less just than men or justice is essentially the human virtue (cf. *Rep.* 335c4). This would mean that the most divine man would not be particularly just. S.'s injustice[R].

6a6–9: S.'s impiety[R]. S. openly confesses his dislike of the popular notions about the gods.

6a9–b4: S.'s injustice[R]. But he does not reject these notions [P]6b2–3[P]—he cannot reject them because he is ignorant of these matters—. In the *Rep.* [378b], he rejects them: his ignorance is feigned. S. does not want to teach E.: he is not φιλάνθρωπος [philanthropic]. Dialogue (cf. ad 4b4–6).
[V]cf. Burnet ad 9c7.[V]

6b5–6: S.'s injustice[R]. E. would reveal the secrets—it is Socrates who does not. S.'s impiety[R]. Why is S. certain that the myths are wrong? 5e6 and 6a1, 6b9, [P]7a11–b4 (εἴρηται [was said]) [P]: there is no evidence to support them except hearsay—mere δόξα [opinion], contradicted by another δόξα [opinion]—does this suffice? Incompatibility of ἀδικεῖν [doing injustice] with divinity > natural theology.

6b7–c4: S.'s justice[R]. The myths rejected assert that there is enmity among gods: justice is peaceableness.

[V]6b9: the poets who say these things are not good poets.[V]

6c1–2: S.'s impiety[R]. These myths νομίζονται [are believed in] by the city of Athens—[P]οἱ ἀγαθοί γράφεις [the good painters] > the bad γράφεις [painters] = the accusers.[P]

[V]S.'s impiety[R]: 6c4–6: S. wants to know what piety is in order to say what piety is—not in order to do it.[V]

6c5–7: A compliment to S.'s justice[R].

6c8–9: S. would not be surprised (for he knows the type, τό εἶδος [the form/idea]), <but> therefore he is not interested.

6c9–d4: S.'s impiety[R]. It is only now that S. points out E.'s fundamental mistake. → E. has said "Zeus is the justest of the gods" without raising the question "what is justice?" There is a criterion higher than the gods for judging of the gods. And if we know this, [V]we do not need stories about the gods.[V] The element of man is the particular, not the universal. (This is the reason why the Bible is "historical"). Man "naturally" understands the universal as a derivation from the particular ("unamerican," "unjewish" etc.).

6d1: not: φίλε [dear]. [P]cf. 5c4.[P]

6d10–e2: Ideas[R]. E. does not see the difference between the two statements. [V]Negative ideas are dropped.[V]

6e7–8: E. does not see any particular difficulty. He thinks it is easier to answer the τί ἐστι [what is] question than to know what actions are pious—in a sense, this is true.

7a7: The problem of piety[R]. Gods cannot be pious
[P]→ this is why he illogically adds ἄνθρωπος [human being]. Contrast 7a7 with 6e10: S. drops plural.[P]
→ ὁμοίωσις θεῷ [assimilation to god] = transcending piety.

7a8–b1: "It is said" that ὅσιόν [holy] is absolutely opposed to ἀνόσιον [unholy]; maybe the notion of [**p. 10**] piety is self-contradictory (the humility of the pious is the greatest arrogance).

7b2–5: στάσις [strife]: the action of Zeus (the subject) against his father (the ruler). διάφοραι [differences]: the differences between equals.
The hostility of the gods: S. rejects these myths—why?

7b6–d6: S.'s impiety[R] What kind of difference of opinion breeds enmity and anger? Difference of opinion, not about number, greater and smaller, heavier and lighter, but about just—unjust, noble—base, good—bad. But: "I agree with my brother Francis, I want the same as he, Mantua [recte: Milan]" (Charles V)[6]: they agree as to the ἀγαθόν [good], and this very fact breeds hostility. Also: νικᾶν [being victorious] is καλόν [noble]: this agreement breeds hostility. It is not S. who makes the assertions: he merely asks E. (c12ff.). Not only disagreement about the ἀγαθά [good things] and καλά [noble things], but desire for them breeds hostility. [P]*Mem.* II 6, 21[P] [P]Most obvious—use of first person plural—S. and E. do not become enemies although they do not agree at all as to the δίκαιον [just]—<ultimately this is due to S.'s justice> (see especially 7d4–5). cf. ad 8d4–e10.[P]
Yet, disagreement about them may breed hostility. Why the emphasis on this reason for hostility? Who disagrees about the good, the noble and the just? Beings who do not know, who are unable to know (d3). The

great πλάνη [wandering] of the πλῆθος [multitude] regarding δίκαια [just things] and ἀγαθά [good things] (*Phaedrus* 263a–b).

The enmity of the gods is then due either to greed or to ignorance, but rather to the former (d4: ὅταν [whenever])—yet: greed is ultimately ignorance. The root of E.'s ignorance is the ignorance of the gods themselves.

7d1–2: Problem of justice[R]. καλόν [noble] central—ὀργή [anger] arising from insult, slighted honor. But also: καλοὺς καλεῖν [to call beautiful]—→ is not πλάνη [wandering] regarding ἀνθρώπινα [human things] founded on the nature of things? If this is so,

a) either we disregard them altogether, turn to μαθηματικά [mathematical things] and follow custom.

b) or we try to reach mathematical knowledge regarding ἀγαθά [good things] and καλά [noble things]. What does S. do in the *Euthyphron*?

[**p. 9 verso**] Summary (up to 7b5)—cf. supra opposite p. 5.

Connection between content (λόγος [account/argument]) and form (ἔργον [action])—

a) content: 'what is piety?'—quest for the idea of piety—the attempts fail → we do not know what piety is—hence, we do not know whether piety is good.

b) form: discussion presented not in the form of treatise, but in that of a dialogue: the general subject (piety) reflected, or immersed, in a particular or individual situation—why?

The question 'what is piety?,' the quest for the idea of piety, is a philos. question. Now, piety is not only the subject matter of philosophy, but it is crucially the element of the act of philosophizing: is the philosopher as such pious or not? If the philosopher as such is not pious, and if the philosopher is the highest type of man, piety would not be a part of man's excellence—piety would not belong to the <species> genus "virtue."

Thus: one cannot answer the question of what piety is without clarifying the relation of piety and philosophy—this relation is not clarified in the *Euthyphron*—hence, the question of what piety is, is not answered.

The problem of the philosopher's piety is reflected in the fact that S. is accused of impiety—is the accusation justified?

In the *Euthyphron*, S.'s piety remains an open question: just as it remains an open question what piety is.

(S.'s piety remains an open question:

a) the expert in piety who vouches for it, is a fool

b) ------------------------------------------- does not know what piety is.

c) ------------------------------------------- is himself suspect of impiety.

d) S. who confesses to be ignorant (and hence in particular regarding piety) seeks a teacher in piety only in his old age when he is accused of impiety.

e) above all: assuming that piety = following πάτρια [ancestral things], customs regarding the gods, S. seems to be pious, since he advises E. not to act against custom—but: in the given case, every sane person, pious or impious, would follow custom, because the case against custom is extremely weak in the given case. ad 4e4–8, 5a3–b7.).

[P]Why does it remain an open question?[P]

<This could easily be understood if the philosopher is as such not pious and if impiety were a dangerous thing (a criminal offence e.g.). However that may be,> what is the purpose of the dialogue?

a) does S. want to learn from E.? No

b) does he want to teach E.? No—ad 6a6–b6.

c) does he want to seek together with E.? It would be futile.

S. wants to prevent E. from committing a grave mistake (S.'s φιλανθρωπία [philanthropy]): that is all that S. can do in the case of a man like E. → Plato wants to present <S.> the wise man in his intercourse with a fool (ad 4b4–6) → he presents the true analysis of piety reflected in the distorting mirror of the conversation of the wise man, suspected of impiety, with an expert in piety. [P]See opposite page 11.[P] **[p. 10 verso]**

c) The thematic question 'what is piety?'—the question of the shape, or looks, or idea of piety—the assumption that there are "ideas" (cf. ad 5c8–d5). "I know a thing"—why? I have seen it—I have seen it; the seeing is in the past, the knowing is now → knowledge ≠ sense-perception. What is that knowledge? "I know Mr. Miller"—i.e., I will recognize him if I would see him, or I would know what to expect of him (again: recognition). I see something: I say, it is a tulip: I recognize it as a tulip. I understand what I see: understanding means to recognize something as something which is not simply identical with it → to recognize something as something else. If I say, "this here is Charles," I may mean only "this man is called Charles"; I reveal only the name by which this man here is generally known. But I may also mean "this here is the Charles with these and these character traits, past, etc. I have told you of—look at whether his behavior does not bear out what I have told you; whether you do not recognize in him the things I told you.["] In all such statements both people take for granted that Charles is a human being—they presuppose knowledge of what a human being is → the basis of all knowledge would thus seem <is> to be knowledge of this kind "this here is a human being," i.e., the recognition of something here and now as something that is not simply here and now. That which is not simply here and now, must be unchangeable or identical with itself; if it were not, it would not function as a center of reference for all other recognitions. The basis of all knowledge is the knowledge of things that are identical with themselves or unchangeable: i.e., knowledge of ideas.

These self-identical things do not depend on any arbitrary convention among men: they are independent of any human arbitrariness: we have to hunt them (we can't look them up in law books, dictionaries, . . .). They are by nature.

Things are naturally divided into classes: horses, cows, houses, laws. . . . Even if houses and laws are purely human inventions, laws are something entirely different from houses, essentially different (essentia = forma); the essential difference is not a human invention (it is impossible to live in laws).

Every horse that I see, has the class-character of a horse. But it has qualities in addition to that class-character. I.e. it is lacking the pure "identity with itself" of "horse." Yet, curiously enough, this horse here, is concerned ultimately, not with its being this horse, but with the class-character horse. For: every living being finds the peak of its being in love, in the consummation of love, i.e., in the perpetuation of the class. The individual aspires to the idea: to the permanence of the idea: his aspiration is life, its life. If life is the aspiration to the idea, the idea is norm or pattern or standard. [**p. 11**]

Let us apply this to man. Every human being has qualities in addition to the class-character of man, i.e., he lacks the pure "identity with itself" of "man." This lack shows itself in the fact of human aspiration or dissatisfaction; man is not being satisfied with being this or that individual: he wants to be happy. Let us assume that happiness consists in coming as near as possible to the pure class-character of man; the good of man's aspiration, or the standard for man, would be the idea of man. The fact that Plato does not speak in that context of the idea of man, but of virtue, and of particular virtues, is due to the fact that a specific difficulty is involved in the pure class-character of man: it is of the essence of man to be the μεταξύ-being [in-between-being], in-between animal and pure mind, and therefore to aspire to something beyond humanity.

It is then impossible to clarify the relation between idea as class-character and idea as norm or pattern without considering "pure mind." Let us assume that pure mind is God: the doctrine of ideas is essentially related to doctrine of God. The proper attitude to God is popularly known by the name of piety. There is an inseparable connection between the doctrine of ideas and the problem of piety.

What did we learn from the *Euthyphron* about this relation? S. seeks the idea of justice as his model just as E. seeks the justest god as his model: the ideas replace the gods, the old gods: the ideas are the new gods which S. is said to have introduced. The justification of S.'s change: before I can take a just god as my model, I must know what justice is; otherwise I cannot know whether the allegedly just god is really just: there is a standard for judging of the actions of god, a standard with which the god must comply, therefore a standard that is higher than the god, and a standard to which man has a direct access. Man does not need then knowledge of the gods in order to know justice: philosophy = knowledge of the ideas is sufficient (ad 5e5–6a5, 6c9–d7, 7a7–b1). Knowledge of the gods is superfluous: S. is impious.

Euthyphron would be right if there were no ideas. Euthyphron's premises (= the mythical notion of the gods as fighting gods) decisive for the implicit denial of the ideas. Let us first consider 7b6–d6.

The alternative to doctrine of ideas is theology (mythology): the highest beings are, not ideas, but "persons"—not universal, but a person, an individual—a being bearing a name (a Thou)—but beings have a name in order to be distinguished from other individuals of the same class → polytheism. Continued: p. 12. **[p. 12]**

[P]Cf. p. 14, 2nd half.[P] These gods would not be subject to, or dependent on, a higher norm—they would not have any standard independent of their arbitrariness—they would not be guided by knowledge—they would be ignorant—they would fight.

[V]Nominalism (Occam): radical denial of essences and universal archetypes → murder etc. is bad, because it is prohibited by God, and it is not prohibited by God because it is intrinsically bad. God could command murder—even that men shall hate Him; God could have been incarnated in a donkey as well as in man, or take on the nature of wood or stone (→ he could have created other gods → polytheism → fights) Gilson *Philosophie au Moyen Âge* 652[7]

Why is Plato so certain that there are ideas? that there is intelligible necessity? That ον [being] = νοητόν [intelligible]? Cf. Parmenides: the impossibility of the being of nothing → the necessity of being. But: to be = to be something = What = to be a part—the Parmenidean ἕν [one] "is" ἐπέκεινα τῆς οὐσίας [beyond being; cf. *Republic* 509b].[V]

What about a theology in agreement with doctrine of ideas? god = pure mind = mind that grasps the ideas which are independent of his will.

S.'s impiety[R]. Human excellence = coming as near as possible to pure mind = ὁμοίωσις θεῷ [assimilation to god]—but the gods are not pious: human excellence ≠ piety.

E.'s first and implicit definition of piety: piety = to imitate the highest and justest god—a divination of the truth by the μάντις [seer].

Before we continue, let us clarify the context: E.'s second definition: ὅσιόν [holy] = to do what is dear to the gods—but the gods fight with each other, i.e. they disagree as to the δίκαιον [just], καλόν [beautiful] and ἀγαθόν [good]—they love opposite things: opposite things are dear to them: ὅσιόν [holy] is self-contradictory. One can imitate only knowing gods, viz. by striving for knowledge; to imitate not-knowing gods, is self-contradictory. 7d1–2 (see p. 10.)

Problem of justice[R]

7e1–3: Omits ἄδικα [unjust things] (cf. the τε in 7d1) → δίκαια [just things] = ἀδικία [unjust things].

7e6–7: ἀγαθά [good things] come to the center—the natural object of φιλία [love/friendship] is ταγαθόν [the good].

7e9–8a2: connection between δίκαιον [just] and self-assertion of ἔχθρα [hatreds]. cf. the limitation in following pages to δίκαιον [just]—ἄδικον [unjust].

8a7–9: S.'s impiety[R]. Piety is self-contradictory, not only on E.'s premises, but also if ἀρετή [virtue] = ὁμοίωσις θεῷ [assimilation to god].

8b4: S. adds Hephaistos and Hera: the injustice of son to mother: the city is the mother (2c8)—[P]no: gods of the now ruling dynasty[P]

8b7–9: Problem of justice[R]. E. seeks something regarding which all gods agree ("whoever does injustice to anyone, must be punished"). [V]His concern with his case: agreement of the gods as to this point would suffice.[V]

8b10–c1: This agreement is utterly irrelevant, because it is at once controversial whether the action at hand is <controversial> unjust.

[P]8b10–c7: Euthyphron addressed by name—his own case: 4d6–8.[P]

8c3–d3: All who commit an unjust action, agree that he [who] commits an unjust action, must be punished, but they deny insincerely that they committed an unjust action. They do not dare to deny the principle (viz., that the ἀδίκων [the one doing injustice] must give δίκη [justice]). Does this mean that they believe in that principle? Certainly not: they pay lip-service to it—the principle to which they agree, is only a social convention. Besides, it is not true that all people admit the principle in question—cf. "the sophists"—but, perhaps, the sophists are not ἀδικοῦντες [the ones doing injustice], but immoral. **[p. 13]**

8d4–e10: Problem of justice[R]. What is controversial, is, not the principle, but the application to the circumstances. More precisely, not daring to question the principle in speech, they limit themselves to questioning in speech the application to the case at hand. Does this mean that they agree with each other as to the principle? They do not agree, in their thought, as to the principle that they profess; they agree with each other as to the principle that they dare not profess—viz. that ἀδικεῖν [doing injustice] is good → they agree as to the ἀγαθόν [good], and this basic agreement is the cause of their mutual enmity.

S.'s impiety[R]. This applies to the gods as well as to men → the gods are consistent models of τελεία ἀδικία [perfect injustice] → piety (= imitation of the gods or doing what is dear to the gods) is injustice (cf. 9a1: φίλε [dear]).

E.'s character[R]. E. who takes the gods as his model, is unjust.

9a1–b3: Even if it is granted that all gods agree that unjust actions must be punished, they will not yet agree as to a) the injustice of the action of E.'s father, and b) the justice of E.'s prosecution of his father.

9a3–6: S.'s rhetorical change of the case: omits "hunger and cold," i.e. criminal neglect by the father of E.—he thus shows that E. could never win his lawsuit. Ultimately, because he would have to make the gods agree regarding the 2 points (stated at 9a1–b3).

The fundamental reason why E. cannot win: if piety = imitating the gods proves to be injustice, E.'s father would be dear to the gods precisely if E. proves that he was unjust. He could win his lawsuit only if he were more unjust than his father, i.e. if he were a perfect pleader.

9b3: the hyperbolic expression: if E. could persuade all gods—but even if he did, he would not yet have proved a thing.

9b4–5: E. does not want to answer—apparently, he does not see how he could answer and thus convince the audience: he becomes doubtful whether he can win his case (contrast with 3e5–6 and 5c1–3). The action[R]: S. induces E. to drop his charge against his father.

The passage is almost in the center of the dialogue.

9b6–8: E. might prove his point to the multitude.—[P]yet: the multitude ridicules him (3c1–2). His prophecy that he will win the lawsuit (3e5–6), is refuted: he is a poor μάντις [seer]. He certainly can no longer foresee the future.[P]

9c1: But for this he would have to be a good speaker > he would have to know.

9c2–8: S. speaks to himself: he imitates the listener to E.'s anticipated speech: he is not "charmed" by E.'s speech—he can think for himself while E. speaks → he would talk to his neighbor while E. speaks in court.

9c3–6: Piety—Justice[R]. Piety is implicitly reduced to justice: pious are all actions between man and man that are considered just by all the gods. [**p. 14**]

[P]9d3–5: This qualification deprives the agreement of the gods of all value as far as the practical problem of E. is concerned.[P]

9e1–3: The corrected definition. → a genuine agreement between all the gods would be possible only if all gods were knowing beings, i.e. if they would know the idea, independent of their will, of justice → the god would love "the pious" because it is "pious."

Summary (up to 8d3)—(cf. opposite p. 10 above).

First (implicit) definition: it is pious to imitate the gods, and especially the <greatest> best and justest god (5e–6a).

Objection: to do this one would have to know first what justice is, i.e. the idea of justice: knowledge, or wisdom, would be the prerequisite of piety. Besides: if we know what justice is, why can't we leave it at imitating the idea of justice? Especially since the idea of justice is higher than the gods: in order to be just, the gods have to comply with the idea of justice; that idea is the pattern or model for the gods → knowledge, or wisdom, would make piety (= imitation of the gods) superfluous.

This would mean: the philosopher is not pious, S. is not pious, his accusers were right.
But: the discussion continues—evidently, there are some points which need further discussion. a) it is assumed that there are ideas—why must there be ideas? b) if piety is superfluous or erroneous, why did it come into being and play such a role? c) knowledge or wisdom seems to be a prerequisite of justice → knowledge is different from justice, and justice is different from knowledge: what is justice? These questions are the subject of the following discussion.
Second definition (= first explicit definition): the pious is what is dear to the gods (6e10–7a1).
The common notion of piety is based on the premise that there is nothing higher than the gods—that in order to act well, the gods do not have to comply with a higher standard: the common notion of piety is based on the implicit denial of the existence of ideas. Now, knowledge is knowledge of the ideas. The tacit presupposition of the vulgar notion is then that the gods are ignorant, ignorant especially regarding justice → the gods fight with each other. In the language of monotheism, if the divine will is not guided by divine intelligence, i.e. if all necessity rests on a basis of arbitrariness, everything is possible, everything is permissible → chaos and fight. But this is absurd: God could kill himself and decree that the world will last forever after his suicide and follow immutable laws. Not everything can be possible: there must be necessity at the bottom of arbitrariness: there must be ideas determining even the will of God.
What is necessary, is unchangeable, is always in the same way: it can be predicted: it is the object of knowledge [**p. 15**]
The ideas are the object of knowledge. Human knowledge is always imperfect, is always ignorance. Only a god can have perfect knowledge. Man must strive for as perfect a knowledge as possible: he must imitate the wise god. If piety = imitation of gods, piety would be philosophy.
[P]S. and E[R].[P] <The common> Euthyphron's notion of piety arises from the divination that to be a truly human being, man must aspire beyond mere humanity; but it misinterprets what it divines. [V]Yet the notion that piety is to imitate the gods, is a heretical notion. Piety in the ordinary sense is worship of the gods with sacrifices and prayers—piety thus understood is superfluous and therefore harmful.

What then is the right attitude to the gods? God = pure mind = mind that grasps the ideas perfectly (p. 12 l. 3). Philosophy = ὁμοίωσις θεῷ [assimilation to god]. God : philosopher = actual philosopher : potential philosopher—but the actual philosopher loves the potential philosophers; ergo God loves the philosophers; the philosophers are θεοφιλεῖς [dear to the gods] → θεοφιλές [dear to the gods] ≠ ὅσιον [holy]. But: do the gods love?[V]

If piety is philosophy, to make people pious = to make them philosophize: but S. does not try to make E. philosophize. What does this mean? This fact indicates the problem of the relation of philosophy and justice. S. is just: he does not accuse people—he does not harm people: but does he help people? He is reputed to be philanthropic, i.e. to teach people all he knows—but he does not teach E. all he knows: is he then not philanthropic? is he unjust?—let us first return to the surface.

Pious = what is dear to the gods—but the gods contradict each other—piety is a self-contradictory notion (8a7–8). E. suggests: there are some things regarding which all gods agree. Comment on 8b7–d3. Continue: 8d4.

10a1–4: pious = what is loved by the gods. Question: is it loved by the gods because it is pious, or is it pious because it is loved by the gods? are the gods subject to a higher norm or are they not subject to it? E. does not understand.

10a5–c12: There are two kinds of actions (γίγνεσθαι [to become] and πάσχειν [to undergo]—c1–7)—in all cases, the object of action as such is posterior to the action itself. Now, the pious = loved is posterior to the act of loving: the pious is loved by the gods because the gods love it, and not for any intrinsic quality it has: the gods' love has no cause, no reason. This is a problem we have discussed already: are the gods inferior to the ideas or are they not? [V]This question is not explicitly discussed. E. grants that the pious is loved by the gods because it is pious, because of its intrinsic character (10d1–11) and he is thus compelled to admit that ὅσιον [holy] ≠ θεοφιλές [dear to the gods], and even that the pious and the pleasing to the gods are opposites (10d12–11a6). Thus there is apparently no progress of the argument.[V]

But there is a new question coming up (alluded to by the examples): the two alternative answers presuppose that the gods love. The gods are supposed to be perfect = self-sufficient beings that do not need anything → would beings that do not need anything, love anything?

Problem of justice[R]. More precisely: pious = what the gods love; but the gods love what they believe to be good, and in particular what they consider just (7e6–7, 9d1). What is justice? φιλανθρωπία [philanthropy]—the gods are said to love men (7a7): do the gods love human beings? → does the superior love the inferior? [P]does the superior serve the inferior? (This is justice.)[P] **[p. 16]**

Problem of justice[R].

| | | |
|---|---|---|
| φέρω | lead, carry, fetch, bring | —inanimate beings |
| ἄγω [lead] | | —living beings |

ὁρῶ [see]

14c4: the questioned ὑπάγειν [leading] the questioner

11d, 15b10: the (φορά [carrying]) of the λόγοι [accounts/arguments]

a) ἄγειν [to lead] central → is the lover superior to the loved? does the higher love the lower?

b) ἄγειν [to lead] central → does love lead away (for the lover's benefit) or lead on (for the loved's benefit)?

c) φέρειν [to carry] and ἄγειν [to lead] ≠ ὁρᾶν [to see] → does love affect ("vary") the beloved or does it leave it unaffected? e.g., does men's love of the gods in any way affect the gods (cf. c6–8)

The gods are said to love men, and the gods are said to be perfect beings.

If the lower (men) loves the higher (gods), it will leave the higher unaffected.

If the higher (gods) loves the lower (men), it will affect the lower—but being perfect, the higher will lead the lower on for the benefit of the lower: it will not lead it away (for the higher's benefit).

But let us assume that the higher cannot love the lower: is it possible that the higher leads on the lower without loving it? That this is possible, is shown by the action of the dialogue: S. leads E. on without loving him (cf. ὦ φίλε [o dear]—9a1 etc.) [P](3c6, 5c4, 10e9, 14a1)[P]

Why? Not for its own sake, but ἀναγκαίως [necessarily] (philosopher > society > sociability . . .).

But there is no necessity for the gods: the gods will not love men.

But (Glaucon, e.g.): the higher leads on the lower while loving it—why? potential philosophers → if the gods love[8] any man, they would love the philosophers. [P]But is not the philosopher in need of fellow-philosophers, whereas perfectly wise beings would not be in need of any help? (cf. 10c1–7).[P]

"The action always precedes the object of the action as such"—this is literally true—but it raises a difficulty: the seen thing must be there before I can see it → there are things which must be before they can be acted upon and there are things which are produced by the action. Difference between δόξα [opinion] and ἐπιστήμη [knowledge]. If ὅσιον [holy] is essentially νόμῳ [by law], it is constituted by the δόξα [opinion]; if it is φύσει [according to nature], it is merely grasped by ἐπιστήμη [knowledge] (cf. *Minos* 313b8–c3).

10d1–e8: The explicit refutation: ὅσιον [holy] ≠ θεοφιλές [dear to the gods]; for: the pious is loved because it is what it is.

the θεοφιλές [dear to the gods] is what it is, because it is loved—[P]and for no other reason.[P]

11a4: The emphasis on the fundamental difference and opposition between θεοφιλές [dear to the gods] and ὅσιον [holy] → θεοφιλές [dear to the gods] = σοφία [wisdom] and σοφοί [pl.: (the) wise]: the love of the gods has a reason independent of their will. ὅσιον [holy] = public worship, public sentiment: by no reason independent of will.

The irony: not piety, but θεοφιλές [dear to the gods] has a standard outside of itself.

[V]Piety and philosophy are incompatible. S.'s impiety[R].

For: piety is based on premises refuted by the experience of the philosopher that the higher would care for the lower (see p. 16)—piety is only νόμῳ [by law][V] **[p. 17]**

11b6–8: E. was never before in such a confusion: the "proof" that pious and θεοφιλές [dear to the gods] are opposites, is responsible for that.

[V]S.'s superiority, his σοφία [wisdom], has become evident—what then does his ἀμαθία [ignorance] mean?

He says: it is no real superiority—every description of the situation as a victory of S. would be a jest—he suggests a jest, but shows that it is not applicable to the case, because not he, but E., is responsible for what has happened. E. replies that S. is responsible all right—that S. is Daedalus. At this point, S. confesses that he does have a τέχνη [art], although against his will—his is the σοφία [wisdom] of Daedalus = production of true opinion—especially of the true opinion that the συνών [companion] does not know (for only if the συνών [companion] would know what knowledge is, would he know that he knows nothing).

Cf. the contrast with E.'s σοφία [wisdom] (11e2, 12a5): S.'s σοφία [wisdom] is precisely the knowledge of his ἀμαθία [ignorance]—the knowledge that there are ideas belongs to his ἀμαθία [ignorance].[V]

11b9–c6: S. wants to help E. a little by giving him an explicitly jocular explanation of his confusion that will be according to E.'s taste. A mythical explanation: tracing the happening to the ancestor. E.'s theses are the work of S.'s ancestor Daedalus; but this must be a joke since E. is the author of his thesis and E. is not a descendant of Daedalus. Or should S.'s ancestor exercise influence through contagion? Is there a kind of μίασμα [pollution] (4c1–2)? S. indicates that the kind of confusion created in E. leads to the accusation against him. [P]S.'s crime[R].[P] E.'s character[R]: E. is really friendly to S.

[V]Question: how would S. have spoken to Meletus? With still greater reserve. [P]S.'s justice[R].[P] Cf. *Rep.* [450d3–451a4]: reasonable friends. [P](This explains why S. attacks the myths openly in the *Rep.* and not in the *Euthyphron*).[PV]

11c7–d2: E. makes S. responsible[R] for the moving around of his thesis, because he, E., would desire it to stay [P]→ 11d3 (ἑταῖρε [fellow]).[P]

11d3–e2: S.: the desire is irrelevant—opinions are bound to run away (*Meno* 97f.: true opinion (≠ knowledge) compared to the works of Daedalus). S. too would wish his opinions to stay—he does not like to have the art of moving the theses—he thus implicitly admits that he does have the art of Daedalus.

S. crime[R]: Therefore, S. is responsible for E.'s confusion—more precisely: for E.'s becoming aware of his confusion.

In the contemporary *Theaetetus,* S. explicitly admits that he possesses an art: that of midwifery. In the *Euthyphron,* he traces his art through his father to Daedalus; in the *Theaet.* [149a1–151d3 and context], he traces it through his mother to Artemis. In the *Euthyphron,* he does not act as a midwife. "S.'s injustice[R].

S. imitates his ancestor Daedalus, just as E. imitates (his ancestor) Zeus (cf. the "kinship" between E., Meletus, and Meletus βασιλικόν [the kingly] > Zeus—cf. ad 2b10–11). Zeus ruins his father, just as E. wishes to ruin his father: but E. fails. <Daedalus ruins his son> Daedalus desires to save himself and his son, but he fails through the deficiency of his

art (*Mem.* IV 2.33)—S. desires to save himself and his son, but he ruins himself and διαφθείρειν τοὺς νέους [corrupting the young] through his ἀμαθία [ignorance] (2c5–7)—but in doing this, he successfully imitates Daedalus. He is Daedalus: he is productive of true opinions: he does not teach. [P]check: *Meno* 97f.[P] In the case of E. e.g., he is productive of the true opinion in the mind of E. that he does not know the pious things.
[P]Daedalus-Uranus.
S. makes true opinions—he is accused of being a maker of certain things (3a8–9).[P] **[p. 18]**

Summary up to 11b5
The first explicit definition of piety (piety = what is beloved by the gods) has been "refuted": θεοφιλές [dear to the gods] and ὅσιον [holy] are contraries—but this statement is followed by the assertion that they are not contraries (but related like πάθος [attribute] and οὐσία [being]), i.e., that they are different (10d13–11b1, 15c2). Shortly afterwards, a new definition of piety, the last one will be suggested which will lead to the result that θεοφιλές [dear to the gods] is identical with ὅσιον [holy]. To understand this contradiction and to understand the sequence in which the two contradictory statements occur, we have to remind ourselves again of the problem as a whole.
The explicit subject of the bulk of the dialogue is the question what piety is. But this universal question is linked up with two particular cases, the case of E. and that of S. S. is accused of being impious, and E. is suspect of being impious because he accuses his father of an impious action. The case of S. is obviously of much greater importance: the problem of S.'s piety is the problem of the philosopher's piety: are philosophy and piety compatible?
Is S. pious? a) at the end of the dialogue, we do not know what piety is—and hence, whether S. is pious.

b) E. vouches for S.'s piety; but, to say nothing of the fact that E. does not know what piety is, he is fool and, in addition, of dubious piety.

c) assuming that piety = following custom, S.'s assistance to custom is ambiguous because of the ambiguous character of E.'s case.

→ S.'s piety remains an open question = the piety of the philosopher remains an open question.

Yet we do learn something about piety from the dialogue. We learn at least what is the problem regarding piety. It is whether piety is identical with, or different from, θεοφιλές [dear to the gods]. But by this very fact we learn something about the nature of piety. The very insolubility of a problem reveals to us the nature of the subject matter with which the problem is concerned (the fallacy of scepticism: all negative arguments use knowledge of the subject matter).

The ordinary view: it is pleasing to the old gods (θεοφιλές [dear to the gods]) that they be worshipped in the customary manner (ὅσιον [holy]) → θεοφιλές [dear to the gods] = ὅσιον [holy].

Therefore: if θεοφιλές [dear to the gods] ≠ ὅσιον [holy], it is not pleasing to the old gods that they be worshipped in the customary manner. That θεοφιλές [dear to the gods] ≠ ὅσιον [holy], has not been proved by the argument which was meant to prove it (10d1–11b). But E. believes that it has been proved—and he is greatly disturbed—and for good reasons.

**[p. 19]**

To understand E.'s situation, we must consider the fact that when he was asked what piety is, he did not give as his answer the orthodox definition. He suggested: ὅσιον [holy] = to imitate the old gods.

Now: ὅσιον [holy] = to worship the gods in the customary manner.

θεοφιλές [dear to the gods] = what is pleasing to the gods—

a) while the gods do not do it;

b) while the gods do it.

Now, the old gods do not worship the old gods in the customary manner. Hence, if θεοφιλές [dear to the gods] = doing what the gods themselves do or imitating the gods, θεοφιλές [dear to the gods] ≠ ὅσιον [holy]. E. is perturbed, because the result is the consequence of his principle.

E.'s first, implicit definition amounts then to a silent rejection of the orthodox view. What is the reason underlying that rejection?

a) how do we know that the gods are pleased by the customary worship? Answer: the city knows it (4e4–6, 6a6–b1, 9a2–3, e4–7). But how does the city know? Through its experts on these matters. Yet, E. is an expert [P](13e8–9)[P]. In other words, the view of the city is a mere δόξα [opinion]; the opposite view (that of E.) is equally plausible.

b) which of the two views is more plausible? or more reasonable? is a reasonable man more pleased by men worshipping him or by men imitating him? does not pleasing, love, friendship presuppose identity of view regarding the good, noble, just (7c10ff.)?
S.'s critique of E.'s view (and implicitly of the orthodox view): if one intends to please the old gods by imitating them, or by doing things that they do not do, there must be agreement among the old gods—but they disagree among each other and they contradict each other—hence, it is impossible to please the old gods. [V]We could imitate only such gods as are in agreement with each other—but genuine agreement is brought about only by knowledge: we could imitate only knowing gods. The imitation would not consist in prayers and sacrifices—for the gods do not pray nor sacrifice: we could imitate them only by actions of justice.[V]

E. suggests therefore that one should please the justest god—he implies therefore that justice is the standard—now to please the justest god, one must know who the justest god is—one must know before what justice is, or the idea of justice—the just god is just only insofar as he complies with the idea of justice: he is subject to the idea of justice; the idea of justice is higher than the god. Furthermore, if we know the idea of justice, we do not need to imitate the justest god; it suffices perfectly if we imitate the idea of justice: piety = imitation of the gods is perfectly superfluous. Quest for the ideas, or philosophy, replaces piety: the ideas are S.'s new gods.

[V]But: we do not know what justice is; we are ignorant (ad 11e4–6)—we have to strive for knowledge of the ideas, i.e. we have to philosophize. But the gods must be wise beings if we are to imitate them: the imitation will consist in philosophizing. If imitating the gods is piety, philosophy is piety.[V] <In other words: one could please the gods, by imitating them or by doing things that they do not do, only if there were agreement among the gods; but agreement presupposes knowledge, and knowledge is knowledge of the ideas → the only imitation of the gods that is possible is philosophy. The new gods are knowing gods. If to do what pleases the gods is piety, philosophy is piety.> [**p. 20**]
But that has nothing to do with piety = worshipping the old gods in the customary manner → θεοφιλές [dear to the gods] ≠ ὅσιον [holy].

The irony of the explicit argument: θεοφιλές [dear to the gods] is presented as entirely dependent on the whims of the gods, whereas ὅσιον [holy] is presented as independent of it.

S. and E. agree as to the implicit principle (θεοφιλές [dear to the gods] = imitatio Dei ≠ ὅσιον [holy]). S. is pious from E.'s point of view. This explains E.'s friendliness. Or, from M.'s point of view, both S. and E. are impious.

[P]The action[R].[P] But is S. really impious? His impiety is said to consist in the fact that he does not worship or recognize the old gods (3b2–3). He cannot understand the absurd accusation (3b1). He turns to E., the expert, in order to learn from him (5a3–b5, c5, 6d2, 10, e3; 7a4; 9a1). What precisely does he learn from him? That piety = to imitate the old gods. Yet it proves to be impossible to imitate the old gods because they contradict each other. Confronted with this difficulty, E. suggests that one should imitate the justest god—and he thus starts on the downward path that leads to the substitution of the ideas for the old gods. The pious S. takes another road, a safer road. If it is pious to imitate the old gods, the safest course in case of conflict among the gods is to imitate the oldest god. The justest god whom E. selects, is not the oldest god—he selects the highest god among the present gods, the gods for the time being (τυγχάνειν [to happen to be] in 5e6, 6d3, 8a11).—He does not thus escape the difficulty because even the gods for the time being contradict each other (S.'s addition of Hera and Hephaistos in 8b3–4)—above all: the gods for the time being do not νομίζειν [believe in] the old gods (5e5–6a3). S. tries to imitate the oldest god. [V]Imitating οὐρανός [heaven] = the right life (*Tim.* 90c–d). In 8b2–4, Uranus is in the center.[V] The oldest god does not try to διαφθείρειν [corrupt] his own father: E. is impious because he punishes his father ([P]5b3–4,[P] 8b1–2). If one wants to be pious, one must try rather to ruin one's sons, as Uranos did → διαφθείρειν [to corrupt], not the old, but the young. I.e.: S.'s διαφθείρειν τοὺς νέους [corrupting the young], and especially his doing this by not recognizing the gods for the time being, is pious precisely if piety = imitating the oldest god. S. is pious on the basis of E.'s principle. And: he is pious on the basis of his own principle (piety = philosophizing). He is indeed impious on the basis of M.'s principle. Now, E. is impious on the basis of both M.'s and S.'s principles. And, which is worse, he is impious on the basis of his own principle. Yet: it is proof that he is impious on the basis of Meletus's principle which gives him the greatest shock, a still greater shock than the realization that he cannot win his law-suit: he is now shuddering at his own boldness [P](cf. ad 12e3–4)[P]. **[p. 21]**

11e1–4: The action[R]. S. has made E. doubtful as to whether he could win his lawsuit [P](ad 9a1–c8).[P]

He has made him shudder at his own boldness (cf. ad 12e3–4).

[P]cf. p. 20 bottom.[P]

He makes him now return to orthodoxy: after having made him realize the danger to which he has exposed himself, he shows him a way back. It is Socrates who now suggests for the first time a definition of piety which expresses less ambiguously the orthodox view. Now it is S. who is teaching E. to teach him (S.).

11e4–6: Problem of justice[R]. Why is it necessary for E. to say that all ὅσιον [holy] is δίκαιον [just]? Because it is necessary for him to trace ὅσιον [holy] = θεοφιλές [dear to the gods] to the justest god (5e6). Furthermore: the gods fight; but fight is (or presents itself as) fight for one's rights (8d8–10 etc.); the gods are then concerned with, or they love, δίκαια [just things] (7e6–8a2). cf. also 5d9, [P]ad 9c3–6.[P]

The deeper reason. How shall we imitate the gods? The next answer: by actions of justice. But why? We do not know—we are ignorant regarding the most important subjects. Now, this very ignorance regarding the most important subjects is the answer to the question of what the most important thing is: the most important thing is to strive for knowledge, i.e., to philosophize. The need for philosophy is more evident than the need for justice. Yet, in the dialogue, S. does not philosophize; he does not learn from E. nor does he seek together with him; still, he somehow takes care of him. This is the problem of justice: why should the higher care for the lower without loving it?

Furthermore: are the δίκαια [just things] knowable? in the way in which numbers etc. are knowable? If not, are they of any interest to the philosopher?

11e6–12a3: Problem of piety and of justice[R]. There are just things that are not pious, that are not required by piety. One may be pious, or pleasing to the gods, or imitate the gods without being just to human beings?

12a5: Critique of orthodoxy[R]. The enormous pretention underlying the common view of θεία [things divine]: the people know that it is pleasing to the gods to be worshipped in the customary manner. Cf. 11e2.

12a9–b1: The meaning of the verses: out of fear of Zeus, you will have awe. The apparent critique of the poet typical of Plato's critique of poetry in general. [**p. 22**]

12b2–3: Presumably: indicating the fact that there are various reasons for disagreeing with the verses. Cf. 15a1–2: the gods responsible for the good things (only).

12b4–c2: Critique of piety[R]. Whereas there may be fear without shame, there is never shame without fear, i.e. there is never fear of bad reputation without other fear. <cf. ἅμα [at the same time] in c1.>

12c3–9: This is now covered over: shame is a subdivision of fear, so that no other kind of fear need be implied in shame. At the same time, shame is compared to the odd (περιττόν: beyond the regular number or size, out of the common, extraordinary, strange, more than sufficient, superfluous, excessive). [P]Piety seems to be superfluous: we need not imitate the gods: it suffices if we imitate the ideas.[P]

12c10–d4: Fear

→ shame

→ other fear

Number

→ odd

→ even

Just

→ pious

→ other just

ὅσιον [holy] ~ περιττόν [odd, superfluous] ~ αἰδώς [sense of shame] —a kind of fear—fear of the gods (15d7)

ὅσιον [holy] = part of justice. Relation of ὅσιον [holy] to justice proper = relation of odd and even → ὅσιον [holy] and justice proper are opposites. Cf. ad 11e6–12a3. [P]Cf. ad 3d6–9.[P]

12d5–11: 50% of the δίκαια [just things] is ὅσιον [holy]. In the ὅσιον [holy], the 3 sides are unequal. In the human δίκαιον [just], there are at least 2 sides equal. ὅσιον [holy] ≠ ἴσον [equal].

12e3–4: cf. 3a1, c4–5 (the common cause of S. and E.). Now, E. is accused of impiety by Meletus! [P]The action[R].[P]

Summary of 11e6–12e4.

The problem of justice and piety[R]. θεοφιλές [dear to the gods] ≠ ὅσιον [holy] = what is dear to the gods is not the customary worship by sacrifices and prayers, but that men imitate the gods or that they do what the gods themselves do. Now, imitation of the gods is possible only if the gods agree among each other, and agreement presupposes knowledge: only wise gods can be imitated. Directly: it is foolish to imitate unwise beings. In what does the imitation of the gods consist? The first answer will be: in actions of justice. But why? We do not know → we are ignorant regarding the most important subject. Now, this very ignorance regarding the most important subject is the answer to the question of what the most important thing is: the most important thing is to strive for knowledge, to philosophize. The need for philosophy is more evident than the need for justice. [**p. 23**]

Furthermore, we do not know whether there are gods, i.e. wise gods, whom we could imitate. Nor do we know whether it is pleasing to the gods that we imitate them. The need for philosophizing is more evident than the need for piety.

We are then confronted with two questions: a) why justice? b) why piety? How can they be answered?

In the dialogue, S. does not philosophize; he does not learn from E., nor does he seek together with E. Still, he somehow takes care of him; he behaves in a philanthropic way. But philanthropy is at least akin to justice. [V]12e7–8.[V] In S.'s action, we may find an answer to the question of why justice is necessary.

But what about piety? Piety is now introduced as a part of justice, the other part being human justice. The problem: it seems to be possible to be pious without being just to human beings, and to be just to human beings without being pious (ad 11e6–12a3, 12c3–d4, e5–8). If justice is necessary, piety may be superfluous (περιττόν [odd, superfluous]).

12e1–8: Action[R]. S. threatens E. with persecution by Meletus—in order to make E. orthodox. Accordingly, E. now says that piety is that part of justice that consists in tending the gods, whereas the other part consists in tending men.

Cf. *Gorg.* 507b1–4: only right behavior to men is just (right behavior to gods is piety). *Rep.* 372a1–3. [P]*Protagoras* 331b.[P]

12e9–13a5 The action[R]: What does tendance mean in the case of the gods? In the case of all other tendance, only the expert can tend → only the expert can be pious; only the expert can know what actions are pious or not (cf. 14d1). This supplies the ironical explanation of the dialogue. That it is ironical, is obvious from the fact that S. meets the expert in piety by accident: he [does] not seek him.

S.'s impiety[R]. S., not being an expert in piety, cannot be pious.

13a7–b3: The problem of justice[R]. The tendance of brutes: the most obvious example, the tendance of human beings, is left out. And yet this example will be of decisive importance, because the tendance of human beings is justice proper. We have to apply throughout to justice proper what is said about the other "half" of justice (viz., piety): only the expert in justice, i.e., the ruler, is just.
*Ap. Socr.* 20a6–b5, *Rep.* 342c1–d1, 345c1–e2.

13a9–10: Central: dogs. Νὴ κύνα [By (the) dog].

13b4–c2: The problem of justice[R]. All tendance is for the advantage of the tended: all justice is for the advantage of the (other) men. S.'s action is for the advantage of Euthyphron. But why should one act for the advantage of others? *Ap. Socr.* 25c5–e6. *Rep.* 335b6–c8. [**p. 24**]
To act for the advantage of one's fellows, of those with whom one lives, is to act to one's own advantage. But: S.'s caring for his fellows makes him hated (3d1–e3). Does he not help his fellows? or does he lack the art of helping (is he inept)?

13c3: The oath: E. is shocked by the implicit suggestion that piety could serve the purpose of harming the gods.

13c4: Problem of justice. Problem of piety[R]. "To the advantage"—of whom? of the tenders? or of the tended? For the other ways of tendance (ἱππική [horsemanship] etc.) are for the advantage primarily of the tenders, only secondarily for the tended.
Both justice and piety primarily serve one's own benefit and only secondarily the benefit of men or gods.

13c6–10: The oath: another shocking suggestion which, in addition, is emphatically applied to E.'s case: does E. not make Zeus worse (more unjust) by confirming him in the principle underlying his unjust action against Kronos?

13c11–d2: Problem of piety[R]. S. knew all along that E. meant by the tendance of the gods the tendance that is to the benefit of men.

13d5–8: Problem of piety[R]. Piety is the tendance supplied by slaves to their masters: tendance motivated by fear. By obeying the masters, they make the masters gracious. I.e., by their tendance, they make their masters better! (cf. ad 13c3).
But is this simply true? By catering to the master's whims, the slave may make the master gracious to him; he will make him at the same time

morally worse. Is not the appeasing of a habitually angry being a sure means for making it morally worse? (ad 13c6–10).

Problem of justice[R]. Apply this to justice: does S. cater to the whims of the people? of E. in particular? Obviously not. He tries to make men aware of their ignorance, thus modest, better, more sociable—hence, better companions to him. But: he does not succeed. 1) the just = the true ruler (ad 13a7–b3), S. is not just. But what if the just = the good slave? Is S. not compelled to take care of his fellows, just as the decent slave is compelled to serve his master and yet refuses to cater to his whims? The compulsion under which the dialogue takes place. But why does S. refuse to cater to the whims of his fellows?

13d9–e5: Piety[R]. Piety is an art serving the gods. As a serving art it must be in the service of something that the gods produce. It has been ruled out that the gods themselves are improved by tendance. It is now suggested that the work of the gods requires assistance by men as a conditio sine qua non. Is this not a serious possibility that there is a divine master-art that uses human ministering arts? Let us look at the arts [**p. 25**] we know, the human arts, e.g., medicine, ship-building, house-building. Do these arts suffice for bringing about their desired result (health, happy sea-voyage, happy living in the house)? The limitation of the arts: τύχη [chance] (cf. 13d10). The divine art would be the control of τύχη [chance], of what is not controllable by human art. The divine art = providence.

Justice[R]. The examples—πλοίον [ship] in the center—the ship of state (cf. *Rep.* 488)—the stormy sea of society—the danger to the philosopher: like a man who has fallen among wild beasts (*Rep.* 496c–d).

13e6–9: Action[R]. E.'s self-confidence has been restored. His strong confidence at the beginning: 4a12–b3; 4e9–5a2; 6b3–6. His serious doubt in the middle: 9b4–10; 11b6–d1 (cf. 11e2, 12a5). The restoration is due to the fact that he is now again approaching the common view.

13e10–12: Piety[R]. As appears from the examples that follow: the gods produce wonderful things for us while they use us as their servants.

Justice[R]. The city produces wonderful things for us while it uses us as its servants.

14a1–8: Justice[R]. The peaceful activity of farming requires less man's serving other men than does the warlike activity (cf. *Rep.* 332e3–5). But what about the human γεωργική [art of farming] (2d2–3)? Is teaching not teaching of friends? Justice (≠ friendship) and compulsion.

14a11–b7: Piety[R] is the human art (ἐπίστηται [know]: b3) of humoring the gods which in its turn controls the divine art of providence and thus supplies the supplement to the ordinary human arts. I.e.: the gods bless only those who humor them.

Justice[R] preserves families (estates) and cities. But philosophy requires cities. Ergo: justice is necessary. It consists in the fair distribution of the advantages and burdens of society. Is a ἱκανὴ κρίσις [sufficient judgment] of what is fair or not, possible? (7c10, d3–4) The problem of ἰσότης [equality] geometric, arithmetic; the dilution of true equality by fictitious equality (consent)—*Legg.* 757—→ νόμος [law]: conventional equality: that the higher serves the lower, is a matter of necessity or compulsion. One has then to follow νόμος [law]. (*Rep.* near the beginning [328b]: ἀλλ' εἰ δοκεῖ, [ἦν δ'ἐγώ] οὕτω χρὴ ποιεῖν [if it is so decided, (I said), that how we must act].) S. refuses to cater to the whims of the people, because in doing so he would ruin the πόλις [city]. The only concession to the people that he makes, is his acceptance of the principle of νόμος [law].

[lines] b8–9: Piety[R]. The work produced by the gods with the assistance of men is σωτηρία οἰκῶν κ. πόλεως [the salvation of households and a city]. **[p. 26]** But is this not achieved by γεωργική [skill of farming] and στρατηγική [generalship] (14a1–8)? Is it not in another way achieved by justice? Yet: the power of τύχη [chance]—it is to be controlled by piety. That control is impossible. But: the fact of τύχη [chance] is the ultimate justification of piety.

14b9–c1: Justice[R]. E. is unjust, if justice = φιλανθρωπία [philanthropy] = teaching everyone indiscriminately → S. is unjust in this sense (ad 3d5–6).

14b9–c5: Justice[R]. S. knows what piety is—but he does not teach it—his questioning E. is not learning from E.

Piety[R]. What is the decisive point which E. has missed? He missed it by the reference to prayer and sacrifice. Piety = recognition of the power of τύχη [chance] without the attempt to control τύχη [chance].

The one thing needful is to philosophize. If there are gods, i.e. wise gods, it will be pleasing to them that men imitate them → "piety" is to philosophize. Yet: philosophy presupposes conditions which philosophy cannot guarantee (healthy mind, natural gifts, leisure . . .). Philosophy must recognize its own limitation. It must recognize the power of τύχη [chance]. If it does not do it, it defeats its own purpose: it will not arrive at a true notion of reality: it will ascribe necessity and intelligibility to the fortuitous. Ultimately, it will deny difference between ideas and ἕκαστα [particulars]. Philosophy is then inseparable from the right attitude to τύχη [chance] while right attitude is intended by common piety. The right attitude to the blows of fortune is ἀνδρεία [courage].

Piety in the ordinary sense (= control of τύχη [chance]) is absurd, as will be shown in what follows.

14c3–4: Justice[R]. S. is the lover (or questioner) and E. is the beloved (or questioned)[9]—S. is led, E. is leading.

cf. 10a5–c8 (ἄγειν [to lead] the central example for clarifying the problem of φιλεῖν [to love]). S. loves E.: he loves E.'s wisdom (14d4–5)—he loves what he needs. But he does not need E. → he does not love him. As little as he is led by E., as little is he a lover of E. His justice consists precisely in his taking care of E. without loving him.

In the perfect city, S. would command E.: he would not converse with him. His conversation with him is due to compulsion.

14c5–d3: Piety[R] = art (ἐπιστήμη [knowledge]) of asking from, and giving to, the gods = art of controlling τύχη [chance].

Justice[R] = art of giving and taking.

14d9–e5: Piety[R] = art of asking from, and giving to, the gods = asking and giving in the right manner = asking them for what we need [**p. 27**] from them and giving them what they need from us. But since the gods do not need anything, sacrifices at any rate are absurd.

14e11–15a2: Piety[R]. All good things which we have, are given to us by the gods. The argument does not make sense if it does not imply that only the good things, and no bad things, are given to us by the gods. For if the gods give us also bad things, the business would not be so bad for the gods after all. Besides, if the gods give, or can give, good and bad things, appeasement of the angry gods will be in order. (But cf. *Crito* 44d6–8 (and Burnet).) (The reason for his not saying "the gods give us only all the good things we have" is precisely to draw our attention to the implicitly rejected possibility—viz., the gods give us also bad things—in which common piety is rooted.) Now, if the gods give us only good things, κακὴ τύχη [misfortune] has nothing to do with the gods—its cause is different from the gods → there is no providence—there is no protection against misfortune.

Justice[R]. S.'s justice = willingness to help his fellows to sociability so that he be benefitted by it—but he is hated—he fails—why? His failure is due to τύχη [chance] (cf. 3e2–3; *Crito* 46b8).

15a2–8: Piety$^{R}$. We understand by gods perfect beings = wise beings; but wise beings are good, and not bad or childish. If they care at all for men, they would be responsible only for good things: there is no need for bribing them. Furthermore: the gods being perfect do not have any needs (cf. 14e1–2); ergo there is no reason for giving them anything.

15a9–10: Piety$^{R}$. The gods desire to be honored—are they ambitious? But if they are, this will lead to fights among men, and this to impossibility of honoring the gods.

15b1–2: Piety$^{R}$. What is not useful, is not φίλον [dear] → since men cannot be useful to the gods, they cannot be dear to them → the gods do not love men, they do not care for men.

<15b3–6: Piety$^{R}$: Ergo—the pious has no other reason than the inscrutable will of the gods. Cannot one leave it at that? One could but for the fact that E. has previously said the opposite. I.e.: an ordinary man who would not have questioned custom at all, would have remained consistent. Action$^{R}$. What is the consistent position? "I obey the city which tells me that I have to worship the gods of the city in a manner pleasing to these gods, i.e., in the customary manner by speech and by deed"—14b3; cf. 11b6–7: νοεῖν [to think] ≠ λέγειν [to speak]—. For this can be done, it is possible. And even necessary: disobedience to the city [**p. 28**] brings ruin to the city and therewith to everyone. Now: to obey means "not to reason why?"

15b7–c12: Action$^{R}$. Reminder of "Daedalus," i.e. of the lowest ebb of E.'s self-confidence. E. shall remember after his return to orthodoxy the gravity of the danger of aberration.

Or: he does not allow E. to come to rest in the orthodox position as a position based on knowledge. He wants him to follow custom in the spirit of obedience, of blind obedience. Custom should be divorced from the alleged ἐπιστήμη [knowledge] (14d1–2).>

Summary of 12–14

Piety$^{R}$. In the *Euthyphron*, S. discusses piety with an expert on piety who is a man of questionable piety. E. expresses his heterodoxy unwittingly by suggesting that piety = imitating the gods, and he is thus led by S. to admit that what the gods love (sc. that men imitate them) is different from the pious (= customary worship of the gods). Shocked by this unforeseen and dangerous consequence, he is now prepared to be led by S., to be led back to the common view according to which it is precisely the ordinary worship that is pleasing to the gods. This ordinary view is suggested by S.: S. is really pious.

Yet, as we have seen, in discussing the ordinary view, S. points out its doubtful character. He thus lets us see why he cannot leave it at piety in the ordinary sense. E.'s view which was discussed in the preceding part, is clearly more sophisticated than the ordinary view; after all, E. is an expert on piety. Only in the discussion of the 2nd explicit definition are we confronted with S.'s critique of ordinary piety. The reasonable order of discussion is then inverted. For: the discussion is not simply reasonable, or concerned with clarifying the subject matter, but it serves a philanthropic purpose: to help E., to protect him against his folly.

The ordinary view regarding piety:

a) piety is a part of justice, the other part being justice to human beings → men may be pious without being pious [recte: just] to human beings and vice versa.

b) piety is the tendance of gods, just as justice proper is tendance of human beings.

Tendance may mean:

α) making the tended better, i.e., ruling or controlling the tended, in the ultimate interest of the tender. Tendance in this sense cannot apply to the gods, if the gods are either good or not controllable by man.

β) serving the tended in the way in which slaves tend their masters—this is more plausible, because it is possible even if the gods are good and not controllable by man. [**p. 29**]

Piety[R]. But what is the reason for piety thus understood? why is piety thus understood good? The slaves fear the masters: disobedience will be punished, obedience will be rewarded: the slaves' well-being depends on their tending their masters. The masters produce the well-being of their slaves, but this depends on the collaboration of the slaves (i.e. on whether the slaves obey or not) → the masters bring about the well-being of their slaves with the assistance of these slaves. Now, one can bring about something either intelligently or without intelligence; in the first case, we speak of an art of bringing about → piety = tending the gods is an art subservient to the divine master-art which brings about the well-being of men: the divine master-art is called providence. But there is this crucial difference between the ministering art called piety and other ministering arts: in the other ministering arts, the ministering artisan does not determine the end, the product; or, the end or the product is *not* the well-being of the ministering artisan. I.e.: in the case of piety, *men* bring about their own well-being by using the divine master-art for *their* purpose. The higher is put in the service of the lower.

Conclusion: regardless of whether tendance is understood as *improving* the tended or as *serving* the tended, men would be the rulers of the gods.

However: the tendance consists in prayers and sacrifices. Piety = the intelligent use of the divine master-art consists in *influencing* the gods by prayers and sacrifices. The gods are then not simply the *servants* of men: there is a relation of *equality*: the equality of beings that exchange *goods*: piety is a kind of art of trafficking. This presupposes that the gods need things from us just as we need things from them. But this is absurd.
For the same reason (sc. because the gods do not need things from men), it is absurd to conceive of the gods as in any way *serving* men.

*Justice*[R]. Now, if need is *the* reason for service and hence in particular for that service that is called justice proper, justice proper is based on *need*. [P]But so is love. If justice is not based on love, it can only be based[P] on *necessity*, on *compulsion*. S.'s taking care of E., his serving him is ultimately due to compulsion. ad 15b1–2.

14e9–15a4: *Piety*[R]. But let us assume that the gods serve men out of sheer kindness or *beneficence*—all the good things which we have, come from the gods. And they would come from the gods without our serving the gods. **[p. 30]**
The notion of service to the gods is based on the premise that the gods give also bad things, or that they give us good things only conditionally (they withhold them if we do not serve the gods).

15a2–b2: See above p. 27.

15b3–6: *Piety*[R]. Ergo: the pious has no other reason than the inscrutable will of the gods. Cannot we leave it at that? *Justice.*[R] To worship the gods in the customary manner with sacrifices and prayers is pleasing to the gods—why?—we do not know—no λόγος [account/argument] is possible—the gods are pleased by it because they are pleased by it (cf. 15c5–6 with 10d). But: how do we *know* *that* the gods are pleased by it?
We cannot accept this assertion merely because someone makes it: 9e7.

Let us start from the only possible premise that the gods give all good things to men, not because the gods need men's service, but out of pure kindness. Why should the gods will that men worship them? Worship is a part of justice. The gods will that men be just to them (i.e., grateful to them) so that they be just to their fellows. Man must be grateful, he must know what he owes to others, in order to be just. Piety is then a kind of education to justice proper: piety serves justice proper. But: δίκαιον [just] = νόμιμον [legal] → the specification of what one owes to the gods, is supplied by the νόμος πόλεως [law of the city], by custom.

What ultimately counts is then justice proper. [V]Cf. the example in 4b8–c2: certain unjust actions lead to religious μίασμα [pollution]—and 4d9–e1. 5d8–6a5. 8b7–9.[V] But: justice proper is independent of piety—one can be just to one's fellows without being pious (= prayers and sacrifices). → a man who is just to his fellows, would not need piety. Only those who otherwise would not be just to their fellows, need piety as an education to justice. But are unjust men likely to be just to the gods? Only if the gods punish for injustice—i.e., only if they fear the gods: fear of the gods is required as a sanction for justice proper.

This means: the gods punish injustice and reward justice → the gods are just. By being just, we imitate the gods → piety = doing what is pleasing to the gods is justice proper. Piety = customary worship is necessary only for those who otherwise would not be just.

Presupposed:

a) the unjust fear the gods—because they fear punishment, i.e. bad things coming from the gods—but do any bad things come from the gods? and is hurting men not tantamount to making men worse (*Rep.* I [335b2–335e5])? But punishment = correction of the unjust: are the unjust really corrected by misfortunes? how do we know that the misfortunes come from the gods? **[p. 31]**

b) the gods care for justice—are the gods as knowing beings concerned with πλανώμενα δίκαια [wandering/changeable just things]?

c) the gods care for men—does the higher care for the lower?

d) what is required for piety, is only deed and speech, not thought (14b3; 11b6–7).

15b7–c10: The action[R]. The pious has no other reason than the inscrutable will of the gods. Why does Socrates not leave it at that? For: he wants merely to bring back E. to the ordinary view. If piety = worshipping the gods with prayers and sacrifices, the case of E. has nothing do with piety. But E., who is not just, can be induced to drop his lawsuit only if his action can be shown to be impious. One could try to lead him to a notion of piety which would cover his own case. Prior to that, one can merely show him that he does not know what piety is and thus induce him to abide by the customary view.

S. reminds E. of "Daedalus": of the lowest point of E.'s self-confidence. E. shall remember ever after his return to orthodoxy the gravity of the danger of aberration.

Piety[R]. S. suggests therefore that E. cannot leave it at suggesting that piety = to do what is pleasing to the gods because he had said before that piety ≠ θεοφιλές [dear to the gods]. But for this inconsistency, S. might have left E. at the view that piety = customary worship of the gods and nothing else. An ordinary man would not have questioned custom at all; he would have been more consistent than E. To obey the city which tells us that one has to worship the gods in the customary manner by deed and by speech: this is possible without contradiction. It is even necessary: disobedience to the city brings ruin to the city and therewith to oneself. Now: to obey means "not to reason why?" Customary practice is to be divorced from alleged ἐπιστήμη [knowledge] (14d1–2). Traditional practice is divorced from traditional reasons (and therefore the difficulties inherent in the myths are avoided)—but traditional practice is not left without reason: the sufficient reason is the law of the city.

15b7: [P]Piety[R].[P] E. is required to wonder (ὦ θαυμάσιε [wondrous]: 3b1, 5a3, 8a10, d11). He knows θαυμασιώτατα [most wonderful things] (6b5, c5–7). But S. will not wonder (6c8). E. wonders about things about which S. does not wonder: S. finds E. much more wonderful than his stories: the root of all wonderful stories is the soul of man—much more wonderful than its products (*Phaedrus* near beginning [234d]). [V]Cf. 3c2, 4a1: μαινόμενος [mad].[V]

15d3–4: S.'s impiety[R]. The man who did not let off Proteus, is Menelaus (*Euthydemus* 288b7ff.)—the husband of Helena. [**p. 32**] What is the tertium comparationis? S. is Menelaus—is Xanthippe Helena? The τύχη [chance] in S.'s life: his failures. *Odyssey* IV 351–479. S. did not sacrifice or give the gods their due—he is thus brought into a situation where he has no choice but to get hold of the elusive soothsayer Proteus-Euthyphron in order to learn from him—his appointed future? S. is so impious that he does not take seriously the μαντική [divinatory art]—no, in order to learn from him what piety is.

15d4–e1: Piety Justice[R]. Only certain knowledge of what piety truly is could induce a man to deviate from customary piety. In the absence of such knowledge, one should follow custom. Why? Fear of the gods (= αἰδώς [sense of shame]—cf. ad 12c10–d4)—? but (ad 15b3–6), this will not influence a just man. Shame of human beings = fear of reputation of badness. *EN* on αἰδώς [sense of shame]: the good man does also the νόμῳ καλά [the noble things by law] so that he cannot be reproached [cf. *Nicomachean Ethics* 4.9]. The fear of reputation of wickedness is not wholly unrelated to ordinary fear (ad 12b9–c1). Cf. *Legg.* 698b2–c3.

15d5–6: S. does not question here that E.'s father was guilty of murder. The principle which he accepts is: that a son must not indict his old father for murder, especially for the murder of a serf. Cf. 4b5–6.

15e1–2: Justice[R]. E. conceals his wisdom (3d5–6, 11b1, 14b9–c1), whereas S. reveals it to everyone—or rather he is reputed to reveal it to everyone.

15e5: ὦ ἑταῖρε [o fellow]—no longer: ὦ φίλε [o dear] as in 3c6, 9a1, 10e9, 14a1, d4.

5c3: ὦ φίλε ἑταῖρε [o dear fellow]. 6d1 and 11d3: ὦ ἑταῖρε [o fellow].

16a1–4: S.'s impiety. Only if he had learned from E., would he have avoided impiety. For: he did not have a teacher of piety before. Hence, anything he knew about piety, would have to be discovered by himself: it will be καινόν [new].

[p. 33]

*Crito*

The problem: why does S. obey the law? The one thing needful is philosophy, not justice. [V]For: our ignorance about the most important things is the compelling reason for the quest for knowledge of the most important things: quest for such knowledge is the most important thing for us.[V] Why justice? What is justice? At first glance, obedience to the law (to give everyone his due—but what is everyone's due, is determined by the law). Why then obedience to the law?

The setting: The philosopher is presented in a situation where obedience to the law would seem to be impossible: S. unjustly condemned to death—on the basis of an unjust law. He is accused of impiety by people who do not know what piety is. Nay, the very law against impiety is the work of men who do not know what piety is.

In this situation, S. has a conversation on this problem with a friend, in the solitude of prison. It is a conversation of μόνος προς μόνον [one on one]. No public display of wisdom. This is safe: in such a discussion we get the pure truth. But: it is safe to say the truth one knows to intelligent friends: not to intelligent enemies, nor to foolish friends. E. is a foolish friend, or rather a fool benevolent to S.

What about Crito? [V]No ἀλαζών [boaster] as E.[V] He is of the same age as S. and his fellow-tribesman. He vouches together with his son Critoboulos, Plato and Apollodorus for S.'s fine (*Ap. Socr.* 33d9–e1, 38b6–7); he offered to go bail that S. would not attempt to escape (*Phaedo* 115d7—cf. Burnet ad Crito, p. 172); he was present at S.'s death; he is the one whom S. ordered to sacrifice a cock to Asclepius.

Crito is a friend all right. But what about his competence? Is he particularly good at law-abiding? Just as E. is an expert in piety? Name: κρίτων > κρίνειν, to judge, to pass judgment (*Euthydemus* 291d5; cf. *Ap.* 41b3, 32b4)—the good judge?—the just judge? Crito's justice[R]. What is justice? a) justice [=] wisdom regarding business—Crito is a χρηματιστής [businessman] (*Euthyd.* 304c, 307a5–6), a wealthy farmer (→ ἐπιεικής [decent]); b) justice = τὰ ἑαυτοῦ πράττειν [minding one's own business], not to be a busybody—cf. *Mem.* I 2.47–48 and III 9. c) justice = law-abidingness. The latter is decisive in the situation: a discussion on law-abidingness with a man of dubious law-abidingness. But less dubious in this respect than E. is regarding piety.

43a1: S. starts—contrast with *Euthyphron*—in the *Crito*, an explicit explanation will be given

[P]43a2: C.'s brief answer: he does not want to keep S. awake.[P]

43a3: The question implies: it is night—thus: what part of the night?

43a4: The time before the first glimmer of daylight. cf. *Protagoras* 310a8—ib. 312a7 (= 71 lines later—corresponds to *Crito* 44d10): already some visibility. No explicit mention of this change in time in the *Crito*, because it is a dramatic dialogue.—[P]Setting[R] → Crito corresponds to Hippocrates: no dialogue with a sophist follows. The discussion remains within the limits of gentlemanship.[P]

43a8: Crito is wealthy—maybe he bribed the jailer—[P]Crito's justice[RP]

[P]43b3: the first oath: "god forbid"—C. feels strongly about it.[P]

43b5–6: Crito's concern with S.'s ἡδονή [pleasure]—his εὐεργεσία [doing good] (43a8). [V]He treats S. as he would wish to be treated by others if he were in S.'s place—the golden rule, ἰσότης [equality]—but it is inappropriate because S. does not suffer from what is [would be] the most terrible thing to C.

Justice = to be good to others (εὐεργετεῖν [to do good deeds]: 43a8)—to do what the others consider good or to do what is good?

What is truly εὐεργετεῖν [to do good deeds], may be κακουργεῖν [to do evil] in the ordinary sense → the highest εὐεργεσία [doing good] to kill or enslave one—?[V] Crito's justice[R] **[p. 34]**

[P]43b10–11: Justice = doing good → what is good? what are the good things? life, health, wealth . . . Are they merely imaginary? Obviously not. S.'s indifference to his dying connected with the fact that he is already old. May be that he would have taken a different attitude if he had been in the prime of life: the ambiguity implied in the setting[R] (cf. *Euthyphron*)[P]

← S.'s piety = justice[R] →

43b10–c3: S. does not revolt against his fate: his patience, his piety: he does not try to control τύχη [chance]. Similarly, he does not revolt against men. If C. were in S.'s place, he would revolt against his fate (b3–4). He calls S. blessed on account of his τρόπος [manner]; but, he finds, τρόπος [manner] alone is not enough. C.'s justice[R].

[P]43c2: ἡλικία [old age] ≠ τρόπος [manner] (b7)—cf. *Rep.* (Kephalos)[P]

43c6–7: Ambiguous: possibly "If I were in your place, I would suffer from this blow more heavily" cf. b3–4.

43c7–8: C. has absolute faith in human messengers. ἄγγελος [messenger] = "one who announces or tells, e.g., birds of augury" S.'s piety[R]—[P]d6–7.[P] For C., what δοκεῖ [is opined], is δῆλον [manifest]; he substitutes consistently[10] the messengers for the fact reported by them.

44a2: The ship will not arrive today; for S. has to die one day after its arrival; and he will die "the day after to-morrow." "I will tell you": S opposes himself to human messengers. S.'s δαιμόνιον [daimonion]: his δαιμόνιον [daimonion]. [P]S.'s piety[RP]

44a5: It is still night (cf. Burnet ad loc.) But consider 43d8.

44a7–8: Not the delay is fortunate, but the pleasing dream. [P]It so happened that C.'s εὐεργεσία [doing good] (his not awakening S.) was appropriate → εὐεργεσία [doing good] can't be trusted. Setting[RP]. [V]C. did not awaken him because he wanted to spare him pain; what he actually did, was not to interrupt S.'s enjoyment.[V]

44a10: The dream: δόξα [opinion].

[P]44a10–b1: Ἀρετή [Virtue]? Cf. *Mem.* II 1.22[P]

44a10–b2: Achilles (*Il.* IX 388 ff.): "If the great shaker of the Earth grant me good journey, on the third day should I reach deep-soiled Phthia." S. is told what Achilles himself tells. Achilles (ib. 400ff.): "For thus my goddess mother telleth me, Thetis the silver-footed, that twain fates are bearing me to the issue of death. If I abide here and besiege the Trojans' city, then my returning home is taken from me, but my fame shall be imperishable; but if I go home to my dear native land, my high fame is taken from me, but my life shall endure long while, neither shall the issue of death soon reach me." <The goddess (?) tells S. that, given certain conditions, he might desert the "army" out of anger with his rulers (cf. *Rep.* 389e) and preferring his quietude to fame—this is what Crito suggests: 45c5ff. (S. is "betraying" himself, his sons—).—but how? by fleeing? or by staying? The latter is suggested by Crito (45c5ff): S. will "betray" himself, his sons by not fleeing. Phthia is in Thessaly—cf. 45c2–4—S. could desert the "army" out of anger with his rulers and preferring his quietude to fame by fleeing to Thessaly → the dream suggests precisely what Crito is going to suggest! The ambiguity of the dream: the guidance has to be expected from λόγος [account/argument] alone.> **[p. 35]**

44b1–3: S.'s crime. S.'s suicide[R]

Achilles says that out of anger with his rulers he will desert the army and prefer a long life to immortal fame. This is ἄτοπον [absurd] if applied to S.; for S. is old and he is not angry (cf. 43b9).

But does the dream not throw light on what a young Socrates would have done? cf. ad 43b10–11. Army ~ city in action: did S. not desert the city by refusing to do τὰ πολιτικά [the political things], and did he then not prefer his security, a long life, to what the city considers immortal fame? cf. *Ap. Socr.* 31d7–32a3; 32e2–3. cf. the problem Achilles-Odysseus in *Hipp. mai.* and the comparison of S. to Odysseus in the *Protag.* and *Mem.* IV 6.

S. is being told in a dream what Achilles tells of his own accord while being awake: S. is not responsible for the statement → cf. his explanation of why he is not doing τὰ πολιτικά [the political things] in the *Ap. Socr.*: he traces it to an oracle.

Still, the dream must be understood in relation to the actual situation—to the old Socrates who is condemned to death, and who is confronted with a choice of staying in prison and dying, or of fleeing and living. The dream tells him that (given certain conditions) he would come to Phthia on the third day.

Phthia = a) Hades → staying and dying

or

b) Thessaly → fleeing and living } flight to Thessaly suggested by C. (45c5ff.)

The dream is ambiguous. It says either: by staying, S. becomes a deserter preferring his security to his fame, or: by fleeing, S. becomes a deserter preferring his security to his fame.

In either case, a beautiful woman in white dress suggests that "security," not "fame," should be considered. This is unambiguous.

The principle is unambiguous; the application is ambiguous: the λόγος [account/argument], and not the dream, must decide that.

S. understands the dream to mean that he should stay (die on the 3rd day: 44a2–b2); this means: it is more expedient, more convenient to stay and to die; flight is more burdensome. cf. ad 44b4.

C. is going to suggest (45c ff.) that by staying S. will be guilty of desertion, of dereliction of duty; that by fleeing he would prefer his fame to his security. C. recommends flight: his principle is, not security, but fame → the problem of fame: of δόξα [opinion]. **[p. 36]**

44b4: Not only the principle, but the application too is evident. For it is possible to come in two days from Athens to Thessaly,—

44b5–6: C.'s impiety[R]: he suggests that S. obey him, i.e., to his reasons, and not to the dream.

44b6–c5: C.'s reasons. [V]He (Crito) will be deprived of his friend and he (Crito) will get a bad reputation.[V] Setting[R].

a) S. should not deprive C. of his best friend. The term used is not φίλος (beloved, dear—which S. applies to C. in 46b1, 54d2, just as he applied [it] to Euthyphron in 3c6 etc.), but επιτήδειος (made for an end or purpose, suitable, convenient, useful, serviceable, necessary, friendly). C. speaks of ἐπιτήδειος also in 43c6, 44e2, 45e1, and only once (44c3) of φίλος [friend]. Cf. *Memor.* II 9 end (one would have to consider also the *Euthydemus* and the *Phaedo*). cf. ad 44c1–9

b) C. will get a bad reputation (δόξα πονηρίας)—the reputation of having preferred money to a friend (φίλος). Here he uses φίλοι [friends] because he states an ἔνδοξον [accepted opinion] which speaks of φίλοι [friends].

44c6–9: S. disregards completely C.'s loss of his best "friend"—he does not even try to comfort C.: the questionable character of that friendship. Justice[R]. He limits himself to rejecting what he obviously considers C.'s chief reason: fear of bad reputation with the many. This he declares to be an utterly irrelevant consideration. He admits that the consideration of the ἐπιεικέστατοι [pl.: most decent] deserves some consideration. I.e., S. rejects what in the *Euthyphron* (12b9–c1, 15d8) appeared to be the motive for justice, [V]or rather, προς Εὐθύφρονα [with a view to Euthyphro], S. did not make this important distinction[V]. Maybe, it is fear of bad reputation with the best which is that motive. Yet the best will approve of everything a man like S. does (cf. Burnet ad 44c8–9). Yet (c6) οὕτω, in this manner → maybe a certain kind of considering of public opinion is essential! We have seen this in analyzing the *Euthyphron*: it is impossible to cater to the whims of the many—but this does not mean that all their opinions have to be discarded.

44d6–10: Justice. The many can't procure the greatest good (φρόνησις [practical wisdom]) nor the greatest evil (folly). What they can do to a man, is indifferent (Burnet)—but: is ἀδικεῖσθαι [to do injustice] indifferent? No—*Gorgias* 469b12–c1. Hence: the many will do what occurs to them, but neither wisdom nor folly can be produced by such a procedure.

Is it true that if the many could do the greatest evil, they could also do the greatest good? The physician who is best at making people healthy, is also best at making them sick: every δύναμις [power, capacity] is τῶν ἐναντίων [of contraries]. But is this universally true? [V]Difference between δυνάμεις [powers, capacities] and ἕξεις [habits] (*EN* 1129a11 ff.) → ἡ τἀγαθῶν ἕξις [the habit of the good (pl.)]—τὸ ἀγαθόν [the good] consists of καλά [noble things] and ὀρθά [right things] (*Rep.* 517c1–4).[V] The gods who are responsible for the greatest goods (*Euthyphron* 15a1), are not responsible for the greatest evils (*Rep.* II). Does S. not mean to say "I wish that the many were gods (as the many understand the gods: production of the greatest goods and the greatest evils)—everything will be wonderful. In this case, I would simply bow to them. But since they are not omnipotent, there is no need for that." [P]cf. Burnet ad 46c5.[P]

[**p. 36 verso**] Summary of—44b6: The problem—the philosopher and the law (or justice). Extreme case: the philosopher willing to undergo capital punishment meted out to him on the basis of an unjust law. But: S. is old: may be a younger man would have revolted. Ambiguity of the setting. The ambiguity: is S.'s obedience not due to prudential considerations? The dream: the woman in white dress seems to advise S. to consider his security, and not his fame. The question: ἀγαθόν [good] ≠ καλόν [noble] (cf. *Rep.*). Crito is concerned with reputation—with reputation with the many → by implication he attributes competence to the many—i.e., equal status with the wise → justice is equality: he treats S. in exactly the same way in which he would wish to be treated by S.
S. implicitly denies that justice = equality.
Connection with practical problem: can one treat the πόλις [city] as an equal?

[**p. 37**] 44e1–45a3: The second reason (taken for fear of bad reputation with the many) is disposed of. C. takes now up a third reason which is implied in the second reason: the spending of money: maybe, S. does not wish C. to ruin himself financially; S., the friend, takes care of C. who wants to take care of S. The loss of his fortune would be a greater blow to C. than the loss of his life would be to S. An example of what justice[R] means.

45a4–5: Setting[R]. S. admits that the welfare of his friends is an important consideration preventing him from fleeing. Justice[R]. Is then his justice in this case loyalty to his friends and nothing else? But, he adds, καὶ ἄλλα πολλά [and many others] determine his choice. However this may be, this passage makes it quite clear that S. does not doubt that the many may do considerable harm, and that this is an important consideration for a sensible man in making his plans.

45a6–c4: Setting[R]. C. makes it clear that he and the others do not incur any danger; especially that he himself does not have to pay a cent. S. should not worry about his friends, not especially about Crito, nor more particularly about C.'s money. Ambiguous: the ξένοι [strangers] who give the money, are less in danger from the sycophants (Burnet). We have to see whether S. shows any signs of having been convinced by this argument (viz., that his friends will not incur any danger).

45c5: It is here that C.'s serious, positive argument starts. The argument taken for "the bad reputation with the many" has been disposed of. The argument taken for the danger or safety of the friends has been disposed of: there would be no inconvenience if S. fled. But why should he flee? Now C. says that it is S.'s duty to flee—that his staying will be cowardice.

45c5–8: a) S. will desert himself

45c8–d6: b) S. will desert his sons

} no word about S.'s deserting the city. C.'s justice[R]

45d6–46a4: c) the principle: one should do the right thing, fearing bad reputation. Justice[R]. Change from previous statement (44b9–c3): the bad reputation feared is not merely that of miserliness, but also of ἀνανδρία [lack of courage]. [P]Also: transition from S.'s ἀνανδρία [lack of courage] to C.'s ἀνανδρία [lack of courage]: the motive of C. is his concern with his own reputation.[P]

Is C.'s concern with bad reputation with the gentlemen? Is this the reason why he does not care for the democratic city? [P]and hence for the city?[P]

46a5–6: C. does not believe in the dream (Burnet). C.'s impiety[R] **[p. 38]**

46b1–6: Here, S.'s βουλεύειν [advising] (46a4–5). The βουλεύειν [advising] not [to] be guided exclusively by λόγος [account/argument]—by that λόγος [account/argument] which comes to sight to him as the test which he λογίζεται [reasons]. No other man, no assent by another is needed. Contrast the ἡμᾶς [us] in b3 with the ἐγὼ [I] in b4 and the μοι [to me] in b5. Yet: he follows nothing of his things but his λόγος [account/argument]—the δαιμόνιον [daimonion]? but also the λόγος [argument] itself is determined by things which are not S.'s own: the truth. This applies, not only to the present case, but to S.'s whole life: his own λογίζεσθαι [reasoning] supplies him with his standard.

46b6–c1: Again, he does not refer to the result of his conversations, but to the λόγοι which he "said." He speaks now of λόγοι [accounts/arguments]: there is no example of a new λόγος [account/argument], as a result of a new λογισμός [reasoning]. He sees no reason to deviate from his previous λόγοι [accounts/arguments]: there will be no βουλή [piece of advice]. The present τύχη [chance] is no reason whatever to jettison the previous λόγοι [arguments]. But must not our action take into considerations new circumstances? S. does not deny that occurrences of τύχαι [chances] may modify the λόγος [account/argument]: σχεδόν τι [just about]—e.g., war. But: εὐδαιμονία [happiness] cannot be made dependent on τύχη [chance], or else εὐδαιμονία [happiness] will be impossible.

46c2–6: More precisely, the τύχη [chance] is now replaced by the power of the multitude: ἐπιπέμπουσα = Divine visitations (Burnet). The power of the multitude and its effect is no reason for jettisoning the earlier λόγοι [accounts/arguments]: if S.'s earlier λογισμός [reasoning] had not taken this fact into consideration, it would have been the λογισμός [reasoning] of a fool.—Still, S. suggests, maybe there is a new point other than the effect of the power of the multitude which we have not considered before: these new points ought to be discussed.

46c4–6: cf. *Euthyphron* 2c7–8: the grown-ups are frightened by the πόλις [city] just as children by their mother → we must not be frightened by the πόλις [city].

46c6–e1: S. turns now to the opinions of the multitude (≠ their power): not all opinions of the multitude are authoritative: some opinions of the multitude are. The authoritative part of general opinions must be presumed to have been integrated into S.'s λόγος [account/argument] so as to take care of the present τύχη [chance].

46d3–4: S.'s reputation is at stake: shall he compromise his whole life by a rash and foolish action now?

46e2: What opinions of the multitude? The opinions about the gods.

47a1: S. accepts Crito's human messenger: he does not take seriously his dream.

47a2–5: Only the opinions of some men have to be considered. The opinions of the Athenians, e.g.? And if the opinion of the wise is not also the opinion of the unwise as to how far the opinion of the many has to be considered?

This criterion is both ἱκανόν [sufficent] and καλόν [noble] (cf. the καλῶς in 46e2).

47a7: The opinions to be considered are the useful or good ones (≠ ἀληθεῖς [the true ones]).

47b1: καὶ τοῦτο πράττων [and doing this] and who makes this his business ≠ who does it παιδιά [in play]. [**p. 39**]

47b9–11: One has to consider the opinions, i.e. the praise and blame, of the expert rather than the opinions, i.e. the praise and blame, of all others, and therefore one has to follow the prescriptions of the expert. No complete disregard of the opinions of the many.

"To drink": one has to drink hemlock on the advice of the expert.

47c1–3: Why must one obey the expert? Not because one fears his praise and blame, but because one is concerned with one's own, substantial good.

47d1–3: Is there an expert regarding δίκαια [just things] etc.? S. always denied that he is an expert. To what can we possibly turn in the absence of experts? To "certain" opinions of the multitude. But to which? Which opinions of the multitude have to be selected? Practically: these which have become laws. But why? No knowledge of δίκαια [just things] → quest for such knowledge = philosophy → philosophy needs πόλις [city] and πόλις [city] needs laws.

a) obedience to law in general; b) obedience to law in the present case.

47d4–6: And later: ψυχή [soul] is not mentioned. cf. 48a3 with 51a9: ψυχή [soul] is replaced by πατρίς [fatherland].

47d7–48a4: If there is something which makes the soul sick, it must be avoided; and if one has contracted a sickness of the soul, by following the opinion of the many, it is preferable to die. We do not know what justice is; but we do know that it is absurd to say that mere life is the highest good: no one can help admiring certain dead people more than quite a few living people.

<48a5–d7: Exclusive consideration of justice—but do we know what justice is?>

48a5–10: As a substitute for the summary—we have to follow, not all opinions, but the useful ones; we have to follow the opinions, not of all men, but of some: of the sensible. → we have to follow the opinions of the expert in the interest of our well-being; we have to follow the opinions of the expert in justice in the interest of our well-being (our soul). But is there such an expert? Can there be such an expert, as long as there is no knowledge of the soul?

48a10–11: In the absence of such an expert, is it now wise to bow to the opinion which rules, out of simple fear of death?

48b3–7: It is absurd to be guided by consideration of fear of death. This would be reasonable only if we knew that death is the greatest evil. Hence, life would be the greatest good. But do we admire people for the mere fact that they are alive? Do we not admire certain dead men more than all men alive?

48b8–10: No proof of it is given here. It was the basis of C.'s argument by which he tries to prove that S. should escape.

48b11–d4: Consideration solely from the point of view of justice. [**p. 40**]

48c3: Yet may it not be a man's duty to take care of his children? What is meant here by justice, does not imply this duty.

48d8–e5: S. makes C. the judge of what would be just for S. to do. It is indeed irrelevant whether the Athenians, οἱ πολλοί [the many], object to his escape or not; just as it is irrelevant whether these utter laymen prescribe a certain drink or not. C.'s consent however is crucial—why? He is the expert on justice.

48e5: ἀρχή [τῆς] σκέψεως [principle of inquiry] = ἀρχὴ τῆς βουλῆς [principle of advice] (cf. 49d6–7)—yet ἀρχή [principle] (only τὸ δίκαιον [the just]) has been laid down before (48b11–d5)—we have to look out for the differences. 49a4ff. is a repetition of the preceding passage.

49a4–b6: Ἀδικία [injustice] first= bad condition of the soul, mental perturbation or sickness. Now: ἀδικεῖν [to do injustice]. Let us assume that ἀδικεῖν [to do injustice] = deceiving, and ἀδικεῖν τρόπῳ τινὶ [to do injustice in a certain manner] = deceiving for the benefit of the deceived (3 questions: the central one!). Ἀδικεῖν is primarily a legal concept: what is its connection with ἀδικία [injustice] = ill health of the soul.

Since death is not the greatest evil, and the good condition of the soul is [a] much greater good than the good condition of the body, ἀδικεῖσθαι [to suffer injustice] is a lesser evil than ἀδικεῖν [to do injustice].

49c7–8: ἀδικεῖν = κακῶς ποιεῖν ἀνθρώπους [to do something bad to human beings]. What has disorder of the soul in common with hurting others? All "aggressiveness" proceeds from weakness of the soul. Note that S. does not say: δικαιοπράττειν [doing justice] = εὐεργετείν [to do good].

49c10–d2: The problem of war, and hence of the πόλις [city]. Yet: the just war = correction of the unjust enemy. But: the πόλις [city] = οἱ πολλοί [the many]. Or are there other rules regarding πόλις [city] and the individual? Ultimately no; but need for a compromise between what the πόλις [city] would actually accept and what is simply just (cf. *Rep.* on war: Socrates ≠ Glaucon).

49d2–3: The emphasis on δόξα [opinion]: the expert on justice is one who accepts a specific δόξα [opinion] regarding justice. But why is this δόξα [opinion] preferable to the opposite one? Ultimately, because it is the only one consistent with φιλοσοφεῖν [philosophizing].

49e6–8: It is not S. who gives this answer. The implication of the fact that this is a second question: ἐξαπατᾶν [deception] is not simply ἀδικεῖν [to do wrong].

49e9–50a1: Not C. must be persuaded, but the πόλις [city]?

50a7–8: The appearance of the Νόμοι [Laws]—cf. the appearance of Ἀρετή [Virtue] in S.'s dream. Ἐπιστάντες [coming upon] used of dreams, visions. <Homer> **[p. 41]**

50a8–b8: The argument: one must do nothing which by implication ruins the whole city—nay, which supplies a precedent for the ruining of any city. For by doing such a thing, one hurts other human beings, and especially the philosophers (= one's friends). But this reason is not used: why? It would not bring out the superiority of the city to Socrates. Why should that superiority be asserted? Because the argument leading up to "absolute obedience to the laws" is not simply true. What should be said if a given πόλις [city] makes impossible the life of the philosopher, perhaps of a young philosopher? What about a law which would impose the duty to commit unjust acts? All questions of this kind are evaded by the assertion of the superiority of the πόλις [city] to S., or by the substitution of inequality [P](πατρίς [fatherland]) for equality (other human beings). In truth, S. (the philosopher) is superior to the πόλις [city] (οἱ πολλοί [the many])—the πόλις [city] is ἀναγκαῖον [necessary] for philosophy: for this reason, is the philosopher concerned with its preservation.[P]

[V]Summary: One must follow the expert regarding the soul; only he can say what is truly just—but is there such an expert? If not, there is no criterion independent of custom. But: why should one follow custom, and not one's desires? The authority of custom needs a non-customary legitimation.

S. is not an expert—he seeks for justice = philosopher. S. knows that he knows nothing: he knows that he knows nothing. He knows what is implied in quest for truth. Quest for truth is most important → the soul is higher than the body (confirmed by absurdity of opposite view). Quest for truth → indifference to bodily goods → no motive for hurting others = for being unjust. Moreover: quest for truth → society → beliefs required for society = justice. Moreover: fundamental difference between non-philosopher and philosopher → justice ≠ equality.
Crito: one must not hurt anyone under any circumstances—one may hurt the πόλις [city] if one is hurt by the πόλις [city] first—contradiction—or: does he not think that πόλις [city] are ἄνθρωποι [human beings]? The cause of his confusion: what does hurting mean? 44d4 → the greatest evil is death, all men are equally killable → justice is equality → tit for tat
S. does not point out the self-contradiction of Crito—why? Dialogue—also: S. does not mention ψυχή [soul] (just as C. does not mention πόλις [city])—C. speaks of ἐπιτήδειοι [the fitting ones] (≠ φίλοι [friends]). S. truly treats C. as an expert in justice.
How does it come that C. can be convinced by S.'s personification of the Νόμοι [Laws]? Justice = equality—the democratic view—but the πόλις [city] is radically democratic (Callicles; Ar.'s *Politics*) → no criticism of the πόλις [city]—C. radically a political man.
Also: C.'s property—rests on law—[V]

50c1–51c5: No reference to the principle that one must not ἀνταδικεῖν [treat unjustly in return] in any case: the principle is limited now to ἀνταδικεῖν [treat unjustly in return] a superior.

51d5–e1: Two questions: only the last is answered → the problem of the *Rep.*: positive duty of the philosopher to the πόλις [city] (τὰ πολιτικά πράττειν [doing the political things]) only in the case of the πόλις [city] which cares for philosopher.

51e4–5: The νόμοι [laws] generated, not only S., but all his ancestors: they generated the whole "tribe" of Athenians: the νόμοι [laws] replace φύσις [nature].

51e4–8: The citizen is compared to a slave: the compulsory character of obedience to the laws.

51c9–d1:—cf. 44d6–10: the many are not capable of producing the greatest good.

51d1–e1: cf. ad 50e4–8: As far as the laws rest on mere compulsion, they would not lay claim to obedience. What about the parents? Are they not imposed on man without his assent? Besides, if no πόλις [city] is fully just, is there actually freedom to emigrate?

52a1–2: The mildness of the νόμοι [laws]. It leaves everyone the alternative either to emigrate, or to persuade or to obey. ^VDid S. ever try to persuade the city that a given law was not just?^V

52a4–8: S.'s decision was taken long before the present conversation. The shame of contradicting oneself merely out of fear: 53a7.

52d2–3: The only reason why S. is obliged to obey the laws is συνθήκη [contract]: there is no natural superiority of the laws and of the πόλις [city], but absolute obedience to the laws is the price which has to be paid for the existence [**p. 42**] of πόλεις [cities].
Only true agreement is binding → contrat social—Rousseau's formulation → the problem of the goodness of laws not soluble that way.

52e1–2: Mere ἀνάγκη [necessity] would not bring about duty/obedience: application to slavery.

52e2–3: A younger philosopher would be in a different position.

52e5–6: Allusion to S.'s μέμψεσθαι [blaming] the Athenian laws without πείθειν [obeying] them (52b7–8). cf. *Apo. Soc.* 37a8ff., *Rep.* 538c5ff.

53a8ff.: Here the argument taken, not from δίκαιον [just], but from ἀγαθὸν [good]. Silent admission of the power of the πολλοί [many] to inflict κακά [bad things].

53b–c: The alternative is: εὐνομοῦνται πόλεις [city with good laws] in the neighborhood or anarchic societies far off—what about εὐνομοῦνται πόλεις [cities] far off? → the setting of the *Laws*: the Athenian Stranger legislates for a new πόλις [city] in which S. could not be condemned to death for impiety.

53e2: λυπεῖν [inflict pain] ≠ κακουργεῖν [do evil].

**Notes**

1. the popular → E.'s
2. murdered → victim
3. After the dash, Strauss had written, but then crossed out: "in the latter case, even more, on account of the sharing of μίασμα."
4. by speech → in thought
5. Harold Cherniss, *The Riddle of the Early Academy* (Chicago: University of California Press, 1945). Strauss's abbreviation "p. m." is short for "penes me" (in my possession).
6. Cf. Kant, *Kritik der praktischen Vernunft*, AA V, 28:

> Es kommt auf diese Art eine Harmonie heraus, die derjenigen ähnlich ist, welche ein gewisses Spottgedicht auf die Seeleneintracht zweier

> sich zu Grunde richtenden Eheleute schildert: O wundervolle Harmonie, was er will, will auch sie etc., oder was von der Anheischigmachung König Franz des Ersten gegen Kaiser Karl den Fünften erzählt wird: was mein Bruder Karl haben will (Mailand), das will ich auch haben. (In this way a harmony may result resembling that depicted in a certain satirical poem as existing between a married couple bent on going to ruin: Oh, wonderful harmony, what he wants is what she wants etc., or like the pledge which is said to have been given by Francis I [of France] to the Emperor Charles V: what my brother Charles wants [Milan], that I want too.)

7. Étienne Gilson: *La Philosophie au Moyen Âge*, vol. 2: *Du XIIIe siècle à la fin du XIVe siècle* (Paris: Payot, 1944, second edition), 652:

> La haine de Dieu, le vol et l'adultère sont mauvais en raison du précepte divin qui les interdit, mais ç'auraient été des actes méritoires si la loi de Dieu nous les avait prescrits. Il va sans dire enfin que Dieu n'a pas de mérites en soi à récompenser chez l'homme, ni de fautes en soi à punir; il peut donc perdre les innocents et sauver les coupables; il n'y a rien de tout cela qui ne dépende de sa simple volonté. On pourrait suivre Ockham plus loin encore et montrer avec lui que Dieu aurait aussi bien pu se faire âne que se faire homme, ou revêtir la nature du bois et de la pierre. A partir du moment où nous supprimons radicalement les essences et les archétypes universels, il ne reste plus aucune barrière qui puisse contenir l'arbitraire du pouvoir divin. (The hatred of God, theft, and adultery are bad because of the divine precept which forbids them, but they would have been meritorious acts if the law of God had prescribed them to us. Furthermore, it goes without saying that God has no merits that he can reward as such in man, nor offences as such that he can punish [in man]; he can therefore condemn the innocent and save the guilty; in these, there is nothing which does not depend on his will alone. We could follow Ockham still further and show with him that God could just as easily have become an ass as he became man, or take on the nature of wood and stone. From the moment we radically remove the essences and universal archetypes, there is no barrier left that can contain the arbitrariness of divine power.)

Gilson's account is based on Ockham's *Commentary on the Sentences of Peter Lombard* (William of Ockham, *Opera philosophica et theologica*, vol. 2/2 [1970], II, qu. 19 O and qu. 5 H).

8. lead → love

9. There is a conflict in the manuscript tradition of the Greek text for 14c3–4. Some have "the lover must follow the loved one," others "the questioner must follow the questioned." The former is the reading adopted by Burnet.

10. rightly → consistently

CHAPTER 2

# Strauss's Lecture "On Plato's *Euthyphron*" (1952)

The subject matter of the *Euthyphron* is piety. For more than one reason the *Euthyphron* does not tell us what Plato thought about piety. It certainly does not transmit to us Plato's final or complete view of piety. Still the work transmits to us an important part of Plato's analysis of piety. Thus, by studying the *Euthyphron* we shall not learn more than part of the truth, as Plato saw it, a partial truth, which is necessarily also a partial untruth. Yet we can be certain that we shall never find the truth about piety as Plato saw it except after having understood and digested the half-truth that is presented to us not so much in the *Euthyphron* as through the *Euthyphron*. The half-truth presented to us through the *Euthyphron* does not belong to the common type of half-truth. The most common type of half-truth tells us the commonly-accepted opinions. The half-truth presented through the *Euthyphron* is not a generally-accepted half-truth. It is unpopular. Since it is unpopular it is irritating. An irritating half-truth is in one respect superior to the popular half-truth. In order to arrive at the irritating half-truth we must make some effort. We must think. Now it is most unsatisfactory if we are first forced to think and then receive no other reward than an irritating provisional result. Plato gives us two kinds of comfort: first, thinking itself may be said to be the most satisfying activity regardless of the character of the result. Secondly, if we should believe that the result is more important than the way to the result, Plato's moral character is the guarantee that the final result, or what he regarded as the complete account of piety, would be absolutely satisfactory and in no way irritating.

The *Euthyphron* is a conversation between Euthyphron and Socrates about piety. Three definitions of piety are suggested and all three of them prove to be insufficient. Having arrived at the end of the dialogue, we are perplexed with regard to piety. We do not know what piety is. But does not everyone know what piety is? Piety consists in worshipping the ancestral gods, but according to ancestral custom. This may be true, but piety is supposed to be a virtue. It is supposed to be good. But is it truly good? Is worshipping ancestral gods according to ancestral custom good? The *Euthyphron* does not give us an answer. It would be more accurate to say that the discussion presented in the *Euthyphron* does not give us an answer. But the discussion presented in any Platonic dialogue is only part of the dialogue. The discussion, the speech, the *logos*, is one part; the other part is the *ergon*, the deeds, the action, what is happening in the dialogue, what the characters do or suffer in the dialogue. The *logos* may end in silence and the action may reveal what the speech conceals. The conversation between Socrates and Euthyphron takes place after Socrates has been accused of impiety. The dialogue abounds with references to this fact, this action. It forces us, therefore, to wonder, Was Socrates pious? Did Socrates worship the ancestral gods according to ancestral custom? The *Euthyphron* then gives us a two-fold presentation of piety. First, a discussion of what piety is. Secondly, a presentation of the problem of Socrates's piety. These two subjects seem to belong to two entirely different orders. The question of what piety is is philosophical. The question of whether Socrates was pious seems to belong to the realm of gossip, rather than to that of philosophy. Yet while this is true in a sense, it misses the decisive point. For the philosophic question is whether piety in the sense defined is a virtue. But the man who has all the virtues to the degree to which a human being is capable of having all the virtues is the philosopher. Therefore if the philosopher is pious, piety is a virtue. But Socrates is a representative of philosophy. Hence, if Socrates is pious, piety is a virtue. And if he is not pious, piety is not a virtue. Therefore, by answering the gossip question of whether Socrates was pious, we answer the philosophic question regarding the essence of piety. Then let us see whether we can learn anything from the *Euthyphron* regarding Socrates's piety.

Socrates is accused of impiety, he is suspect of impiety. Now Euthyphron, who is a soothsayer, is an expert in piety, and he is convinced that

Socrates is innocent. Euthyphron vouches for Socrates's piety. But Euthyphron does not know what piety is. Still if we assume that piety consists in worshipping the ancestral gods according to ancestral custom, everyone could see whether Socrates was pious, whether Socrates did or did not worship the ancestral gods according to ancestral custom. Euthyphron, in spite of his philosophic incompetence, could be a good witness as regards the decisive fact. But the truth is that Euthyphron is not likely to pay much attention to what human beings do. Above all, Euthyphron's own piety is, to say the least, open to suspicion. Therefore, let us dismiss Euthyphron's testimony and see what we ourselves can observe.

We hear from Socrates's own mouth that, both prior to his accusation and after it, he regarded it as important to know the divine things. Apparently in consequence of his quest for knowledge about the divine things, the accuser thought that Socrates was an innovator, that is to say, a producer of error. The accuser naturally thought that he himself knew the truth. He charged Socrates in fact with ignorance of the truth about the divine things. The charge presupposed that Socrates's alleged or real ignorance was careless, but that ignorance could not be criminal except if truth about the divine things was easily accessible to every Athenian citizen. This would indeed be the case if the truth about the divine things were handed down to everyone by ancestral custom. Was Socrates criminally ignorant of the divine things? He seems to grant that he is ignorant of the divine things. But he seems to excuse his ignorance by the difficulty of the subject matter. His ignorance is involuntary, and therefore not criminal. Now if Socrates was ignorant of the divine things, he did not believe in what tradition or ancestral custom told him, as well as everyone else, about the divine things. He did not regard these tales as knowledge. As a matter of fact, he suggests that one ought not to assent to any assertion of any consequence before having examined it. He makes it rather clear that the ancestral reports about the ancestral gods are not more than bare assertions. If Socrates was really ignorant, radically ignorant, he does not even know whether the ancestral gods exist. How then could he worship the ancestral gods according to ancestral custom? If Socrates was really ignorant, and knew that he was really ignorant, he could not possibly be pious. Of course, he could still go through the motions of worship, he could outwardly conform. But this conformity would no longer be pious, for how can a sensible man worship beings whose very existence is doubtful? Socrates's outward conformity would not have been due to any fear of the gods but only to being ashamed of what human beings might think of nonconformance, or to the fear of bad reputation. Fear of bad reputation is fear of reputation for badness. People who did not believe in the ancestral gods were thought to be simply bad men, men capable of every kind of wickedness, and this stigma attached especially to philosophers. In the circumstances, Socrates would seem to have been forced to conform outwardly, if not for his own sake, at any rate for the sake of philosophy. Still, if Socrates conformed outwardly, how could people know that he was not pious? They could know it from what he said. But did Socrates say everything he thought to every human being? He himself feared that he was believed to say profusely everything he knew to every real man out of philanthropy, and to say it not only without receiving pay, but even gladly paying money himself, if he had any, provided people would only listen to him. We have the impression that what the Athenians really resented was not so much his cleverness, or the deviationist character of his thought, as his alleged missionary zeal. His real crime, the crime that killed him, was then not so much his impiety as his apparent philanthropy, or what is called in the charge, his corrupting the young.

Hitherto, we have taken at its face value what Socrates said in regard to his ignorance with regard to the divine things. But if we look again into the *Euthyphron,* we find that Socrates is in fact not altogether ignorant in this respect. Towards the end of the conversation, he says that all good things which he has have been given by the gods. Earlier in the conversation he indicates that he loathes the current stories about the gods committing unjust actions or their having dissensions and fights with each other, and that he does not believe that these tales are true. He seems to believe to know that the gods are good and just and, therefore, both the givers of all good things and only of good things to man and incapable of fighting with each other. But precisely this knowledge would make him impious, for the current tales about the gods which he rejected were not merely the invention of good painters and not so good poets. It is much more important that they supplied the rationale of important elements of the ancestral worship. The fact that he did not accept the current tales about the fights of the gods would explain why he was accused of impiety. He himself suggests this explanation. But did he profusely say to every real man that these tales are untrue? Was he guilty of excessive philanthropy?

In his conversation with Euthyphron he does nothing of the kind. He does not go beyond indicating an unbelief in regard to these tales, or his being displeased with these tales. He says that he accepts the tales with some feeling of annoyance. In addition he did not seek the conversation with Euthyphron. He did not approach Euthyphron with the intention of enlightening him. On the contrary, the conversation is forced upon him by Euthyphron. Without Euthyphron's initiative, Euthyphron might never have heard that one could or should doubt the current tales about the gods. Socrates does not show a trace of missionary zeal.

To this, one might make the following objection. In the second book of the *Republic*, Socrates develops his theology at great length. But, in the first place, the characters with whom Socrates talks in the *Republic* and even the audience which is present are a select group. Euthyphron does not belong to the same type of man. He belongs firstly to the majority of Athenians who condemned Socrates to death. And, secondly, in the *Republic* Socrates does not explicitly mention, as he does in the parallel in the *Euthyphron*, the fact that the wrong notions of the gods were, as it were, embodied in the official cult of the city of Athens. The outspoken criticism of the *Republic* is directed against the poets who were private men and not against ancestral custom. I draw this provisional conclusion. Socrates was indeed impious in the sense of the charge. But he was not guilty of that excessive philanthropy of which he feared he might be thought to be guilty. I have said the conversation with Euthyphron was forced upon Socrates. Certainly Socrates did not seek that conversation. The reference to Socrates's favorite haunts at the beginning of the dialogue is most revealing. That reference reminds us of the opening of the *Charmides* and the *Lysis* where Socrates himself describes how gladly he sought those places where he could converse with the young. Socrates does not gladly talk to Euthyphron. He talks to him because he cannot help it, out of duty, or because he thought it was just to do so. This conversation was an act of justice. Socrates shows by deed that he is just. Here the deed bears out the implicit testimony of Euthyphron. Whereas Socrates's piety remains, to say the least, doubtful, his justice becomes perfectly evident. But what is justice? According to the *Euthyphron*, justice, in the strict sense, seems to be identical with skillfully tending human beings. By virtue of such skillful tending, herding, human beings are benefited or become better. Whatever may have been the success of Socrates's skillfully tending Euthyphron, he is certainly trying hard to make Euthyphron better by showing him, who believes to be extremely wise, that he is extremely stupid. Or by trying to make him somewhat reasonable, in acting justly, by trying to make people better, Socrates believes to act prudently. For every sane man would want to live among good and hence helpful persons, rather than among bad and hence harmful people. But just as a man who tries to appease vicious dogs might be bitten by them, or just as a father who takes away from a child harmful toys might provoke the child's anger, Socrates, in trying to better people, might have provoked their resentment, and thus have come to grief. Was it then prudent of him even to attempt to better the Athenians? In spite of this difficulty, Socrates's attempt was rewarding to him and to his friends, and ultimately even to us. For in talking to people, however silly, he was learning, he was studying human nature. Without this study the Platonic dialogues could never have been written.

But let us come back to the main issue, Socrates's impiety. Socrates was impious because he knew, or believed to know, that the ancestral reports about the ancestral gods which were underlying ancestral custom are wrong. This knowledge is perfectly compatible with the possibility that Socrates was ignorant in regard to the divine things. He may have had sufficient knowledge of the divine things to know that the current tales about the gods are untrue, and therefore that the worship of the ancestral gods according to ancestral custom is not good or, if you wish, that to worship the ancestral gods according to ancestral custom is not true piety. But he may not have had sufficient knowledge of the divine things in order to know what true piety positively is. In that case, he could not know whether he was truly pious or not. And assuming that other men are not likely to be wiser than Socrates, no man could know whether Socrates was pious or not. In that case one could say no more than he ought not to have been punished for impiety. I personally believe that this would have been a wise decision. It is just possible that this is the most obvious message of the *Euthyphron*: that it would be wonderful if the crime of impiety could be wiped off the statute books. But from Plato's point of view that message could not express more than a pious wish, a wish that cannot be fulfilled.

Let us now turn to a somewhat more exact analysis of the *Euthyphron*. Let us first try to establish the place of the *Euthyphron* within the cosmos of the Platonic dialogues. The *Euthyphron* deals with piety, i.e., with one particular virtue. It belongs therefore together with the *Laches* which deals with courage, the *Charmides* which deals with moderation, and with the *Republic* which deals with justice. Now there are four cardinal virtues—courage, moderation, justice, and wisdom. There is no Platonic dialogue devoted to wisdom, which, I add, is only true if you assume that the *Theages* is spurious, because the *Theages* is devoted to wisdom. Instead we have a Platonic dialogue on piety. Is then wisdom to be replaced by piety? The dialogue in which the four cardinal virtues are set forth most clearly is the *Republic*. In the *Republic* Socrates seems rather to replace piety by wisdom. When speaking of the nature of the philosopher, i.e., on the most exalted level of the discussion of morality in the *Republic*, Socrates does not even mention piety. In spite or because of this, there is no Platonic dialogue devoted to wisdom. Yet wisdom is a kind of science, and there is a dialogue devoted to science, the *Theaetetus*. Now the *Euthyphron* and the *Theaetetus* belong together, not merely because they deal with particular virtues, but also because they are contemporaneous: the two conversations take place about the same time, after the accusation and before the condemnation. They belong to the end of Socrates's life. Accordingly, they contain explicit references by Socrates to his father and his mother or, more precisely, to the skill of his father and the skill of his mother or, still more precisely, to the skill of his ancestor on his father's side and to the skill of his mother. He compares his own skill to the skill of his mother. He denies that his own skill has any kinship with the skill of his ancestor on his father's side, with the skill of Daedalus. The relation of his own skill to the ancestral, to the paternal, remains doubtful. His attitude toward the ancestral or paternal remains doubtful.

The *Euthyphron* deals with piety and it leaves open the question of what piety is. The *Theaetetus* deals with science and it culminates therefore in a description of the philosophic life. That description in its turn culminates in the thesis that one must try to flee from here thither as quickly as possible, but that flight is assimilation to god as far as it is possible. And that assimilation consists in becoming just and pious together with prudence. Here in this most solemn and central passage, almost literally central, the question of whether piety is a virtue is answered in the affirmative. Yet this passage is not altogether free from ambiguity as would appear from a consideration of the context. One cannot settle any Platonic question of any consequence by simply quoting Plato. This much about the place of the *Euthyphron* within the cosmos of the Platonic dialogues. Let us now turn to the setting.

The aged Socrates is accused of impiety by young Meletus. Euthyphron takes Socrates's side over against Meletus. But Euthyphron, the young Euthyphron, has accused his own aged father of impiety. Euthyphron's action parallels Meletus's action, the young man accusing the aged one.

Euthyphron occupies a middle position between Socrates and Meletus. What kind of a man is he? What kind of man is he who is the only interlocutor in Plato's only dialogue dealing with piety? Euthyphron is well-disposed towards Socrates and he is a boaster. He is a harmless boaster. There is a connection between his boasting and his harmlessness. What makes him side with Socrates? Socrates has a power of divination, the demonic thing that happened to him. And Euthyphron is a professional diviner. Both Euthyphron and Socrates are different. Both have superior gifts. And superior gifts of the same kind. On account of this superiority they are envied by the many. Euthyphron believes that he and Socrates are in the same boat. Euthyphron is a diviner. He boasts that he has superior knowledge of divine things. Because he has such knowledge he can predict the future in an infallible manner. Yet the people will laugh at him as at a madman. They do not take him seriously. They regard him as harmless. But he is so certain of his superiority that such ridicule does not affect him. He is proud to appear to be mad. For he knows somehow that the divine is bound to appear as madness to those who have at best only human wisdom. He speaks of himself and the gods in the same breath. He draws a line between himself and human beings. He is certain that only an expert in the divine things, a man like him, can be pious. By implication he denies the ordinary citizens the possibility of being pious. He has a great contempt for the many. He keeps the most marvelous part of his knowledge for himself, or for an elite. He conceals his wisdom. He does not conceal, however, his claim to wisdom. Therefore, he is sometimes driven to reveal his wisdom too. One does not know whether he conceals his wisdom voluntarily or because it does not find any takers. Being versed in the divine things, he despises the human things; hence he knows next to nothing of human things. He seems to believe that all conflicts are conflicts about principles, about values. He doesn't seem to be aware that most conflicts presuppose agreement as to principles, that most conflicts arise from the fact that different men regard the same thing as good, and want to have it each for himself. He seems to believe that men who are accused of a crime defend themselves by denying the principle that criminals ought to be punished instead of denying the fact that they committed the crime. Euthyphron is harmless, within the limits of his knowledge of divine things. If this knowledge should force him to harm human beings, he will not for a moment hesitate to do so. He would not hesitate for a moment to accuse them of impiety even if they are his father or mother, his brother or sister, his children, his wife or his friends. In striking contrast to Socrates who would not accuse anyone of anything. At the beginning of the conversation, Euthyphron believes that he is in the same boat as Socrates. Socrates draws his attention to the fact that whereas Euthyphron is ridiculed on account of his superior gift, Socrates is persecuted on account of his. Socrates suggests, as an explanation of this difference, that Euthyphron conceals his wisdom and therefore is safe, whereas Socrates is thought to broadcast his wisdom and therefore is in danger. At this point there does not seem to be another difference between Socrates and Euthyphron than that Euthyphron is more reticent than Socrates. After Euthyphron had proudly told the surprised Socrates of his feat which consists in accusing his own father of impiety, and Socrates has indicated a doubt in regard to the wisdom of this act, Euthyphron might seem to become aware that he is wiser than Socrates. Whereupon Socrates suggests that he wishes to become a pupil of Euthyphron, who claims to know everything about the divine things, in order thus to bring about his acquittal of the charge of impiety. He suggests more particularly that he would like to use Euthyphron as a lightning protector against Meletus's bolts. He wishes to hide behind Euthyphron's back and his well-concealed wisdom. He draws Euthyphron's attention to the fact that by teaching Socrates Euthyphron is going to leave the sheltered position which Euthyphron enjoyed hitherto. All this does not make any impression on Euthyphron. All this does not make him realize that he is not in the same boat as Socrates, or that a gulf separates him from Socrates. He becomes aware of this gulf only after Socrates has indicated his doubt of the truth of the current tales about the gods. For after this he puts, however unwittingly, Socrates into the same category as the many. From that point on he knows that Socrates is not in the same boat as he. Yet he still apparently regards Socrates, in contradistinction to the many, as educable, i.e., as willing to listen to Euthyphron's wisdom. Socrates, however, disappoints his expectations. Very curiously, Socrates is chiefly interested in less worthy, less divine and, in fact, trivial subjects. He is much more interested in the definition of piety than in wondrous stories about what the gods did or what they demand of man. Socrates seems to have a desire for a kind of knowledge which Euthyphron does not regard very highly, which, however, he condescends to gratify. In the sequel it dawns upon Euthyphron that he might lose his lawsuit which, after all, he would have to win on earth before a human jury, before a jury consisting of the many; but Euthyphron pays too little attention to human things to be upset by that prospect. On the contrary, Socrates's strange familiarity with human things, and with the manner in which the low conduct their low affairs, has convinced Euthyphron that Socrates belongs with the many not only for the time being but altogether, that Socrates is not educable, that his unwillingness to listen to Euthyphron's wisdom is due to incapacity to understand that wisdom. Socrates, in a word, is a worldling. Somewhat later, Socrates succeeds in bringing it home to Euthyphron that he grossly contradicts himself. Although he knows that self-contradiction is a bad thing, and although he appeals to the principle of self-contradiction when arguing against others, Euthyphron is in no way perplexed by the weakness of his own speech. In fact, he would seem to have expected something like it. His self-contradiction merely proves to him that he cannot say or express to Socrates what he thinks, or has an awareness of. How indeed can one express experiences like those of which Euthyphron can boast to someone who has never tasted the divine things? Is one not bound to contradict oneself when trying to communicate the incommunicable? Still later, Euthyphron almost openly refuses to tell Socrates the true secrets regarding the divine things, although Socrates urges him to do so. He suggests that Socrates must rest satisfied with the simple verities which even the vulgar know sufficiently. Socrates's strange remark regarding these simple verities—they concern sacrifices and prayers—apparently reveals to Euthyphron an abyss of ignorance in Socrates. When Socrates asks Euthyphron shortly before the end of the conversation not to regard him as unworthy, he is quite serious to the extent that he is convinced that Euthyphron does regard him as unworthy. The conversation comes to an end because Euthyphron gives it up as hopeless, and he gives up the conversation as hopeless because he has learned in the course of the conversation that Socrates is a hopeless case. Euthyphron is immune to Socrates's conversational skill. He suffers as little change during the conversation as Socrates himself. He learns in his own way something about Socrates, just as Socrates learns in his way something about Euthyphron. This is all. In a sense, then, he is really in the same boat as Socrates. For the similarity which we have mentioned amounts to a fundamental similarity. Euthyphron is a caricature of Socrates. Just as Socrates, Euthyphron transcends the dimension of the ordinary arts and virtues. But whereas Socrates goes over from the ordinary arts and virtues to philosophy, Euthyphron goes over from them to a spurious kind of knowledge of the divine things. Euthyphron, as it were, replaces philosophy by a spurious kind of knowledge of the divine things. Although Euthyphron believes to be superior to both Meletus and Socrates, he in fact occupies a middle position, between Meletus and Socrates. We must now try to define that middle position.

Meletus accused Socrates of not believing in the gods in which the city believes. Meletus identifies himself with the belief of the city. Meletus calls Socrates before the tribunal of the city. Meletus identifies himself with what we may call the orthodox view. What the orthodox position is will become somewhat clearer after we have clarified Euthyphron's deviation. Euthyphron himself knows that he is different, that he deviates from what "the human beings" regard as pious. What does he understand by piety? In his first answer to Socrates's question as to what the pious is, he gives a formally defective answer. He gives an example instead of a definition. His second answer is formally adequate and so is his third and last answer. But neither the second nor the third answer expresses that view of piety which is underlying the formally defective first answer. Now only the first answer has a direct relation to Euthyphron's taste, to his action, to his accusation of his father. Only the first answer is a speech of Euthyphron in harmony with Euthyphron's deed, with his life, with the principle animating his life. It is therefore the only answer given by Euthyphron which throws a light on that view of piety which is characteristic of him. Plato has killed three birds by making Euthyphron express his true view of piety in a formally defective answer. In the first place, he thus characterizes Euthyphron as insufficiently trained. Furthermore, he thus lets us see that Euthyphron never made fully clear to himself the full meaning of his deviation from the orthodox or accepted view. And thirdly, he thus prevented a real discussion of the real issue: no solution to the problem of piety can be given in the circumstances, and no solution to the problem of piety shall be given lest the reader be prevented from seeking the solution for himself. What then would be a formally adequate expression of that view of piety which Euthyphron indicates in his first and formally defective answer? We shall say: piety consists in doing what the gods do. And we shall contrast this view with the orthodox view, according to which piety consists in doing what the gods tell us to do. For to worship the ancestral gods according to ancestral custom means, since the custom must ultimately be conceived of as divinely instituted, to do what the gods tell us to do. Euthyphron expresses his view of piety by deed, rather than by speech. Contrary to ancestral custom, he accuses his father of impiety. Yet piety is said to consist in worshipping the ancestral gods according to ancestral custom. His deed amounts to a denial of the accepted view. His deed expresses a view that piety consists in doing what the gods do. Euthyphron's view of piety is heretical. Or, to use a more up-to-date term, it is deviationist. This can be easily seen from the following considerations. According to the orthodox view, piety consists chiefly, not to say exclusively, in praying and sacrificing. But the gods do not pray and sacrifice. By imitating the gods or the actions of the gods, by doing what the gods do, one will not pray or sacrifice. The gods are not pious. By imitating the gods, one ceases to be pious. A more adequate formulation of Euthyphron's view would therefore be that what pleases the gods is if men do what the gods do, and therefore that what pleases the gods is something entirely different from the pious. But Euthyphron shrinks from admitting to himself this implication of his view. In his second answer, he identifies the pious with what is pleasing to the gods. Yet Socrates shows him that what he really means is that the pious and what is pleasing to the gods are altogether different things. It is true Socrates shows this to Euthyphron in a somewhat different manner than I just indicated, but we shall gradually see that Socrates's explicit argument is only the apparently simplified but in fact the immensely telescoped formulation of his implicit argument. Euthyphron holds then the view that piety consists in doing what the gods do. How does he know what the gods do? From what the human beings believe about the gods, from what the human beings agree upon in regard to the gods, from the current tales about the gods which he takes to be true. But those current tales also say that men ought not to do what the gods do, but rather what the gods tell men to do. Euthyphron's position is therefore untenable. The authority to which he appeals refutes him. He ought to return to orthodoxy.

But can one return to orthodoxy? Can one accept a position which is based on mere tales? Yet, if we abandon the tales, what can we say about the gods and about piety? Still we divine that the gods are superhuman beings, and therefore that the highest human type gives us an inkling of what the gods might be. But the highest human type is the wise man. The analogy of the wise man will therefore be the best clue at our disposal in regard to the gods. Now the wise man loves more the people who do what he does than those people who merely do what he tells them to do, and who do not do what he does. Accordingly, we may then be inclined to think, considering that we understand by gods superhuman beings, that the gods do not rule at all by telling people what they should do, or by issuing commands. However this may be, the analogy of the wise man, which is our only guide to knowledge of the gods or of what would please the gods—this analogy leads us to realize that Euthyphron's view of piety is a half-hearted attempt to transcend the orthodox view of piety in the direction of a higher view. Euthyphron does occupy a middle position between Meletus and Socrates. It is impossible to return to Meletus. We have no choice but to go forward to Socrates.

The direction of the road and even the end of the road is indicated by Euthyphron's half-way position and by the difficulty with which it is beset. Yet Euthyphron's view is superior to the orthodox view and Euthyphron knows it. His boasting is not altogether unfounded. Euthyphron transcends the orthodox view because he aspired to something higher than is visualized by the many. Yet he has no right to this observation. He really is a boaster. Euthyphron contradicts himself by saying that what pleases the gods is the pious, and by meaning that what pleases the gods is not the pious. To solve the contradiction, one must leave it at simply denying the identity of what pleases the gods and the pious. One must have the courage of holding the view that one cannot please the gods except by being impious in the sense in which the city understands impiety. Or, more precisely, one must have the courage to be impious in a certain manner. In what manner? Euthyphron had meant that it is pleasing to the gods if men do what the gods do. But the different gods do different and even opposite things. By pleasing one god one will displease the other. It is impossible to please the gods if the different gods are pleased by different things, if the different gods disagree with each other, if they fight with each other. Euthyphron admits this in a way. He is doing what the best and justest god, Zeus, does. He chooses the justest god out of the many gods for his model. But in order to make this choice, he must know justice. He must know what justice is. He must know the idea of justice. For the justest god is the god that imitates the idea of justice most perfectly. But if one knows the idea of justice, there is no reason why one must imitate the most perfect imitation of the idea of justice. Why not imitate the idea of justice itself? There is no reason for imitating any god. Imitating the gods, doing what the gods do because the gods do it, and hence piety, proves to be superfluous. We must go a step further and say there is no need for any gods. If we doubt the current tales about the gods, if we try to think for ourselves, we are led to the conclusion that what general opinion assigns to the gods actually belongs to the ideas. The ideas replace the gods. From here we can understand and judge Meletus's charge.

Meletus is right to this extent. Socrates really does not believe in the gods of the city. And he really introduces different beings. But Meletus is wrong in assuming that the different beings which Socrates introduces are gods or demonic things. In fact they are the ideas. If we want to speak of gods, we would have to say that the different gods which Socrates introduced are the ideas. One can also say that Meletus erred grossly in speaking of Socrates's introducing novel things. For the ideas, being prior to any beings which imitate the ideas, are prior to any gods. They are the first things, the oldest things. Following a clue given by Euthyphron, Socrates formulates Meletus's charge as follows: Socrates is accused of making gods (the Greek, *poiein*, "inventing"). Socrates's defense can be stated as follows. Socrates is the only one who recognizes as first things such beings as can in no sense be conceived of as having been made and as making other things. His view is the radically unpoetic view, poetic in the sense of "making." His accuser was a poet. If one were to deny that the first things are the ideas, one would be forced to say that the first things are the gods, and that the gods made the ideas. (Tenth Book of the *Republic.*) One would be forced to conceive of the first things as making or productive beings. The alternative suggested by the *Euthyphron* is so extreme that one would be very glad if it could be evaded. How can it be avoided? Let us return to the point where Euthyphron unwittingly left the right way.

Euthyphron had divined that doing what the gods do is superior to doing what the gods tell or command us to do. But he became perplexed when he realized that the different gods do different things, opposite things. He was forced to choose among the gods, and therefore he had to appeal to a principle of choice or preference. That principle proved to be the idea of justice, i.e., something which is superior to the gods. But is there no way of choosing among the conflicting gods without having recourse to the ideas, without undermining piety? Indeed there is. From the point of view of ancestral custom, the good is identical with the ancestral, with the old. The best gods will be therefore the oldest gods. In order to find out what the oldest god is, we do not have to refer to any ideas. We simply have to consult the records of the past. If we accept the current stories as such records, we learn that the oldest god is Uranos, the grandfather of Zeus. The only possible way of being pious, in the sense of doing what the gods do, the only way of being safely pious along Euthyphron's lines, is to do what Uranos did, or to imitate Uranos. But what did Uranos do? He hurt or damaged his children. He damaged the young. In Greek this is the same as he corrupted the young. That is to say, precisely by corrupting the young would Socrates be pious. Or the other way around, the pious Socrates chooses the only pious way, of picking the oldest god as his model, and therefore corrupts the young. Yet Uranos is not only a personal god, he is also heaven. And we know from other Platonic dialogues that virtue can be identified with imitating heaven. Meletus on the other hand, who accuses the aged Socrates, and more particularly Euthyphron, who tries to destroy his own aged father, imitate Zeus, a relatively young god. They are impious. In addition they are inconsistent, for Zeus did not respect the old gods. Hence not Meletus and Euthyphron who respect the old gods, but Socrates who does not respect the old gods, imitates Zeus. Socrates seems to be pious from every point of view, except that of simple orthodoxy.

One may say that these are jokes. These statements are certainly exposed to quite a few difficulties, one of them being that while Uranos may be said to be the oldest god, he certainly is not the oldest divinity. Certainly mother earth is older than Uranos. And Socrates would probably not admit that a man's virtue is incompatible with imitating a female god or a female being in general. Was not his own skill a woman's skill? Let us therefore repeat our question, whether we cannot avoid the alternative, either the ideas or the gods. In other words, why is it necessary to assert the primacy of the ideas? The *Euthyphron* suggests an alternative. Either the highest beings are fighting gods, or else the highest beings are ideas. If one denies the primacy of the ideas, one arrives at the belief in fighting gods. Why? Why do the gods fight? Ultimately, because they do not know. But knowledge, genuine knowledge, is the knowledge of the unchangeable, of the necessary, of intelligible necessity, of the ideas. That of which knowledge is knowledge, is prior. The ideas are prior to knowledge of the ideas. There cannot be knowledge if there is no primacy of the ideas. Therefore if one denies the primacy of the ideas, one denies the possibility of knowledge. If the ideas are not the primary beings, the primary beings or the first things cannot be knowing beings. Their action must be blind. They will collide, they will fight. In other words, if the primary beings are the gods, and not the ideas, whatever is good or just will be good or just because the gods love it, and for no other reason, for no intrinsic reason. The primary act is not knowledge or understanding but love without knowledge or understanding, i.e., blind desire. But is this alternative not overcome in monotheism? It is impossible to decide this question on the basis of the *Euthyphron,* in which I believe the singular "god" never occurs. Still the *Euthyphron* seems to suggest that even the oldest god must be conceived of as subject to the ideas. It is true if there is only one god, there is no difficulty in thinking that piety consists in imitating God. One must know that god is good or just or wise, i.e., that God complies with the rules of justice. If that rule were subject to God, or dependent on God, or made by God, if it could be changed by God, it could no longer serve as a standard. God must be thought to be subject to a necessity, an intelligible necessity, which He did not make. If we deny this, if we assume that God is above intelligible necessity, or not bound by intelligible necessity, He cannot know in the strict sense, for knowledge is knowledge of the intelligible and unalterable necessity. In that case, God's actions would be altogether arbitrary. Nothing would be impossible to Him. For example, He could create other gods, and the many gods, who of course cannot have knowledge, would fight.

If piety is superfluous, if the gods are superfluous, why then do almost all men believe that piety is necessary and that the gods are necessary? Why do men need gods? The answer to this question is suggested in the discussion of the third definition of piety. According to that definition, piety consists in tending the gods. More precisely, piety consists in a kind of tending of the gods which is similar to that which slaves practice towards their masters, in prostrating oneself and doing the master's bidding. Piety is a kind of serving. Socrates interprets it as follows. Piety is an art of serving, a serving art, a ministering art. As such, it necessarily serves a ruling or architectonic art. Piety presupposes then that the gods are practitioners of the ruling art. But every art is productive of something. What then does the gods' ruling art produce—while using human arts as its ministerial arts? Euthyphron merely answers, the gods produce many fine things. He refuses to explain to an uninitiated man like Socrates what these many fine things are. And there can be no doubt that the many fine things which Euthyphron has in mind would not have satisfied Socrates. But Socrates also says in the context that, by answering the question as to what the products of the gods' ruling art are, one would have reached an adequate understanding of piety. The examples which Socrates gives in the immediate context make it clear what he regards as the specific product of the art of the gods. Socrates uses as examples of the ministering art, generalship and farming. The fine things which men try to acquire and produce by generalship and farming are victory and good harvest. Yet generalship and farming are not enough for producing victory and good harvest. For these arts cannot guarantee the outcome, and the outcome is what, in these arts, is the only thing that matters. Whether the outcome of the use of generalship and of farming be good or bad depends upon chance. Chance is that which is in no way controllable by art or knowledge, or predictable by art or knowledge. But too much depends for man on chance to get resigned to the power of chance. Man makes the irrational attempt to control the uncontrollable, to control chance. Yet he knows that he cannot control chance. It is for this reason that he needs the gods. The gods are meant to do for him what he cannot do for himself. The gods are the engine by which man believes he can control chance. He serves the gods in order to be the employer of gods, or the lord of gods. Yet there is one particular art, the most architectonic of all human arts, whose outcome particularly depends on chance, and which absolutely requires gods or piety as its complement. This is the legislative art. The legislative art is concerned with the just, the noble, and the good, i.e., with objects regarding which genuine knowledge is much more difficult than regarding numbers, measures and weights, and which are therefore the natural domain of disagreement. The primary object of the legislative art is the just. And it is as a part of justice that piety is defined in the third and last definition. Piety is justice towards the gods, just as justice in the narrower sense is justice towards men. Justice towards men is good. We have already seen that. What is doubtful is the status of piety, or justice towards the gods. It would seem that the need for piety can best be understood from the deficiency or the limitation of the justice towards men. Now the most serious deficiency of justice towards men is that it does not have sufficient sanction in the eyes of irrational people. It is this sanction that is supplied by piety and by the gods. But in order to fulfill this function, piety must be in the service of justice in the narrower sense. Justice in the narrower sense is primarily law-abidingness, or obedience to the law. Piety therefore must be a part of justice in this sense, that it must be a part of obedience to law. But law is primarily ancestral custom. Therefore piety stands or falls by obedience to ancestral custom. It is here where Socrates agrees with orthodoxy over against the heretic, Euthyphron. Euthyphron disobeys ancestral custom by accusing his own father of impiety. Socrates shows Euthyphron *ad hominem* that he has no right to disobey ancestral custom. Now no wonder that he appears to Euthyphron as one of the people, as a vulgar man. We may say that both the orthodox and Socrates have common sense, whereas Euthyphron lacks common sense. By this I mean that a society is possible on both orthodox and Socratic principles, whereas society is not possible on Euthyphron's principles. For society is not possible if ancestral custom is not regarded as sacred as far as practice is concerned. It is for this reason that Plato insisted on the necessity of laws punishing impiety. Liberals like ourselves are tempted to argue against Plato on the basis of Plato's own testimony. Does not Plato show us that in the eyes of all men of common sense, of both the many and of Socrates, Euthyphron is a ridiculous being? And is not the ridiculous a harmless deficiency? Why then not tolerate Euthyphron? But I hasten back to the dialogue.

The *Euthyphron* is a very paradoxical dialogue. So indeed is every Platonic dialogue. The specific paradoxy of the *Euthyphron* consists in this. The normal procedure in a Platonic dialogue in the type to which the *Euthyphron* belongs is that the interlocutor gives first a definition which expresses the most common view on the subject under discussion and then gradually is led to a higher view. But the first definition suggested in the *Euthyphron* is in the decisive respect superior to the last definition, which merely formulates the popular view of piety, meaning piety consists in sacrifice and prayer. More generally expressed, whereas the normal procedure in the Platonic dialogues is ascent from the lower to the higher, the procedure followed in the *Euthyphron* is descent from the higher to the lower. One can explain this paradoxy in two different ways. In the first place, Euthyphron the heretic must be brought back to where he belongs, namely, to orthodoxy or to conformity. In the second place, the *Euthyphron* is an unusually radical dialogue. It suggests the most uncompromising formulation of the problem of piety. Therefore, the structure of this dialogue has this character: A) exposition of the truth; B) explanation of the basic error. Shortly before the end of the dialogue, Socrates compares Euthyphron to Proteus. Proteus was a wily sea-god who could only with great difficulty be seized. He could turn into all kinds of shapes—bearded lions, dragons, leopards, huge boars, liquid water, branching trees. Euthyphron resembles Proteus because he cannot easily be seized, but changes his position all the time. Moreover, Euthyphron resembles Proteus because Proteus is unerring: he can tell all the secrets of the gods. Now Socrates tries to seize Euthyphron, to force him to tell the truth. Who tried to seize Proteus in the myth, to force him to tell the truth? Menelaus. Just as Euthyphron imitates Proteus, Socrates imitates Menelaus. Socrates resembles Menelaus. What does Socrates have in common with Menelaus? Menelaus is the husband of Helen, just as Socrates is the husband of Xanthippe. This does not lead very far. Let us see in what context, or for what reason, Menelaus tried to seize Proteus (*Od.* IV / 351ff.). Menelaus himself says, "At the river of Egypt, eager as I was to hasten hither, the gods still held me back because I did not make the offering due. And the gods wish us ever to be mindful of their precepts." Menelaus tried to seize Proteus because only Proteus could tell him how he could get out of the trouble into which he had come because he did not make the offering due. Socrates tried to seize Euthyphron because only Euthyphron could tell him how he could get out of the trouble into which he had come because he did not make the offerings due. It seems that this state of things throws some light on Socrates's last word to Crito in the *Phaedo*: "We still owe Asclepius a cock," as one might well understand the passage. However this may be, Socrates failed where Menelaus succeeded. The reason is obvious. Socrates did not ask his Proteus what he, Socrates, should do, but he asked him a purely theoretical question, What is piety?

I said at the beginning that the *Euthyphron* conveys to us an irritating half-truth. That irritating half-truth is that piety is superfluous and that the gods are superfluous except for the many. Why is it a half-truth? Because we know that the gods exist. Not indeed the gods of the city of Athens, but the living gods. How do we know it? By demonstration. By demonstration starting from what phenomena? From the phenomena of motion, of self-motion, life, of the soul. Plato has indicated the half-true character of the message conveyed through the *Euthyphron* by never using that word, the term "soul." Through the emphasis on the ideas, and the silence about the soul, Plato creates the appearance that there is no place for the gods. Plato probably would have justified this half-truth by the consideration that the ideas are at any rate above the soul.

In conclusion, I would like to say a word about what might have been offensive to some of you, the somewhat jocular character of the argument, that is devoted to the most serious of all subjects. I remind you of the end of the *Banquet*, which I take to mean that philosophy fulfills single-handed the highest function of both comedy and tragedy. Both the traditional and current interpretation of Plato may be said to bring out the tragic element in Plato's thought, but they neglect the comic element except where it hits one in the face. Many reasons can be given for this failure. I mention only one. Modern research in Plato originated in Germany, the country without comedy. To indicate why the element of comedy is of crucial importance in Plato, I read to you a few lines from the only Platonist I know of who had an appreciation of this element. Sir Thomas More. I quote: "For to prove that this life is no laughing time, but rather the time of weeping, we find that our Saviour Himself wept twice or thrice, but never find we that He laughed as much as once. I will not swear that He never did, but at the leastwise He left us no ensample of it. But on the other side. He left us ensample of weeping." If we compare what More said about Jesus with what Plato tells us about Socrates, we find that "Socrates laughed twice or thrice, but never find we that he wept as much as once." A slight bias in favor of laughing and against weeping seems to be essential to philosophy. For the beginning of philosophy as the philosophers understood it is not the fear of the Lord, but wonder. Its spirit is not hope and fear and trembling, but serenity on the basis of resignation. To that serenity, laughing is a little bit more akin than weeping. Whether the Bible is right or philosophy is of course the only question which ultimately matters. But in order to understand that question, one must first see philosophy as it is. One must not see it from the outset through Biblical glasses. Wherever each of us may stand, no respectable purpose is served by trying to prove that we eat the cake and have it. Socrates used all his powers to awaken those who can think, out of the slumber of thoughtlessness. We ill follow his example if we use his authority for putting ourselves to sleep.

APPENDIX 1

# Selections from Strauss's Notes on the *Euthyphro*

**Note 1**

S.'s piety is vouched for by an expert in piety—but E. is a fool
in addition, he is impious.
by his deed—but the deed is ambiguous.
→ his piety remains an open question

The speech → can a man be pious who does not know what piety is?
can any man be pious?
→ S. as well as all others are impious.
the critique of "what ἡ πόλις νομίζει [the city believes]"
→ S. is impious.
the ignorance of the gods
the πλάνη [wandering] regarding δίκαια [just things], καλά [noble things], ἀγαθά [good things]
→ knowing gods would not have any desires for δίκαια [just things], καλά [noble things], ἀγαθά [good things], because they would be self-sufficient.

Comments in square brackets [ ] are editorial insertions; those in angular brackets < > are notes crossed out by Strauss; those surrounded by superscript V's have been inserted by Strauss on a verso page; those surrounded by superscript P's have been inserted by Strauss in pencil; and those marked by a superscript R have been underlined by Strauss with red pencil.

Now, the ideas are higher than the gods and the ideas are accessible to ἐπιστήμη [knowledge]—ergo: if the gods are knowing, ὁμοίωσις θεῷ [assimilation to god], i.e. (since the gods are not pious) transcending piety. → S. is impious in his thought, but not λόγῳ καὶ ἔργῳ [in speech and in deed]

not ἔργῳ [in deed]: his advice to Euthyphro

not λόγῳ [in speech]: he keeps his knowledge to himself—he is not φιλάνθρωπος [philanthropic].

But this precisely <u>is</u> φιλανθρωπία [philanthropy] = justice = piety.

**Note 2**

S.'s φιλανθρωπία [philanthropy] consists, not in <u>teaching</u>, but in <u>questioning</u>, in cross-examining or perplexing others

—should <u>this</u> explain S.'s unpopularity? or is the explanation supplied in the *Apol.* doubtful?

<u>S.'s crime</u> his <u>injustice</u>

—he never attempts the <u>big</u> job of διώκειν ἄλλους [to prosecute others] (ad 3a2–5)

—he does not teach—he lacks φιλανθρωπία [philanthropy] (ad 3d6–9)

ad 5c4–8

ad 6a6–b6

his <u>justice</u>—his φιλανθρωπία [philanthropy]—he wants to prevent E. from committing what may well be a grave mistake.

The <u>constant</u> reference to E.'s wisdom and his unwillingness to divulge it—cf. ad 3d5–6—and E. openly boasts of his wisdom. Yet: S. boasts of his ἀμαθία [ignorance]—is <u>he</u> not the one who does not divulge his wisdom?

**Note 3**

cf. Xen. and *EN*.

ἀνθρώπινα ≠ μαθηματικά [human things ≠ mathematical things]

1) the former are essentially controversial so that even gods would fight with regard to them
2) the gods are concerned with the former and not with the latter
The solution:
a) the gods are not concerned with ἀνθρ. [human things], but with μαθημ. [mathematical things] (cf. 10d12–13)
b) mathematization of the ἀνθρώπινα [human things] etc.—cf. *Protag.* in fine.

> the gods are concerned with ἀνθρ. [human things] qua μαθηματικά [mathematical things]

On what principle does S. act? Certainly not on a) and b)[1]—he remains within ἔνδοξα horizon [accepted opinion horizon]
—he suggests we do not know what ὅσιον [holy] is and therefore have to follow ἔνδοξα [accepted opinion].
He suggests that we just do not happen to know what τὸ ὅσιον [the holy] is, whereas possibly τὸ ὅσιον [the holy] is unknowable because it is essentially νόμῳ [by law]—or the fundamental infiniteness of our knowledge of ideas—?

**Note 4**

For summary of *Euthyphron*—with a view to *Theology and Politics*.[2]
The basic problem of philosophy—a) philosophy as matter of faith, not of insight—philosophy makes certain special assumptions—

cf. Nietzsche's critique of the philosophers—the decisive assumption is "necessity."

b) contingency at the bottom of necessity (cf. my notes to Shestov).

The need for philosophizing is more evident than the need for justice and piety. But why justice and piety?
Why justice? Justice = θεραπεία [τῶν] ἀνθρώπων [care of (the) human beings]

→ not teaching everyone everything one knows

→ φιλανθρωπία [philanthropy] → teaching everyone everything one knows.

The just man = he who knows to teach human beings = the ruler—he gives everyone what is due to him for the sake of preservation of πόλις [city]—ultimately for the sake of his own benefit (the philosopher lives in society) but S. derives no benefit: he is hated. Why? The limitation of his art and of all art: τύχη [chance]

<Why piety? Piety and τύχη [chance]     cf. *Tim.* on τύχη [chance].

The understanding of τύχη [chance] by philosophy and the understanding of τύχη [chance] by piety.

| τύχη [chance] cannot be controlled | τύχη [chance] can be controlled. |
|---|---|

What leads to the view that τύχη [chance] can be controlled? ἀλαζονεία [boastfulness] or μανία [madness]. Denial of τύχη [chance] proper: no essential difference between ἕκαστα [particulars] and εἴδη [forms]—denial of εἴδη [forms]—gods would not be guided by knowledge—fighting and unjust gods—gods who can be bribed with sacrifices and presents—

The compromise view: wise and just gods concerned with man's justice—presupposes that the higher takes care of the lower without loving it –

Is the assertion of "negative ideas" not another form of expressing the denial of τύχη [chance] and of μὴ ὀν [nonbeing]?>

**Note 5**

Ad *Euthyphron*

—explain what denial of τύχη [chance] means for Platonic dialogue—

the philosopher is Socrates—all unessential features of Socrates, all ἴδια [peculiarities], are necessary with a view to his ἔργον [work].

his dialogue with Euthyphro = the dialogue of the philosopher with the expert in piety on piety.

E. happens to be a man of dubious piety → the expert in piety, at least the expert who is friendly to S, is necessarily a man of dubious piety.

Every good work of art is perfect—no τύχη [chance]—nothing can be added and nothing can be subtracted.

But the good work of imitative arts communicates the intrinsic necessity to its subject matter—they commit the fundamental lie.

**Note 6**

Ad *Euthyphron*

the problem of the justice of the gods –

ἀγαθόν [good] = πάτριον [ancestral]—the ancestors the source of all blessings → the gods are good—why then is this denied by the myth? It does not suffice to say that the poets invented this theology –

The question of the first things—they are the causes of the evil as well—power rather than beneficence.

This must be integrated into my "deduction" of revelation –

the custom as way—our way = the right way—the right way = the ancestral way—the ancestors must be gods or sons of gods—the right way has its origin in the first things –

the first things are responsible for all other things—also for the evil things—the right way is devised precisely in order to cope with the evil things—in order to placate the gods.

The right or holy way as distinguished from the evil way—yet in the origin of the right or holy way, the distinction between holy and evil cannot be made—yet: the gods are models → destruction of morality.

Alternatives:

a) the gods are good ינא שודק יכ ויהת םישודק [Leviticus 20:26: "Be holy because I am holy"]
b) holiness = pleasing the gods ≠ justice: the gods themselves are neither holy nor just—the gods are not good.

(a) does not account for evil—except if man is responsible for evil—or fallen angels—)

—but how do we know that the gods are good? τί ἐστι θεός [what is (a) god?]; a superior being—we know something of superiority among human beings, the σοφός [wise]—the σοφός [wise] is not evil—ergo, the gods will be still less evil.)

----

Problem of piety   Piety = right attitude to the gods—but anthropomorphic gods are essentially hostile to each other → they are unjust → piety and justice are incompatible.
But what about non-anthropomorphic gods? No piety possible or required.
Above all: they would be just by participating of justice—hence be less just than αὐτόν το δίκαιον [the just itself].

**Note 7**

piety = awareness of the power of τύχη [chance].
piety = imitation of the gods = philosophy.

awareness of the power of τύχη [chance] is the proper substitute for philosophy and the only guarantee against ὕβρις [arrogance] or μανία [madness]. Men should ascribe all ἀγαθά [good things] to the gods and all κακά [bad things] to their own faults (*Rep.* II).

But this does not explain why the city must recognize gods?

The myth transforms the unpredictable τύχη [chance] which therefore provokes the gambler (*Republic* 374c), into the predictable action of the just gods—

**Note 8**

What is the justification of piety? Fear of the gods and sense of shame (= fear of bad reputation) = εὐσχημοσύνη [gracefulness]

Cf. 8c10, e1: οὐ τολμῶσι [do not dare] cf. EN on αἰδώς [sense of shame]

Since the philosophers do not have fear of gods, only fear of bad reputation remains.

What is the justification of piety? The view that piety consist in not imitating the old god is superior to the view that we shall imitate them.

But: it is preferable only on account of its practical consequences.
Yet: it is inconsistent as is shown by the argument in *Rep*. II.

**Note 9**

The ἔνδοξα [accepted opinions] presupposed by E.
a) the gods are concerned with δικαία [just things]—in order to be δίκαιοι [just], we have to follow their example—this is our knowledge of δικαία [just things]—(cf. Aristophanes alicubi [somewhere] on the gods as models of action—possibly note to Introduction ch. 4)
The gods fight each other? They contradict each other? But the highest god, the king's father, Zeus, has to be the model—and he is the model for E.
The revolutionary character of E.: he does not follow the example of human beings as told by the stories, but the example of God as told by stories. (Kinship between myth and philosophy.)
<The objections: 1) are the stories true? 2) how do we know that the authentic actions of Zeus are just? Only if we know what justice is—but if we know this, we would not need any stories.
b) Can we know what justice is? The explicitly controversial character →

α) either we disregard it altogether and turn to mathematics

β) or we try to reach mathematical knowledge of justice>

In the *Euthyphron*, S. does neither one nor the other—what he does is that he follows the non-mythical ἔνδοξον [accepted opinion] (honor the father)—the controversy is finished by δόξα πόλεως [opinion of the city]—(cf. the ambiguity of the controversy: it is not so much about the law as about the fact (cf. Ar. *Rhetoric*))
E. is impious because he does not follow the δόξα πόλεως [opinion of (the) city]—S. is pious because he follows it.
E. is impious because he follows Zeus (he harms the father)—S. follows Daedalus and harms the son (note that E. is younger than S.)

→ S. is impious too
for he doubts the δόξα πόλεως [opinion of (the) city].

Both are impious because they doubt the δόξα πόλεως [opinion of (the) city].

But E.'s doubt, because it is not radical, leads to action—S.'s doubt, because it is radical, does not lead to action—but is this correct?

## Note 10

Why piety? We have seen (p. 12 Heft [notebook]) that "either ideas or gods"—which means that primacy of the gods, and hence piety, is due to ignorance. But this [is] no explanation why ignorance (of ideas) takes this particular direction, i.e. ascribing of guidance to gods?

We have therefore to go somewhat deeper.

In other words, we have shown that the assumption that the ultimate is arbitrary will, will not bound by any necessity independent of it, leads to absurdities (the one god may create other gods who also will do what they please → fight and impossibility of piety = pleasing the gods; he may kill himself and decree that the world would go on forever ruled by necessary laws).

The theistic (polytheistic or monotheistic) position stands and falls by admission of necessity at the bottom of arbitrariness.

Yet: why theistic position? why not rule of τύχη [chance] (Hesiod: first Chaos arises) Omnia quae sunt ex nihilo, de nihilo facta sunt.[3]

Now, if there is no necessity at the bottom of arbitrariness, everything is possible and nothing is impossible.

But: certain things are impossible—we all admit this—the doubt that they may be possible (e.g. that man is immortal) is a mere assertion if it is not shown that it is possible.

Generally: "first Chaos arises"—before it arose, it is possible—how? is it possible that something jumps into being out of nowhere? is not space presupposed? empty space? But how can there arise something out of nothing?

If there is no necessity at the bottom of arbitrariness, there can be no knowledge, but only report, "history," i.e. myth.

Yet: the use of words (≠ proper names)—the universals which are understood

Necessity and prediction.

Now, if there is necessity at the bottom of arbitrariness, not everything is necessary—before S.'s trial, it was not necessary that he should be condemned—there are contingent things—things that are not determined in advance, which cannot be predicted: I may stand or sit—whether I will stand or sit, depends on circumstances which no one can foresee—I may

be in the habit of sitting—but, when I try to sit, the chair breaks down and no other chair is available—the chair breaks down because it has been overburdened; besides, the other chair usually available is in use elsewhere in the house—as far as my standing or sitting is concerned, my standing to-day is chance. On the basis of contingency, chance becomes possible. Chance as chance cannot be controlled.
(Philosophy = ideas ≠ ἕκαστα [particulars] → insight into necessity of unmitigated chance.)

Chance decides on the fate of the philosopher e.g.
Now, men rebel against this state of affairs: they want to control chance. Μαντική [divinatory art] (3b5–6, c1–3, e2–3)—S. does not attempt to find out what cannot be found out.[4] Ἀλαζονεία [boastfulness] and μανία [madness]. Denial of τύχη [chance] proper: no essential difference between ἕκαστα [particulars] and εἴδη [forms]—denial of εἴδη [forms]—the causes of all things are arbitrary beings—they are superhuman, i.e. their perfection is to be understood in the light of human perfection, but human perfection is to get what one wants → powerful and happy gods who do not know—fights and unjust gods—gods which can be bribed with sacrifices and prayers—[V](The compromise view: wise and just gods concerned with men: justice presupposes a) that justice is important to gods b) that the higher cares for the lower without loving it.)
Also: the myth transforms the unpredictable τύχη [chance] which therefore provokes the gambler into the predictable action of the just gods.[V]

**Note 11**

S. suggests to a fool that the best thing is to follow custom regarding piety –

a) it is doubtless best in the given case
b) it is doubtless best for this man and his type in general, because he is certainly unable to produce anything better than the custom –
c) it is best for all who do not know what piety is –
but S. himself does not know what piety is—is it knowable?
d) if S. knows what piety is and is knowingly pious, he concedes the difference between his piety and proper piety.
In other words: ignorance → refraining from action—such action is indispensable, based on νόμος [law]

The possibility of action without knowledge: need for action—following the νόμος [law]—if the νόμος [law] proves to lead to manifest unpleasantness to the whole community, necessary changes.

**Note 12**

ad piety: piety is threatened by its justification (the myths = explanation why sacrifices and prayers are pleasing to the gods)—piety must be divorced from its justification—it becomes mere action

**Note 13**

It must be made perfectly clear that Socr. did not believe in the gods of the city.
Hence: the difference between the noble lie and the base lie
—the base lie: Socr.'s respect of popular religion because he was a religious man.
the noble lie: Socr. expels the lie from his soul—as ruthlessly as a Hobbes—
Athena and Zeus are merely products of imagination, and not of ruthless imagination—
but, he answers to Hobbes with a ἄθυμος πρόρρησις [nonspirited address] (*Laws* X [888a])
these popular views are superior to your view in so far as they see that man is not, and cannot be, the measure of all things, μαντεύονται τὴν ἀλήθειαν [divining the truth]; and it is good for them to believe it

**Note 14**

the δαιμόνιον [daimonion]—connection with consciousness as warner—warns of guilt—but all action is essentially guilty (der Handelnde ist immer gewissenlos)[5] ergo δαιμόνιον [daimonion] warns of all action.

**Note 15**

The fundamental problem: primacy of gods or primacy of ideas

—primacy of gods → ὅσιον [holy] = θεοφιλές [dear to the gods] → gods love men in a devastating manner
—primacy of ideas → ὅσιον [holy] ≠ θεοφιλές [dear to the gods] → gods do not love men—except perhaps the philosophers
This is somehow connected with the problem of love; the relation of ἕκαστα [particulars] to ideas being ὀρέγεσθαι [desire]: it is a love of the lower for the higher—a love which does not affect the higher.
The examples in 10a5ff.:

1) φέρειν [to carry], ἄγειν [to lead], ὁρᾶν [to see] are actions which do not affect the object
2) φέρειν [to carry] and ἄγειν [to lead] affect the object to the extent that they change its place—φέρειν [to carry] κ. [and] ἄγειν [to lead] = devastating ≠ ὁρᾶν [to see] leaves the object absolutely unchanged
→ love of the lower for the higher has the character of ὁρᾶν [to see]—but what about the love of higher for the lower?
3) ἄγειν [to lead] is central → the higher affects the lower by leading it

ad action: Does S. lead E. out of love? No—then out of ἀνάγκη [necessity]—philosopher takes care of the πόλις [city] ἀναγκασθείς [having been compelled] *Resp.*—yet no ἀνάγκη [necessity] for gods to care for men whom they do not love → the gods love only the θεοφιλές [dear to the gods]—the philosophers (*EN* X)

10cff.—the examples given by S. in 10a5–b are all examples of πάσχειν [to undergo], i.e. of pre-existing things being acted upon—but the ὅσιον [holy] = θεοφιλές [dear to the gods] which E. has in mind comes into being through the gods' loving—whereas the ὅσιον [holy] ≠ θεοφιλές [dear to the gods] (what S. has in mind) is pre-existing and merely acted upon through the gods' loving.
The deeper meaning: the ὅσιον [holy] (= θύειν [to make sacrifices]) is not θεοφιλές [dear to the gods] (if the gods are knowing beings).

ὅσιον [holy] = to do what the gods tell us to do is not what the gods love—if the gods are wise—if there are ideas (φύσις [nature]—*Odyssey* X)
ὅσιον [holy] = to do what the gods tell us to do is what the gods love—if the gods are ignorant masters—if there are no ideas

E. is not certain whether ὅσιον [holy] = or ≠ θεοφιλές [dear to the gods]
PTO [please turn over]

[V]The first explicit definition: ὅσιον [holy] = θεοφιλές [dear to the gods]

a) if there are many gods who fight among each other, it is impossible to be pious while being impious at the same time → E. is likely to lose his lawsuit and E. gets frightened

b) if the gods agree, or if there is only one god, ὅσιον [holy] ≠ θεοφιλές [dear to the gods] (for: wise god would not demand sacrifices etc.) → to do what the gods do requires abandonment of what the gods command → E. gets still more frightened

11b3–4: the absolute primacy of the ideas ≠ the gods' attitude toward the ideas

action— 11b6–8—E. extremely bewildered
11b9—our ancestor—not "our" fault (11b7–8), sc. of E. and S., but of S. and his people—

<S. Daedalus? son of Hephaestus, son of Zeus cf. *Theaet.*—contemporary with *Euthyphron*>

<ὁσιότης [piety] ἐπιστήμη [knowledge]>
<—father: subject of the dialogue>
<πάτριον [ancestral]>

<11c5: τὸ ἄλλο σκῶμμα [another jest]: namely, μαιευτική [midwifery] (Benardete)>

11b9–c6—E. and S. have inverted their roles or changed their places—by this very fact, they have not lost from their συγγένεια [kinship]—they are in the same boat—S. too is impious

11c4–7—in the case of S., the false λόγοι [accounts/arguments] will run away—whereas they are not abandoned by E.—περιέρχεται [move about] (b9) περιιέναι [go about] (c7) 15b10 (S. speaks of E.)

11c—if S. is the descendant of Daedalus, his ἐν τοῖς λόγοις ἔργα [deed in speeches] would ἀποδιδράσκει [run away] (*Protagoras* 317a)

11b8—E. becomes suddenly aware of the independent movement of the λόγοι [accounts/arguments]—which is not subject to any human or divine control—

11b8–c6—S. seems to trace this apparently independent movement to human agency—to a τέχνη [art]
11c7–d2—E. accepts S.'s "correction': S. is the λόγου τεχνίτης [the craftsman of the argument]
11d3–e1—no, S. says, the λόγοι [accounts/arguments] really have a movement of their own
[note connecting all comments from 11b8 to 11d3–e1:] Cf. Jascha [Jacob Klein]: are the λόγοι [accounts/arguments] moving by themselves or is this due to the fireworks of the sophist?

To the extent, to which the λόγοι [accounts/arguments] move by themselves, there is no human responsibility, no guilt—but S. wants to warn E.—he has therefore to bring in the possibility of guilt—he makes E. responsible—E. makes S. responsible—S. playful hostility in d3 (ἑταῖρε [fellow]) and e2 (τρυφᾶν [dissipated, sluggish]).[V]

**Note 16**

1) History of ideas is the account, in chronological order, of the changes in human thought concerning the whole of human life or concerning the whole *tout court.*
History of ideas deserves methodical priority before sociology of ideas or any other explanation of ideas. For one cannot explain a thing before one knows what the thing to be explained is. Interpretation has to precede explanation.
History of ideas deals with human thoughts concerning the whole, and so does history of philosophy. But history of philosophy deals with a particular kind of human thought—viz. methodical thought. Now, methodical thought is less susceptible of arbitrary interpretation than is unmethodical thought: methodical priority of history of philosophy.

2) If the history of ideas is centered around history of philosophy, the question arises: what is the relation of history of philosophy to philosophy itself? What is philosophy? The attempt to replace opinions about the whole by science, or evident knowledge, of the whole. This

means: philosophy itself is a-historical; the question of what this or that individual thought about the world is not a philosophic question. Now, the fundamental difference between history and philosophy was recognized until a short time ago; today we are confronted with a fusion of philosophy and history which makes the distinction between the two increasingly difficult; today, it seems impossible to carry through the distinction between philosophy and history. If one tries to understand this fact, one is eventually driven to assume a fundamental difference between modern thought and pre-modern thought—the difference which accounts for the fusion of philosophy and history in modern thought, and the separation between philosophy and history in pre-modern thought. This means: if we do not take for granted that history of philosophy and history of ideas are important and meaningful human activities, if we try to understand our own doing, we are confronted with the fact that the difference between modern thought and pre-modern thought is of basic importance for the understanding of all our thought.

We have discussed the question of the difference by criticizing [A. J.] Carlyle's and others' thesis that there is no fundamental change in political thought in particular between the Stoics and the French Revolution. We can show that such a difference exists.

3) To establish the fact of that difference and to understand its purport, we have to know the characteristics of pre-modern thought, of pre-modern philosophy: the first example we discussed was Machiavelli. Machiavelli confronts us with a difficulty that is totally absent from the literature of the 19th and 20th centuries. As Mr. [J. W.] Allen puts it, M. "writes between the lines." Hence we have to read between his lines in order to understand him. We have to acquire some knowledge of how he wrote, of his technique of writing, in order to begin to read his works. We have assigned two major reasons for his technique:

a) he writes as a republican under a monarchic government

b) he writes as an unbeliever in a believing world.

As regards the technique of reading, we have said that reading between the lines, far from being arbitrary, is identical with the most exact consideration of every feature of the author's work: a first-rate author leaves nothing to chance.

4) The question of whether and how far these observations apply to pre-modern thought as such.

Pre-modern philosophy: the Aristotelian tradition > Plato > Socrates.

Socrates a turning point: he brought philosophy down from heaven to earth and introduced it into the cities and houses of men; he turned from the universe, from the divine things to the human things.

And he did this for reason of piety: he was the founder of an emphatically pious, 'religious' tradition. Edelstein 207–9.[6]

Yet, Socrates was indicted and condemned and executed for his impiety.

Should there be a connection between the emphatically pious presentation of his teaching and the fact of his condemnation? The question is usually not even raised: the prevalent teaching is to minimize the importance of the impiety charge and to assume that Socrates was persecuted for reasons of no fundamental nature.

Xenophon's refutation of the impiety-charge—extremely brief—no quotation of the speech of the accusers—cf. *Mem.* I 1 20, II 1.

Plato's *Apology*—S. did not believe in the gods worshipped by the city of Athens—but this is somewhat disguised by the story of the oracle in Delphi.

This does not mean that Socrates was an atheist, of course—but it certainly means that he was not a martyr for his convictions, a religious zealot. His relation to the public was totally different from that of a religious zealot.

Xen. *Mem.* IV 2, 11–17 Plato's concept of the noble lie

Connection with the essence of philosophy: the attempt to replace opinions by knowledge—but opinion is the element of νόμος [law].

Ar. *Pol.*, p.m. p. 129 f.

**Notes**

1. A note at the bottom of the page reads: "<cf. parallels in *Phaedrus* etc.>"

2. Fragment of MS with the same title can be found in Leo Strauss Papers, box 18, folder 17, Special Collections, Regenstein Library, University of Chicago. On p. 5 (the outline of the Introduction), Strauss notes that the introduction was written from October 1, 1947 to October 16, 1947.

3. "Omnia . . . quae facta sunt, mutabilia sunt, quia de nihilo facta sunt, id est, non fuerunt, et Deo faciente, sunt, et bona sunt" (All things that are made are mutable because they are made out of nothing, that is, they were not and, God making them, they are and they are good), Saint Augustine, *Incomplete Work Against Julian* V, 60 (PL 45, 1495), in *Augustinus: Contra Iulianum opus imperfectum*, vol. 2, books 4–6 (Corpus Scriptorum Ecclesiasticorum Latinorum), ed. Ernst Kalinka and Michaela Zelzer (Vienna: Hoelder-Pichler-Tempsky, 1974–2004), 272.

4. Added at bottom of page.

5. LS refers to one of Johann Wolfgang Goethe's *Maxims and Reflections*: "Der Handelnde ist immer gewissenlos, es hat niemand Gewissen als der

Betrachtende." (The one who acts is always without conscience; no one has conscience but the one who observes.)

6. Perhaps "Greek Medicine in Its Relation to Religion and Magic," *Bulletin of the Institute of the History of Medicine* 5, no. 3 (March 1937): 201–46.

APPENDIX 2

# Strauss's Draft for His First Lecture on the *Euthyphro* (1950)

Ad lecture on *Euthyphron*.

The problem of the Platonic dialogue in general:

a) Plato does not teach in his own name—this is due to the problematic character of teaching: to the essential limitation of teaching: what is that limitation?

b) the dialogue is meant to overcome this limitation and this obstacle: how does the dialogue achieve this feat?

c) we have no direct access to Plato's teaching—how can we get an access to it?

Excursus of *Theaetet*[*us*]: philosopher concerned with the truth, with the nature of things, and in particular with the nature of man, and not with people—he does not even know whether his neighbor is a human being—so much is he preoccupied with finding out what a human being is.
But: Plato imitates people—even his Socrates is amazingly well informed about people—sometimes he almost approaches the character of a gossip. Obviously, Plato considered quest for the truth and concern with people inseparable, although of course distinct—

On this lecture, see the introduction to this volume, p. 6. Comments in square brackets [ ] are editorial insertions; those in angular brackets < > are notes crossed out by Strauss; those surrounded by superscript $^{V}$'s have been inserted by Strauss on a verso page; those surrounded by superscript $^{P}$'s have been inserted by Strauss in pencil; and those marked by a superscript $^{R}$ have been underlined by Strauss with red pencil.

[Obviously, Plato considered] theory and practice [inseparable, although of course distinct—]

Theory—knowledge, quest for knowledge

Practice—virtue—"people" → social virtue = justice

→ philosophy and justice are inseparable, although distinct.

While in itself philosophy is primary, πρὸς ἡμᾶς [for us] justice is primary: in every dialogue, S. performs an act of justice (= helping people): he does not in every dialogue embark on a quest for knowledge: what could he learn from Euthyphron? What philosophic truth could he teach Euthyphron? The primacy of justice: philosophy requires a certain preparation, a moral preparation, in fact, a conversion of the whole soul → all Socratic dialogues present this preparation (various stages) or rather they assist us in our preparation: how we can acquire a philosophic attitude—what obstacles we have to overcome in order to become philosophers—from what claims we have to liberate ourselves if we want to become philosophers.

Answer to question a)—the essential limitation of teaching consists in the fact that it cannot be understood without a previous conversion of the whole soul.

Philosophizing presupposes the overcoming of the obstacles to philosophy—i.e., the prejudices nourished by the passions, by our self-assertiveness. The dialogues present these obstacles and also the process in which they can be overcome—

These obstacles cannot be overcome by teaching, by speech—cf. Callicles—a certain φύσις [nature] is required; and they cannot be shaken but by individual measures—by change of the atmosphere as it were.

Answer to question b.

ἔτι [besides]: there are prejudices which ought not to be shaken in most men: καλὸν ψεῦδος [noble lie].

→ the surface of the dialogue (= content) does not transmit Plato's teaching—for his teaching is intelligible only to those who have already undergone the conversion. The explicit "teaching" of S. is rather a means for bringing about this conversion: to serve this purpose, it cannot possibly be simply true.

How then can we get hold of Plato's teaching if that teaching ≠ "content"? Through the "form"—more precisely, through understanding content in the light of the form.

a) Content: doctrine of ideas—the form does not throw light on that. But: idea and ψυχή [soul]—the dialogue presents people in their relation to the truth, i.e., to the ideas—i.e., it presents souls—this presentation (Plato's μίμησις [imitation]) is based on his understanding of the soul → it reveals silently his teaching concerning the soul.

b) λογογραφική ἀνάγκη [logographic necessity]

Answer to question c). PTO
[please turn over]

E. was a fool—S. a wise man. We cannot help loving S., and the divine Plato—we applaud them. Of course, S. did not believe in the old gods, and he did this of course out of piety. He was a martyr: he was unjustly condemned. The *Euthyphron* illustrates this fact most clearly: it holds up the impiety of those who killed S.

But: the first lesson we ought to have learned from Plato, is never to applaud, never to admire before we have understood. From Plato's point of view it is infinitely better to oppose S. on rational grounds than to be an Apollodorus, the prototype of the caricature Platonist.

"S. did not believe in the old gods—and he did this out of piety"—now, S. is accused of not believing in the old gods, i.e., of not believing in the existence of the old gods: he denied the charge; at least, he evaded it: he did not honestly say that he did not believe in the existence of Zeus, Athena, etc. But a pious man, especially a martyr is supposed to die for the profession of his faith → S. is not a martyr for a higher form of piety. S. did not admit that he was guilty in the sense of the charge: he justified his innocence → he believed in the existence of the old gods: either he believed in the existence of the old gods (and hence was not a representative of the higher form of piety) or he did not believe in their existence (in that case, he was dishonest or polite and hence not a representative of the higher form of piety).

For: to say that he understood "the old gods" in a metaphoric sense, and he believed in them in that metaphoric sense is a dishonest way of saying that he did not believe in the old gods. It is dishonest because it conceals the fact that on his way from the popular notion of gods to the philos[ophic] notion, S. had to commit an act of rejection, of intellectual iconoclasm: a specious continuity conceals an intransigent and clear decision. S. wanted to awaken people: we do not follow his example, if we use his authority for putting ourselves to sleep.

No result. We do not know what piety is. For all we can see, S. does not know what piety is. But: λόγος [speech] ≠ ἔργον [action]—twofold presentation of piety—a) speech, b) action: action by S. Two questions: a) what is piety? b) was S. pious? Philos[ophic] significance of this historical question: does piety belong to philosopher, to human excellence? // S.'s action.
<S.'s action: he tries to induce E. to abide by the customary practice out of fear of the gods.>

[1]Why then S.'s return to popular notion of piety?
The τόπος [topic/place] of piety—what gives rise to piety? What is its legitimate meaning?
1) ideas → ideas ≠ ἕκαστα [particulars]—dualism → τύχη [chance], uncontrollable: the fact of τύχη [chance] is ultimate justification of piety: τὰ μεγίστᾳ ἐν πράξει [the greatest things in action] do not depend on human power. Piety arises out of recognition of power of τύχη [chance]. But it is connected with an attempt to control τύχη [chance] via the gods—i.e., it refers τύχη [chance] to ἐπιστήμη [knowledge] or τέχνη [art] which is absurd.
The right attitude is to recognize the power of τύχη [chance] and not to attempt to control it: the virtue in question is ἀνδρεία [courage] (steadfastness in the face of ἀτυχίαι [misfortunes] and εὐτυχίαι [good fortunes]: the high place assigned to ἀνδρεία [courage] in *Rep*[*ublic*].
2) second definition of piety (arrived at with S.'s assistance): ὅσιόν [holy] a part of δίκαιον [just] (the part referring to the gods) → one may be pious without being just to humans and one may be just to humans without being pious.
Now, justice is evidently necessary → piety is superfluous.
Yet: the action shows that piety is not superfluous: S. refers E. to fear of the gods → S. trying to reinforce just action → piety = reinforcement of δίκαιον [just] necessary for those who do not appreciate the claim of justice.

<u>S.'s action</u>
<u>First step</u>: S. makes E. doubtful whether he will win his lawsuit (9a1–c8)—disagreement among <u>gods</u> whether E.'s action is just, but the strongest god is on E.'s side—yet: E. will have to win his lawsuit in <u>Athens</u>: a strong force (a majority) is <u>against</u> him. Piety is ἀνθρώπινον [human].
<u>Second</u> step: this means that his will be considered <u>impious</u>—he will lay himself open to the charge of <u>impiety</u>. In this situation, S. makes E. admit that θεοφιλές [dear to the gods] ≠ ὅσιόν [holy] → θεοφιλές [dear to the gods] = ἀσέβεια [impiety]
<u>Third</u> step: S. suggests the common view of piety: return to εὐσέβεια [piety]: θεοφιλές [dear to the gods] = ὅσιόν [holy].
<u>Fourth</u> step: S. <u>reminds</u> E. of previous discussion that led to "θεοφιλές [dear to the gods] ≠ ὅσιόν [holy]" → E. shall indeed return to customary practice, but he shall do it in realization of his <u>ignorance</u>: for his belief in his wisdom led him astray.
To sum up: S. tries to induce E. to abide by the customary practice out of fear of the gods and fear for his reputation with <u>men</u>—i.e., without knowing a <u>reason</u> of customary practice—E. shall submit to <u>authority</u>.

The issue: is it pious or impious to sue one's own father for the murder of someone who does not belong to one's own family? E.: it is pious. S.: it is impious. S. <u>knows</u> then that a certain action is impious—and yet he does not know what piety is: he is as <u>dogmatic</u> as E.
What is the implicit notion of piety that underlies S.'s <u>action</u>? He emphasizes the fact that the murdered man is a mere menial—can't a menial be <u>better</u> than E.'s father (Meno's παῖς [(slave-)boy])—he refers to an ἔνδοξον [accepted opinion] → piety = to behave toward the gods, the customary gods, in the customary fashion.
This notion of piety underlying the charge against S. → the action of the *Euthyphron* shows, and it is <u>meant</u> to show, that S. was pious in the sense of the charge.
This notion of piety is the most <u>common</u> one, the most <u>obvious</u> one.
In Socratic discussions, the first suggestion of the συνών [companion] frequently is the most obvious notion (*Laches*, *Charmides* etc. ≠ *Rep*[*ublic*]).
The surprising thing is that <u>E.'s</u> first suggestion is <u>not</u> the most obvious

one. Only after *another*, *less* obvious definition has *failed*, and after some prodding by S. does E. reproduce the most obvious notion. Why? E. *deviates* from custom—not only in the particular *case*, but in his very notion of piety. He is a heretic: he does not share the vulgar notion of piety.

*Euthyphron* *continued*.

E. is a fool—granted. But he knows *more* about piety in the traditional sense than the average man: he is an expert in piety. He does not accuse S.—he is friendly toward S.—S. and E. belong together in opposition to Meletus etc. E., the μάντις [diviner], divines, if very dimly, the truth. What then is *E.'s view of piety*? He does not state it in his formal definition: he reveals it *rather* ἔργῳ [in deed] than λόγῳ [in speech]—what is the notion of piety underlying E.'s *action*?

5e5–6a3 piety = *imitating* the gods—imitating what the gods *do*. This implies a rejection of the *popular* notion: according to which piety = *obeying* the gods = doing what the gods *command* = worshipping the gods (cf. 14b2ff.)

If we identify piety with worshipping the gods, the popular view is: the gods are *pleased* by worship and obedience → θεοφιλές [dear to the gods] = ὅσιόν [holy].

E. on the other hand asserts *implicitly*: θεοφιλές [dear to the gods] ≠ ὅσιόν [holy]—the gods are *pleased*, not by worship and obedience, but by *imitation*—not by our doing what they *say* but by our doing what they *do*.

E. is shocked when S. tries to show him that his definition (θεοφιλές [dear to the gods] = ὅσιόν [holy]) leads to θεοφιλές [dear to the gods] ≠ ὅσιόν [holy]—he wants to stick to the accepted equation—but by *his deed* he questions that equation.

His implicit *reason*: imitation is superior to obedience—for it is *wiser* than obedience or worship—a wise man wants to be imitated rather than to be obeyed or worshipped.

E.'s folly = half-heartedness: if the right thing is to imitate the gods, piety is *not* the right thing and the gods are not pious (E. takes as his model Zeus, the *justest* god ≠ the most pious god) → piety is not a virtue.

There are many gods who hold different views—E. picks the justest god—he *knows* then what justice is *prior* to his knowing that Zeus is just.

<→ there is no need for imitating Zeus: imitation of the idea of justice is enough> the just god is just only to the extent to which he complies with, or imitates, the idea of justice: he is subject to the idea of justice; the idea of justice is higher than Zeus. Now, if we know the idea of justice, we do not need to imitate the justest god; it is perfectly sufficient to imitate the idea of justice. Piety = imitating the gods is superfluous. Except: the gods are wise (= have adequate knowledge of the ideas) and we can only strive for wisdom = philosophize—philosophizing = assimilation to the gods = imitation of the gods.

The ideas are the "new gods" of S. // Cf. relation of theology in *Rep*[*ublic*] II with *Rep*[*ublic*] VI–VII.

E.'s heresy, consistently followed up, will lead to S.'s heresy.

What is E.'s πρῶτον ψεῦδος [original error]? From the point of view of piety proper, it would seem to consist in the fact that he is disobedient: he picks his god—he chooses Zeus—for: in choosing, E./one must behave rationally: he chooses Zeus as the most just god—he knows what justice is—he does not need Zeus.

How could one pick a god without being forced to admit the ideas? The gods are the old gods—their claim to reverence rests on their oldness → in case of conflict: pick the oldest god: no problem arises.

The oldest god is Uranus → piety = imitating the Heaven (*Tim.* 90c–d). ἔτι [besides]—Uranus eats his own children, he destroys the young ones—διαφθείρειν τοὺς νέους [corrupting the young]—even on the level of mythology, S. is more consistent than E. But this ὡς εν παρόδω [as it were in passing].

E. is impious from every point of view: from that of Meletus as well as that of S.—and indeed from his own point of view—

Is then the popular view preferable to E.? Is the popular view consistent? Or is E.'s deviation from the popular view not superior to the popular view?

Could one avoid E.'s mistake by remaining within the popular view—by not even thinking of imitating the gods? Piety = to obey and worship the gods according to custom without reasoning why? But why should one worship and obey the gods? Because of their superior power. But can the gods be powerful if they lack wisdom? This is tacitly admitted by the popular view itself: the gods who are powerful rather than wise, can be controlled by man (by means of sacrifices and prayers) → they are dependent on man. The gods must be wise if they are to be powerful. But if they are wise, they will wish to be imitated rather than to be worshipped. And: if they are wise, they are wise by knowledge, i.e., knowledge of the ideas—and hence the highest beings are, not the gods, but the ideas.

The vulgar view is untenable, it is absurd. Yet it is not an arbitrary invention: it is a necessary consequence of the denial of the ideas. Ultimately, there exists only this alternative: doctrine of ideas or absurdities of mythology.
Why? Let us assume the highest beings are, not ideas, but persons—not universals, but individuals—or even one individual—an individual bearing a name (a Thou)—but a being bears a name in order to be distinguished from other individuals of the same class→ polytheism.

The being in question will not be subject to higher norm—their rule of action will be their arbitrary will—they would not be guided by knowledge—they will be ignorant—they would fight—they would be unjust, intemperate, etc.

Occam: primacy of will and yet monotheism—God could command murder—his absolute freedom—(but if he is absolutely free, he could create other gods→ polytheism → fight—or: commit suicide and decree that atheistic universe will last forever—)

either: primacy of intelligible necessity ruling the universe or absurdity.

(the modern alternative: intelligible necessity created by man → Thing-in-itself.)

**Note**

1. Using the phrase "Continuation 2," Strauss inserted here the following two paragraphs (up to "shall submit to authority"), which are written on a separate sheet.

APPENDIX 3

# Strauss's Outlines for a Lecture on the *Euthyphro*

Plan of exposition of idea of *Euthyphron.* Restate the whole argument with a view to monotheism.

I. Connection between "what is piety" and S.'s piety.

II. S.'s piety remains an open question.

III. The problem regarding piety: is θεοφιλές [dear to the gods] = or ≠ ὅσιον [holy] (customary worship of the gods)—

It is safe to assume that S. rejects the equation and therefore that the discussion leading up to θεοφιλές [dear to the gods] = ὅσιον [holy] serves the purpose of leading E. to it and indirectly of explaining customary piety rather than of showing its insufficiency—or of showing its necessity after its claim to truth has been disposed of.[1]

IV. Critique of θεοφιλές [dear to the gods] = ὅσιον [holy] = customary worship of the gods (with prayers and sacrifice)

a) How do we know? The city—but the city laughs at it (cf. Crito: city = Athenians).[2]

the city-recognized expert questions custom.

The most important part of piety is prayers and sacrifices (cf. Xen. *Mem.* on S.'s piety).[3]—presupposes: men control the gods possible reduction of piety to ordinary justice—but: ordinary justice is introduced as an independent species—and S.'s justice is manifest, whereas his piety is not.

V. Critique of θεοφιλές [dear to the gods] ≠ ὅσιον [holy].

The gods do not need any worship of men—that worship is unreasonable—the right attitude is to imitate the gods. Only by imitating the gods, can one become just.

But: the gods fight → we cannot imitate but wise gods.

the justest god > idea of justice.

Relation of ideas and gods.

The problem of τύχη [chance]—the way to ὁσιότης [holiness] = control of τύχη [chance]

τύχη [chance] > ἄπειρον [infinite] / εἶδος [form/idea]

μὴ ὄν [nonbeing] / ὄν [being]

|| absolute μὴ ὄν [nonbeing] is interpreted as θάτερον [the other], negative ideas?

Denial of εἴδη [forms/ideas] + only ἕκαστα [particulars] → τὸ πρῶτον ἕκαστον [the first particular]—history-myth instead of philosophy

But how do we know that justice is good → the need for philosophizing more evident than the need for justice.

I. Connection between "what is piety" and S.'s piety.

The question of what piety [is] inseparable from the question of whether piety is a virtue.

The piety of S. = the piety of the philosopher = relation of piety and philosophy. Let us assume that philosophy is identical with human excellence or virtue—if the philosopher is essentially pious (not pious), piety would be (not be) essentially a part of virtue: the definition of piety depends on clarification of the relation of philosophy and piety—and therewith on answer to question of whether S. is pious.

The question of what piety is, is not answered, because the question of whether S. is pious is not answered. ad 15d5–6 ad 16a1–4

ad 15b7–c10—in the light of 2nd definition, E.'s case has nothing to do with piety, but only with justice proper—

II. S.'s piety remains an open question.

His piety is vouched for by the expert in piety; S.'s piety is shown by his action: he defends piety against a deviation.

But: E. is a fool and in addition a man of questionable piety; not M., who is in accord with public sentiment regarding piety, but E., who disregards public sentiment regarding piety, is friendly to S.; S. starts to learn piety from an expert only after he has been accused of impiety—he apparently did not have teachers in piety previously (not having learned, he must have found out by himself—ἐξευρεῖν [to find out] (12d6) = καινοτομεῖν [mint new]—*Alc.* I 106d and *Laches* 186)— ad 12e9–13a5

above all, we do not know what piety is—hence, we do not know whether piety is not folly.

III. The problem regarding piety.

Probably every reader of the *Euthyphron* thinks he has learned something about piety in spite of the negative result of the discussion. It has been suggested: piety is not "a special department of morality, but only the religious aspect of it"[4] or it "is no specialized art but a condition of soul"[5] or it is "assimilation to god as far as may be"[6] (Burnet 57). Yet this begs the decisive question: is there any connection between piety thus understood and piety as understood by the city of Athens? If the 2 notions of piety are not identical and perhaps even incompatible, the notion of piety allegedly suggested by the dialogue, would imply that S. is not pious in the ordinary sense of the term and therefore guilty.

Yet we do learn something about piety. We learn at least what is the problem of piety. The fallacy of scepticism. Is ὅσιον [holy] = or ≠ θεοφιλές [dear to the gods]? The first answer is: they are different; it seems the last answer is: they are identical. The first answer is asserted not under the leadership of S.—the second answer under the leadership of S. (11e2–4). What does this mean?

a) the case of S.: the accusation of impiety implies that ὅσιον [holy] = νομίζειν θεούς πόλεως [to believe in the gods of the city] = νομίζειν ἀρχαίους θεούς [to believe in the ancestral gods] = the customary gods = customary worship of customary gods <is pleasing to the gods>

If S. believes that something different from the customary worship is pleasing to the gods, he implies that θεοφιλές [dear to the gods] ≠ ὅσιον [holy].

b) the case of E.: he doubtless questions the identity of the pious with the θεοφιλές [dear to the gods] by questioning one special custom. But he questions the equation implicitly. S. brings him to question it explicitly. Confronted with the shocking implication of the apparently trivial deviation from custom, he is prepared for the return to θεοφιλές [dear to the gods] = ὅσιον [holy] (the customary notion).

[V] IV. E.'s thesis or the critique of orthodoxy. Heft [notebook] p. 19.

To worship the gods in the customary manner with sacrifices and prayers is pleasing to them—why?—we do not know—<no λόγος [account/argument] is possible>—they are pleased by it because they are pleased by it (cf. 15c5–6 with 10d)—no λόγος [account/argument] is possible. But—how do we know that the gods are pleased by it?

To worship the gods in the customary manner is pleasing to the gods. Why? The city tells us (ad 12a5). I.e.: hearsay (ad 6b5–6, c1–2).

a) a part of this is μαντική [divinatory art]—but the people (i.e. the city) laughs at μάντις [diviner] (ad 3b5–c5, e1–2) Cf. the "we" in 3a1.

b) the city declares that it is unjust to harm one's father

but at the same time they say that the justest god has harmed his father (5e5–6a5)

This is E.'s explicit argument.

c) the city-recognized expert questions custom—

E.: to establish what is pleasing to the gods, we cannot start from what people say, but from what the gods do: it is pleasing to the gods that we imitate them.

The hidden reason: a reasonable man wants to be imitated in his actions rather than worshipped.

<The difficulty: the gods contradict each other—to imitate the justest god> we have to know what justice is → imitation of the idea of justice—imitation of the gods is superfluous.>

<But how do we know that justice is good?—the need for philosophizing more evident than the need for justice.>

But:
a) the gods fight (contradict each other)—imitation of the gods presupposes agreement among the gods = knowledge.
We cannot imitate gods who are not wise (fighting gods are ignorant and unjust gods: ad 7b6–d6, 8d4–e10).
b) in what would imitation consist? In actions of justice: we have to imitate the justest god.
Idea of justice—we have to imitate idea of justice—knowledge of, or imitation of, the god is superfluous—relation of ideas and theology: Heft [notebook] p. 11–12. Piety superfluous: merely νομῷ [by law] (Heft [notebook] opp. p. 16)
c) But how do we know that we have to be just or that justice is good? → the need for philosophizing more evident than the need for justice.
Conditional: if imitation of gods has any meaning, it is imitation of gods who know = who know the ideas = striving to become like wise gods = philosophize.
d) ironical: the mistake of E. was to pick the justest god—
he should have picked the oldest god = Uranos—to imitate Uranos—

V. Yet in the dialogue S. does not philosophize—his philanthropy and his taking care of human beings = justice.

S.'s justice: he does not accuse (ad 2a3–4; b1–6; 6b7–c7) ad 11e4ff.
an outcome of his ἀμαθία [ignorance] (ad 2c3–8)
he teaches what he knows (3c6–d9)
But: he does not engage in politics (3a2–5). He does not teach what he knows (ad 4b4–6; 5c4–8; 6a6–b6; 11b9–c6, d3–e29.
He does not defect: *Ap. Socr.* 20e8–21a3.
Heft [notebook] p. 15 p[aragraph] 2 and p. 15u–16 ["u" refers to "unten" (bottom)]
By imitating the gods, he does not practice the human virtue of justice (ad 5e5–6a5)
the πλάνη [wandering] regarding the δικαία [just things]: ad 7d1–2.
his not accusing a sign of his not loving τὰ δικαία [the just things]: 7c10ff., esp. 7e6–7, ad 7e1–8a2

The compulsion underlying the dialogue—ad 2a5–6
S. is hated (3d1–e3).
The action (ad 11e1–4) Heft [notebook] p. 20 ad 12e3–4[V]

---

Plan.
5) E.'s heresy— <a) E.'s thesis.>
<b) why is it heretical? Because it makes impossible piety proper: the gods are not pious>
<cf. 5e5–6a3 7a7 cf. 6e10>
<→ θεοφιλές [dear to the gods] ≠ ὅσιον [holy].>
<c) how is it proved? what is its basis? 5e2–6a5.>
<d) it is a half-way house—between Meletus and Socrates—an indefensible position.>
<Either one must return to orthodoxy or one must go on to Socrates's view.>
<→ for: πάτριον [(the) ancestral] says that one must do what the gods tell us to do—>
<6) Why one cannot return to orthodoxy? Our insufficient knowledge of the gods—the fables are not knowledge—the analogy of the σοφός [wise man]: he likes more the people who do what he does than those who merely do what he tells them to do.> <Ar. *EE* 1249b14.[7]>
<Superiority of E.'s view.> [see paragraph 13 of "On Plato's *Euthyphron*" (1952), pp. 86–87]
<7) The end of the road—the gods contradict—one cannot imitate all the gods—one has to choose—how does E. choose? He chooses the best and justest god—primacy of ideas. The gods superfluous—piety περιττόν [odd, superfluous].> [see paragraph 14 of "On Plato's *Euthyphron*" (1952), p. 87–88]
<8) Uranos—S. more pious than E. according to E.'s view of piety.—E. and Meletus διαφθέρειν τοὺς παλαιούς [corrupting the old]: they imitate Zeus> [see paragraph 16 of "On Plato's *Euthyphron*" (1952), pp. 88–89]
<Ἑστία [Hestia]>
<9) S.'s new gods—the ideas vs. the gods.> < ποιητής [maker, poet]>
Daedalus and the λόγος [account/argument] move by themselves—E.'s unawareness of the ideas → the moving of the λόγοι [accounts/arguments] is S.'s fault. (Daedalus.) [see paragraph 17 of "On Plato's *Euthyphron*" (1952), pp. 89–90]

10) E.'s understanding of the ideas. No fundamental difference between ideas and particulars → μαντική [divinatory art] [see paragraph 17 of "On Plato's *Euthyphron*" (1952), pp. 89–90]

11) The meaning of piety: τύχη [chance]
cf. 3e2–3 with *Ap. Socr.* 42a2–5 (cf. *Euthyphron* 15e4ff.)
Burnet ad 13e9–10 *Laws* 709–710 (esp. 710a7–d2) 879b2–3. 798b *Euthydemus* 279c5ff.
δουλεύειν [to be a slave]: 13d—motivated by fear: 15d7
13a–b (central): piety—imitating of dogs (≠ gods)
→ Νή κύνα [by (the) dog]
14b1–7: σωτηρία [τοῦ] οἴκου [καὶ] πόλεων [salvation of (the) household (and) the city]. [see paragraph 18 of "On Plato's *Euthyphron*" (1952), pp. 90–92]

12) The need for piety: supplement of νομοθετική [legislative art]
Application to E.'s <u>case</u>: Cic. *Off.* III 90 cf. Plato *Rep.* II: parents—gods
Both the multitude and the philosopher have common sense → obey the νόμος [law]
E. lacks common sense → disobeys νόμος [law]
Why? The natural element of <u>E.</u>'s "νόησις" [intellectual perception]—cf. <u>his</u> θεῖα [divine things] [see paragraph 18 of "On Plato's *Euthyphron*" (1952), pp. 90–92]

13) The paradoxes of the *Euthyphron*: descent from the higher opinion to the lower
a) practically: E. might be brought <u>back</u> to orthodoxy and to conformity 4e4–8; 15d—Objections to this—14c3–4: sacrifice and prayer are brought up by <u>E</u>—and as a jab to Socrates.
b) philosophically: א) truth; ב) explanation of error. [see paragraph 19 of "On Plato's *Euthyphron*" (1952), pp. 92–93.]

15) The half-truth is the decisive omission of ψυχή [soul]. Consider *Leges* X.
Also omission of ἀνδρεία [courage], σωφροσύνη [moderation], φρόνησις [practical wisdom]. [see paragraph 20 of "On Plato's *Euthyphron*" (1952), p. 93]

14) "Proteus" [see paragraph 19 of "On Plato's *Euthyphron*" (1952), p. 93] ["15" precedes "14," ed.]

---

Plan

<1) Captatio: irritating half-truth. That is infinite task of understanding a Platonic dialogue> [see paragraph 1 of "On Plato's *Euthyphron*" (1952), pp. 75–76]

<2) The problem—no answer to the question of what piety is—>

<2a) Place of *Euthyphron* among the dialogues: *Euthyphron* and *Theaetetus*. ὁσίως [in a holy manner]—cf. "Protagorean" context. ὁσιότης [holiness] replaced by ἐπιστήμη [knowledge] (cf. *Rep.* 395c, cf. list of qualities of philosophers 487a etc.)> [see paragraphs 9–10 of "On Plato's *Euthyphron*" (1952), pp. 80–81]

<3) The characters and their intentions— a) S.>

→ <S. tries to show to E. that he does not know—he wants to attack his father—which is just as well as prudent>

<b) E.>

– the 3 positions: orthodoxy, E. and S.

<4) The action> <4) The character of E.: harmless boaster—his lack of knowledge of ἀνθρώπινα [human things]>

<5) E.'s heresy: a half-way house διαφέρειν [to differ]: 5a1> <5) His heresy>

<6) The implicit criticism of orthodoxy

7) The end of the road: the ideas—the gods superfluous—piety superfluous.

Ideas vs. gods—the central point. → Daedalus → τέχνη [art]

μαντική [divinatory art] → φύσις [nature]

8) The meaning of piety: τύχη [chance]> [see paragraph 18 of "On Plato's *Euthyphron*" (1952), p. 91]

---

Captatio: irritating half-truth. [see paragraph 1 of "On Plato's *Euthyphron*" (1952), pp. 75–76]

2) The problem—λόγος [account/argument]: we do not know what piety is.

ἔργον [action]—S.'s piety—why this gossipy question is identical with the phil. question regarding the essence of piety. [see paragraph 2 of "On Plato's *Euthyphron*" (1952), p. 76]

a) E. vouches for S.'s piety—irrelevant. [see paragraph 3 of "On Plato's *Euthyphron*" (1952), pp. 76–77]

b) S. admits his ignorance of divine things → he is not pious—he could still conform, of course yet: conflict between conformity and philanthropy → his philanthropy his real crime [see paragraph 4 of "On Plato's *Euthyphron*" (1952), pp. 77–78]

c) But S. knows → he was impious, but not philanthropic[R].—yet: he was just—was he?[R] [see paragraphs 5–7 of "On Plato's Euthyphron" (1952), pp. 78–80]

d) yet: S. may have been pious in the true sense of piety—but: we do not know what piety truly is [see paragraph 8 of "On Plato's *Euthyphron*" (1952), p. 80]

3) The place of the *Euthyphron* in κόσμος [cosmos] of the dialogues—*Euthyphron* and *Theaetetus*. [see paragraphs 9-10 of "On Plato's *Euthyphron*" (1952), pp. 80–81]

4) The setting . [see paragraph 11 of "On Plato's *Euthyphron*" (1952), pp. 81–85]

5) E.'s heresy: a half-way house between Meletus and Socrates—we must go beyond Euthyphron toward Socrates. [see paragraph 12 of "On Plato's *Euthyphron*" (1952), pp. 85–86]

6) Socrates: the ideas replace the gods—piety is περιττόν [odd, superfluous]. [see paragraph 14 of "On Plato's *Euthyphron*" (1952), pp. 87–88]

8) Why is it necessary to assert the primacy of the ideas?

Primacy of the ideas = primacy of necessity—vs. primacy of contingency [see paragraph 17 of "On Plato's *Euthyphron*" (1952), pp. 89–90]

Now, blind necessity is not distinguishable from contingency (*Leg.* X: τύχη [chance] = φύσις [nature]).

→ primacy of intelligible necessity—vs. primacy of contingency

Primacy of contingency: everything has come into being out of nothing and through nothing (Hesiod)

At the beginning, there was nothing—nothing was—nothing can be. But: nothing cannot be—nothing cannot have been → everything must have come into being out of something and/or through something.
The only pre-Socratic philosopher mentioned in the title of a Platonic dialogue: Parmenides. His discovery.
There might be nothing. I can think there is nothing—I can think nothing, and I can think Being—both equally but: I cannot think nothing—to think means to think something—nothing is impossible → Something or Being is necessary: the Being which I think and which, apparently, I merely think, is—and it is necessarily. By a miracle which no one has ever fathomed, man is capable to <grasp> reach the outer rims of everything possible, the whole—to grasp the absolute necessity which holds the whole in its iron grip. This is Plato's starting point. His disagreement with Parmenides: Parmenides says Being is One—precisely because nothing cannot be, and all difference, all otherness consisting in nothing. Plato: to be = to be something = to be a What = to be a part → the Whole is not in the sense in which the parts "are": it is beyond being.

---

<1. The λόγος [account or argument] of the Euthyphron does not tell us what piety is = it does not tell us whether piety = worshipping the ancestral gods according to ancestral custom is good—>
<2. The ἔργον [action] is ambiguous: S. is certainly not φιλανθρώπως [philanthropic]. Why does S. take care of E.? justice = θεραπεύειν ἀνθρώπους [to take care of human beings] = appeasing savage beasts—or: in more theological context—>
<3. E.'s heresy: piety = to do what the gods do → S.'s new gods: the ideas. Piety is superfluous (περιττόν [odd, superfluous]).>

<E.'s halfway house: no fundamental difference between ideas and particulars → μαντική [divinatory art].>

<but: awareness of ideas → denial of particulars: all fight is about principles—>

<The implicit criticism of orthodox view.>

<→ harmless ἀλαζών [boaster]>

<4.> 11. How does piety arise? Negatively: from ἄγνοια [ignorance, unawareness] of ideas → capricious

gods who must be appeased—toward whom one must behave like dogs to their human masters.
Positively: from desire to control τύχη [chance]: the gods tell us to do (they have the ἄρχικὴ τέχνη [art of ruling]) what will bring about εὐτυχία [good fortune] → function of piety is to control the uncontrollable = τύχη [chance] without the need of self-restraint and/or philosophy.

12. Why is piety necessary? a) for non-philosophers = men ruled by ἔθος [custom] and νομός [law]—the distinction of τέχνη νομοθετική [legislative art] and πολιτική [political art]—sanction for δικαιοσύνη [justice]—people who do not believe in these sanctions, who do not fear the gods, are capable of anything (*Leges* 886a, 887b5–c2, 967c). Men cannot be just without fearing the gods (contrary to definition of piety as suggested in *Euthyphron*).

application to our case: respect of old age and parents = control of ὕβρις [arrogance] and ἀκράτεια [incontinence] by sobriety

b) for philosophers—fear of δόξα πονηρίας [bad reputation] → conformity.

---

*Euthyphron.*

I <Introduction—the twofold presentation of piety → we have to understand the speech about piety in the light of the deed>

II The characters

<a) S.: suspect of impiety—suspect of philanthropy
his piety vouched for by E—but E.'s piety itself is doubtful—and: no one knows what piety is . . .
his philanthropy—the compulsory character of the conversation—he advises E. against an imprudent action—his justice.>

<b) E.: ἀλαζών [boaster] includes secret knowledge
γενναιότης [nobility of birth]
inferior justice>

III The action—

E. accuses his father of impiety—he must know what piety is—it is pious to do what the gods do—yet the different gods do opposite things: there is enmity among gods—enmity > difference of opinion—but: difference of opinion leads to enmity regarding δίκαια [just things], ἀγαθά [good things], καλά [noble things] → the gods have different opinions regarding δικαία [just things] → they do not know what δικαία [just things] are—if the gods do not know what δικαία [just things] are, human beings do even less: one cannot anticipate in any way what an Athenian jury will judge δίκαιον [just] → it is imprudent to engage in lawsuit. [in the margin: "harsh: threat with Meletus"]

Yet: pious = to do what the justest god does → no difference of opinion regarding δίκαιον [just]—but: controversy does not concern δίκαιον [just], but application to present cases—doubtful character of application → it is imprudent to engage in law suit.

Peripeteia.

**Notes**

1. Strauss put a question mark next to the entire paragraph.

2. Cf. "On Plato's *Apology of Socrates* and *Crito*," in *Studies in Platonic Political Philosophy* (Chicago: University of Chicago Press, 1983), 60: "Previously Socrates had spoken of going away without the permission, or against the will of the Athenians (48b2–c1, e3); now he replaces 'the Athenians' by 'the city,' because 'the Athenians' are 'many' or even 'the many.'"

3. Probably referring to Xenophon, *Memorabilia* 1.1–10. For Strauss's final analysis of this passage cf. *Xenophon's Socrates* (Ithaca: Cornell University Press, 1972), 4–11.

4. Edward Caird, Preface, in Benjamin Jowett, *The Four Socratic Dialogues of Plato: Translated into English with Analyses and Introductions* (Oxford: Clarendon Press, 1903), vi: "The dialogue ends with the apparently negative conclusion that, if we exclude the absurd idea that men can help the gods, piety can only consist in doing what is pleasing to them—the very definition which has already been rejected as unsatisfactory. But the attentive reader will recognize that the discussion has brought us to a point of view from which piety is seen to be not a special department of morality, but only the religious aspect of it." Parts of this passage are quoted by Burnet in his commentary on 13d9 (*Plato's Euthyphro, Apology of Socrates and Crito* [Oxford: Clarendon Press, 1924], 137).

5. "If there were any definite ἔργον which the gods could produce with our help, it must indeed be something 'mighty fine.' But in fact there is none, since ὁσιότης is no specialized art but a condition of the soul (ἕξις ψυχῆς). That is the positive result which the *Euthyphro* is meant to suggest to those who know the true Socratic doctrine, though it is nowhere explicitly stated." Burnet, *Plato's Euthyphro*, 137.

6. "There is, indeed, no product or ἔργον which the gods require our help to produce; but, on the other hand, it is our whole duty so to care for our souls that they may be as wise and as good as possible (*Ap*. 29 d 7 sqq.), and this means that man's chief end is 'assimilation to God as far as may be' (ὁμοίωσις θεῷ κατὰ τὸ δυνατόν), and, as is at once explained, 'assimilation to God' means 'to become righteous and holy with wisdom' (ὁμοίωσις δὲ δίκαιον καὶ ὅσιον μετὰ φρονήσεως γενέσθαι *Theaet*. 176 b1 sqq.). From that point of view the true nature of ὁσιότης becomes intelligible." Burnet, *Plato's Euthyphro*, 137.

7. Cf. Aristotle, *Eudemian Ethics*, 8.1249b14: οὐ γὰρ ἐπιτακτικῶς ἄρχων ὁ θεός, ἀλλ' οὗ ἕνεκα ἡ φρόνησις (for god is not a ruler who give commands, but that for the sake of which practical wisdom commands).

APPENDIX 4

# Strauss's Marginalia to the Greek Text of the *Euthyphro*

Next to title: Cf. Andocides, *De mysteriis* 19: the accusers had said that Andocides had denounced his own father (Leogoras) concerning the mysteries—crime—the denouncer of the father was Lydus ὁ Φερεκλέους (the slave of Pherecles)—the trial of Andocides because of ἀσέβεια was in 399! Andocides calls that special charge: λόγον οἶμαι πάντων δεινότατόν τε καὶ ἀνοσιώτατον λέγοντες. Meletus was one of the accusers of Andocides. But Anytus sided with Andocides. cf. ad *Protag.* 330c2–6.

2a1: 3b2–5, 16a2 [as a footnote referring to "νεώτερον"]

2b3–5: S. not anxious to talk.

2b10: cf. the horses of *Phaedrus.*

2c6: for the construction cf. 3b6–7. [as a footnote referring to "ὥς"]

3a7: *Cratylus* 401c–d *Phaedrus* 247a1

3a8: no doubt of S.'s justice—cf. 2a4–5 b1–2 [as a footnote referring to "σέ"]

3b3: for the sake of the old gods or for the sake of the young? "the old gods" are the young ones—[as a footnote referring to "ἕνεκα"]

In his copy of the first volume of John Burnet's *Platonis opera* (Oxford: Clarendon Press, 1900), Strauss made extensive annotations to the Greek text of the dialogue. We include them here, primarily for the readers of ancient Greek who will consult the Burnet text (also included in the translation by Seth Benardete below, pp. 187–217). All of his notes and references in the margins and in the footnotes are written in pencil. He also underlined hundreds of words in pencil and about two dozen in black ink (not included here).

3b6: The expert sees that S. is not ἀσεβής. S. a fellow-μάντις [as a footnote referring to "γίγνεσθαι"]

3c8–9: Important for *Ap. Socr.*, *Memor.* [in left-hand margin]
S. a teacher of wisdom. [in right-hand margin]

3d1: *Rep.* 517a1–6 [in a footnote]

3d7: *Mem.* I 2

4a1: 3c2

4a6: *Gorgias* 480b8ff.—

4a6: *Cratylus* 396d5 [footnote to "πατήρ"]

4b1: LS deletes the square brackets from "ὀρθῶς"

4b7–8: Cic. *Fin.* IV 27 76

4c4: 2d3

4c4: cf. Burnet ad loc. [footnote to "Νάξῳ"]

4e4–5: 2c3–8

4e9: μοί

5a4: 9c3–5

5a6: cf. σοφία—2d6, 16a2 [in the margin]

5a6: ≠ περὶ πλείστου [footnote to "περὶ πολλοῦ"]

5c7: 3a7–b4

5d4: 11a7f.: οὐσία [footnote to "ἰδέαν"]

5e5–6: cf. 8b

6a1: *Rep.* 365d7–e3, 366bf. Cf. "theology"—Rep. II–III where Socrates (≠ Adeimantus) refers to πόλις in criticizing the popular views. [footnote to "δικαιότατον"]

6a6–7: καινοτομῶν [a line connects this word to 6b2–3]

6b5: 3d5–6

6c1: *Theages* 126e1, *Apol.* 22d5–6

6c2: [After "Παναθηναίοις" LS, again, refers to the footnote for 6a1]

6c8: S. not interested.

6d11–e1: No ideas of στερήσεις—cf. Cherniss

7b1: LS deletes the editor's square brackets of "εἴρηται γάρ"

7d9 ad 7e–8d: *Alk.* I 112, *Hipp. Mai.* 294d, *Phaedrus* 263aff. 250b, *Polit.* 285e–286a, Xen. *Mem.* I 1, 9, IV 4 7–8.

7e2–4: omits ἄδικα, 7d1, cf. 8a7–8

7e7: *Rep.* 412d4 [in the margin]

7e7: ὅσιόν–θεοῖς προσφιλής = δίκαιον, καλόν, ἀγαθόν [footnote to "φιλοῦσιν"]

8b3: 5e5ff.

8c9: —not: νοοῦσι [between the lines, just above "λέγουσι"]

8c9: ergo the "sophists" are not really ἄδικοι. [footnote]

8d4: i. e. the ἄδικον itself is not controversial [footnote]

8d6: ἔν εἰρήνῃ ἢ ἔν πόλεμῳ

8d11: cf. c9–10

8d11–e1: Polus

9b2: cf. 8e6

9c3: 9a1, b6–7, d8

9e3: omits qualification of 9d3–5

10a1: the problem:
if ὅσιόν is νόμῳ or δόξῃ, then act of δοκεῖν-δοξάζειν precedes
[if ὅσιόν is] φύσει, the act of δοξάζειν follows [footnote to "πειράσομαι"]

10a2: ad 7e6–7

10a5: —he brings remote examples which however somehow will point to the basic difference. [footnote to "πειράσομαι"]

10a5–7: *Minos* 313b8–c3 [in the margin]

10d13 ad 10b–d: cf. *Phaidon* 96, 103B

11b1: 3d5–6

11b9: 4a1–4

11e1: 12a5

11e5: 5d9

11e6: 7e6–7

12a5: 11e2

12c10: c3–4

12d5: cf. *Protag.* 330c2–6

13a9: central—νή τον κύνα [in the left-hand margin]

Silence about ἄνθρώπων θεραπεία [in the right-hand margin]

δίκαιον = ἄρχων [footnote to the note in the right-hand margin]

13b13: *Rep.* 335b6ff.

13c4: —omits θεραπευομένου—also not θεραπευομένος

14a1–2: war—πόλις

14a5–6: peace—οἶκος

14c1: 3d5

15b7: 11b9–e1

15e2: 3d5–6

16e4: —sc. than before the instruction given to him by E.

# PART II
# Interpretive Essays

CHAPTER 1

# Reading Strauss's Notebook on Plato's *Euthyphro*

HANNES KERBER

## STRAUSS'S FIRST IMPRESSION AND HIS FIRST STATEMENT ON THE *EUTHYPHRO*

The first sentence of Strauss's notebook on Plato's *Euthyphro* reads: "In the *Euthyphron*, piety is discussed in the form of a conversation between two individuals that takes place in a specific setting" (p. 19). The thing most noteworthy about Strauss's opening statement seems to be that there is nothing particularly noteworthy. In naming the *Euthyphro*'s subject matter and its literary form, the brief summary reiterates what virtually every reader already knows. In doing so, Strauss lightly scratches the surface of Plato's dialogue. However, it is precisely the fact that he begins his notebook on the *Euthyphro* with a rather superficial statement that is significant in and of itself. As Strauss reminds us in his published writings: "The problem inherent in the surface of things, and only in the surface of things, is the heart of things."[1] First impressions and common opinions are the proper starting point of any investigation.

In keeping with this principle, Strauss immediately interrogates his opening statement on the *Euthyphro* by posing a series of questions: "a) why 'piety'? b) why is piety treated conversationally? c) why this specific setting?" (p. 19). Throughout the notebook, Strauss returns again and again to his opening statement and to these three questions. The pages thus abound with the words "piety," "action," and "setting," often underlined with a pencil or a thick red crayon. Periodically, Strauss interrupts his line-by-line commentary on the *Euthyphro* to take stock and summarize how continually refined answers to the three questions have changed the impression expressed in the summary statement at the start of the notebook. As a consequence, Strauss's notebook is structured by six restatements of the notebook's opening lines, each of which attempts to interpret Plato's *Euthyphro* as a whole (see pp. 25–26, 32–36, 38–40, 44–47, 49–50, and 55–57).[2] The six restatements show that, over the course of writing his notes, Strauss has continuously and substantially revised his understanding of Plato's *Euthyphro* without ever forgetting the point from which he started.

The three questions Strauss raises at the notebook's beginning, and to which he regularly returns, serve a common purpose: They point to what Strauss calls in the notebook the "connection between content (λόγος) and form (ἔργον)" (p. 32) and what one of his closest students later called "the argument of the action."[3] By asking why the problem at issue in the *Euthyphro* is piety, why this problem is discussed in a dialectical back-and-forth between the philosopher Socrates and the prophet Euthyphro, and why the conversation takes place in a specific historical setting, Strauss emphasizes that understanding why and how Plato uses the dialogue as a literary form is crucial to understanding Plato's teaching. Since Plato chose to present his teaching not in his own voice in a treatise, but indirectly through a conversation between Socrates and Euthyphro, Plato's teaching cannot be gleaned by merely reading the pages of his *Euthyphro*. "We can get hold of Plato's teaching" only, as Strauss puts it in a set of notes on the *Euthyphro* closely related to the notebook, "through the 'form'—more precisely, through understanding content in the light of the form" (p. 112, cf. pp. 20 and 32).

## STRAUSS'S FINAL RESTATEMENT AND HIS ANALYSIS OF THE *EUTHYPHRO*

Rather than going through all six of Strauss's restatements or following the many twists and turns of his notebook—which include fascinating exegetical detours and bold experimental readings of specific passages of Plato's dialogue—I will jump to Strauss's last restatement, which contains his most comprehensive interpretation of the *Euthyphro*. Then, I will retrace the steps that led Strauss from the first impression with which he begins the notebook to the reading at which he ultimately arrives in his sixth, and last, restatement of the notebook's opening lines. Even though this last restatement is by no means Strauss's last word on the *Euthyphro*, it contains a challenging analysis of Plato's *Euthyphro* as well as an original argument regarding the nature of the gods.

In the last restatement of his notebook, Strauss reformulates its first sentence as follows:

> In the *Euthyphron*, S. discusses piety with an expert on piety who is a man of questionable piety. E. expresses his heterodoxy unwittingly by suggesting that piety = imitating the gods, and he is thus led by S. to admit that what the gods love (sc. that men imitate them) is different from the pious (= customary worship of the gods). Shocked by this unforeseen and dangerous consequence, he is now prepared to be led by S., to be led back to the common view according to which it is precisely the ordinary worship that is pleasing to the gods. This ordinary view is suggested by S.: S. is really pious. (pp. 55–56)

By returning over and over to the three questions he posed near the beginning to interrogate the notebook's opening statement, Strauss continuously adjusts and deepens his first impression of the *Euthyphro*. As a result, he arrives here at a condensed restatement that contains an explanation of the dialogue's movement from beginning to end. This explanation includes, as we will see, some of the crucial features of the opening statement while radically transforming their significance.

The most important, if maybe not the most striking, fact about the final restatement is that Strauss identifies what is often called Euthyphro's First Definition (5d8–9) as the dialogue's hidden center of gravity. According to Strauss's last restatement in the notebook, Euthyphro's initial suggestion that "piety = imitating the gods" acts in complex ways on the other parts of the dialogue. For example, the realization that his claim amounts to a "heterodoxy" is responsible for Euthyphro's state of shock, which then triggers the dialogue's movement toward what Strauss calls the "ordinary" or "common view" of piety (which is restored at the end of the *Euthyphro* when piety is defined in more or less plainly traditional terms as "a certain kind of knowledge of sacrificing and praying" [14c5–6]). According to Strauss, we cannot simply take the remarkable resurrection of "ordinary worship" in the dialogue's closing exchanges as Plato's or Socrates's last word on the issue of piety.[4] Rather, we have to understand it as the result of the effect Euthyphro's own First Definition had on him and the development of his conversation with Socrates. If Socrates is indeed “really pious,” as Strauss claims at the very end of his final restatement, he is so primarily by virtue of initiating Euthyphro’s renunciation of his “heterodoxy” and guiding the “shocked” prophet on his return to what we may call the “orthodox” view. In a crucial (if, of course, not yet fully transparent) respect, all of the dialogue’s actions and speeches are linked to the First Definition.

Let’s explore the interpretation compressed in Strauss’s last restatement by turning to the passage in the *Euthyphro* in which we find Euthyphro’s First Definition:

> Socrates: Say then, what do you say the pious is, and what the impious?
> Euthyphro: I say that the pious is just what I’m doing now, prosecuting him who is unjust in murder, robbery of sacred things, or being at fault in anything similar, whether he be father, mother, or anyone whatsoever, and not to prosecute is impious. (5d7–e2)[5]

As numerous scholars have pointed out, Euthyphro’s ad hoc answer to the “What is?”-question typical for Socrates’s elenctic procedure in the Platonic dialogues is formally defective.[6] For Socrates made clear immediately before posing his question that a proper answer cannot consist in an example, however exemplary, but has to take the form of a general, unitary, and explanatory definition (cf. 5d1–5).[7] The answer Euthyphro gives, however, falls short of providing a proper definition because his specific example lacks the explanatory generality demanded by Socrates’s question.[8] When Strauss first comments on this passage in the notebook, he makes basically the same observation: Euthyphro’s answer shows, according to Strauss’s commentary on 5d8–e2, an “obvious misunderstanding of the meaning of S.’s question.” This misunderstanding becomes evident, as Strauss writes, when Euthyphro provides a “particular instance instead of [a] universal” (p. 29). In the notebook, Strauss illustrates Euthyphro’s mistake with an unrelated but similar case: The question “What is ‘bird’?” is not adequately answered if one says, “A goose is a bird” (p. 29).

Almost all scholars who have commented on this passage of Plato’s *Euthyphro* content themselves with exposing Euthyphro’s failure to fulfill the definitional standards demanded by Socrates’s question and acknowledging the formal flaw of Euthyphro’s First Definition. Typically, scholars take Euthyphro’s mistake as proof that, contrary to his name, which roughly translates to "Straight-Thinker," Euthyphro is nothing but an arrogant fool.[9] As a result, Euthyphro's initial attempt at defining piety is usually seen as worthy of an intellectual blowhard and unworthy of closer philosophical scrutiny.

Unsurprisingly, almost all scholars dealing with the *Euthyphro* have effectively ignored the substance of the First Definition because of its formal flaw and have focused instead on the two subsequent and formally more adequate definitions of piety. Much attention has been paid, for example, to the Second Definition—which says that the pious is what is dear to the gods (6d10–7a1)—as well as to the notorious "Euthyphro Dilemma" as it arises from this view of piety.[10] Similarly, the last, or Third Definition—which claims, as I have already noted, that piety consists in a certain kind of knowledge of sacrificing and praying (14c5–6)—has been regularly adduced to elucidate Socrates's supposed religious beliefs or what is commonly known in the critical literature as "Socratic Piety."[11] While both the dilemma the *Euthyphro* is famous for and the question regarding Socrates's piety eventually do play a role in Strauss's reading of the dialogue, he looks at both issues from the vantage point of Euthyphro's First Definition.

As we saw, Strauss, like the majority of commentators, acknowledges the formal flaw of Euthyphro's first answer to Socrates's question and initially also calls Euthyphro a "fool" for failing to provide a formally acceptable answer. In an early restatement of the notebook's opening lines Strauss writes that "S. discusses what piety is with a fool who claims to be an expert regarding piety—what can be the significance of such a discussion? S. cannot possibly learn from E., nor can he possibly teach that conceited idiot—what can Plato wish to teach us by presenting S.'s discussion with that fool?" (p. 26).

What distinguishes Strauss's interpretation from the bulk of contemporary scholarship on the *Euthyphro* is his refusal to content himself with blaming the First Definition's formal flaw on the logical incapacity or dialectical inexperience of a "conceited idiot" and "fool." Put differently, Strauss's reading of the *Euthyphro* is characterized above all by the remarkable philosophical attention he pays to Euthyphro's First Definition as well as to Plato's choice of dialogue as a form.[12] When Strauss asks: "What can Plato wish to teach us by presenting S.'s discussion with that fool?" (p. 26), he acknowledges the strange setting of the conversation without immediately resorting to an explanation that fails to explain the authorial intention responsible for that very setting.

By taking the problem posed by the dialogue's literary makeup seriously, Strauss allows himself to reconsider Euthyphro's First Definition and to reassess Euthyphro's character. In contrast to the early restatement of the notebook's opening lines, which describes Euthyphro as "a fool who claims to be an expert regarding piety" (p. 26), the last restatement no longer writes him off as a "fool." Instead, Euthyphro here has recovered his status as an "expert on piety" at least to a certain extent (cf. pp. 55–56). The First Definition's formal flaw is now attributed not to Euthyphro's lack of intelligence but to his lack of reflectiveness: Euthyphro "unwittingly" expresses a heretical opinion about piety and he is "shocked" by its "unforeseen" implications (p. 55). As Strauss thus highlights, the "heterodoxy" implied in the First Definition is by no means intended by Euthyphro.

## THE IMPLICIT THEOLOGY OF EUTHYPHRO'S FIRST DEFINITION OF PIETY

Strauss's reason for eventually abandoning his early denouncement of Euthyphro as a "fool" becomes apparent if we pay attention to how Strauss is able to keep going where most scholars stopped. By paying unusually close attention not only to the dialogue's speeches but also to its literary setting, Strauss notices what usually remains overlooked because it is not discussed explicitly in the dialogue: the principle underlying Euthyphro's first answer to Socrates's question is a rare expression of Euthyphro's character and differs theologically in a crucial respect from the later definitions of piety that are discussed in the *Euthyphro*.

As Strauss points out when commenting for the first time on Euthyphro's justification of his First Definition in 5e5–6a5, the underlying principle becomes apparent when we consider the function of Euthyphro's claim in the context of his conversation with Socrates: "Setting: E.'s character. E.'s proof of the piety of his action: it corresponds to Zeus's action; he imitates Zeus, the justest of the gods, the model of justice" (p. 29). Euthyphro's first answer to Socrates's question "What is piety?" is, as Strauss shows, his attempt to justify the pious nature of his seemingly impious prosecution of his own father for murder (see 3e7–4a10)—a scandal in the eyes of all or most of those who are traditionally pious (4c11–12; see Cicero, *De officiis* 3.90). In bringing charges against his father, Euthyphro knowingly imitates Zeus, "the justest of the gods" (see 5e6–6a1), who also did not spare his father, Kronos, when Kronos committed an injustice (see Hesiod, *Theogony*

154–210 and 459–506).[13] Euthyphro's belief in the virtue or duty of such imitation is "E.'s proof of the piety of his action." Insofar as the principle underlying the First Definition—and only the First Definition—explains Euthyphro's "action," it alone is an expression of his "character."[14]

According to Strauss, Euthyphro's simple, if not simpleminded, appeal to Zeus as a "model" conceals—even from Euthyphro himself—the bold theological claim that "piety = imitating the gods" (see pp. 29–30, 36–39, 43–50, 53, 55, and 58). Because Euthyphro voices this claim "unwittingly" (see, again, p. 55) and because Socrates does not explicitly discuss it in the conversation, Euthyphro as well as many readers of the *Euthyphro* fail to notice that the imitative or mimetic notion of piety is at odds with the theological tendency of the Second and Third Definitions.[15] For while the Second and Third Definitions are in agreement with, or can easily be brought into agreement with, the "ordinary" or "common view" of piety, this is, as I will show in the next section, not the case for the First Definition. For this reason, Strauss in his last restatement characterizes the view that "piety = imitating the gods" as a "heterodoxy" (p. 55, cf. p. 39).[16]

## THE TENSION BETWEEN THE FIRST AND THE SECOND DEFINITION

To understand the nature of Euthyphro's not immediately obvious "heterodoxy," let us step once again into his shoes. According to Strauss's last restatement of the notebook's opening lines (pp. 55–56), Euthyphro's realization of the difference between what is "pious" (ὅσιον) and "what the gods love" (θεοφιλές) eventually allows him to grasp the "unforeseen and dangerous consequence" of the view he expressed "unwittingly" when Socrates first asked him to define piety. This difference is first discussed in the *Euthyphro* in 6e10–7a8, a passage that deals with what is often referred to as Euthyphro's Second Definition of piety:

> Euthyphro: The pious, then, is what is dear to the gods, and what is not dear is impious.
>
> Socrates: Very fine, Euthyphro, you've answered in just the way I was asking you to answer. Whether you answered truly, however, I do not yet know about that, but you will obviously go on to teach that it's true what you say.
>
> Euthyphro: Of course I shall.

> Socrates: Come then, let us examine what you mean. What is dear to the gods and a human being dear to the gods is pious, and what is hateful to the gods and he who is hateful to the gods is impious: they are not the same, but most contrary, aren't they, the pious to the impious.

When commenting on this passage in the notebook, Strauss refers for the first time explicitly to "the problem of piety" and, in doing so, picks out one single line. He notes that Socrates "illogically" (p. 31) adds the word ἄνθρωπος (human being) when in line 7a7 he repeats Euthyphro's second attempt to define piety. Where Euthyphro said "the pious, then, is what is dear to the gods" (6e10–7a1), Socrates says, "what is dear to the gods and a human being (ἄνθρωπος) dear to the gods is pious" (7a6–7). According to Strauss, the seemingly small addition of the word ἄνθρωπος puts "the problem of piety" in a nutshell and reveals the implicit tension between the First and the Second Definition: For if what is "pious" is "what is dear to the gods," the gods themselves "cannot be pious" (p. 31), and if the "gods cannot be pious," the imitation of the gods, or, as Strauss puts it, ὁμοίωσις θεῷ, the "assimilation to god" (cf. *Theaetetus* 176b1) amounts to "transcending" the limits set by conventional piety (p. 31; cf. pp. 36, 40, and 96).

Now we are in a better position to understand why Strauss's last restatement of the notebook's opening lines calls Euthyphro's First Definition a "heterodoxy" (p. 55; cf. pp. 39, 117, 124, and 126–28). In the city of Athens, piety was commonly expressed through the "customary worship of the gods," traditional prayers and cultic sacrifices that were said to be pleasing to the gods.[17] By claiming that "piety = imitating the gods," Euthyphro deviates from the traditional view because he tacitly, albeit decisively, denies one of its underlying theological assumptions. The gods, Euthyphro's First Definition implies, are beings that want to be imitated, not worshipped. Unbeknownst to Euthyphro, his First Definition of piety—which he proudly seems to think of as a humble expression of unquestioning obedience—is essentially "heretical" (p. 39).

### THEOLOGY AND THE DOCTRINE OF IDEAS

At this point, we have to return once again to the question of why Strauss in the notebook eventually stops referring to Euthyphro as a "fool." For even if the formal flaw of his initial answer does not warrant calling the self-declared prophet a "fool," the fact that he fails to notice the implicit "heterodoxy" of his First Definition would certainly seem to suffice as the basis for such a verdict. To better understand why Strauss nevertheless retracts his early denouncement of Euthyphro and why he even reinstates, however playfully, Euthyphro's status as an "expert on piety" in the last restatement of the notebook's opening lines (see pp. 55–56), we have to further develop the philosophical and theological implications of Euthyphro's First Definition. For even though the principle implied in Euthyphro's flawed first attempt at a definition of piety has to be described as "heterodox" from the standpoint of traditional piety, it is in a certain respect superior to the theological assumptions expressed in the dogmatically and formally more adequate Second and Third Definitions.

Strauss's most clear-cut statement in the notebook on the superiority of the First Definition shows why he ultimately does not conceive of Euthyphro as a "fool." According to Strauss, Euthyphro should not be called a "fool" for the simple reason that, in a way, he is right: "E.'s first and implicit definition of piety: piety = to imitate the highest and justest god—a divination of the truth by the μάντις" (p. 36, cf. p. 39). Euthyphro's tacit understanding of piety is, according to Strauss, decisively superior to that of the common man on the street: "E.'s view . . . is clearly more sophisticated than the ordinary view; after all, E. is an expert on piety" (p. 56). Strauss shows by deed that instead of "fool," Euthyphro can ironically but not untruthfully be called what he calls himself—a μάντις, a "seer," "diviner," or "prophet" (cf. 3c4 with 3e3). While Euthyphro's unsuspecting suggestion that piety means "to imitate the highest and justest god" goes against the traditional understanding of piety, it "arises," according to Strauss, "from the divination that to be a truly human being, man must aspire beyond mere humanity" (p. 39). In short, Euthyphro is an "expert on piety" not *despite* but *because of* the fact that he is "a man of questionable piety" (cf. p. 55).

Why, then, is the claim that piety means "to imitate the highest and justest god," according to Strauss, "a divination of the truth"? By appealing to Zeus in this way, Euthyphro not only unintentionally suggests the notion of piety as imitating the gods but also introduces a standard based on which a hierarchy among the many gods worshipped by the city of Athens can be established: Zeus is the "highest" god because he exceeds all other gods in justice. From Euthyphro's perspective, establishing such a divine hierarchy might seem indispensable because the mimetic notion of piety forces him to choose one god as a model among the many Greek gods. Without any further explanation, Euthyphro chooses justice as the standard to account for his decision to imitate the actions of Zeus and not, for example, the actions of the older gods Kronos or Uranus.[18] More generally, one may wonder whether the appeal to some standard of divine perfection is not indispensable for belief as such. Is it possible to take a god as one's model or even to truly worship a god without being able to recognize in some way this god's perfection? Is it possible, in other words, to rest one's faith on a hidden, fundamentally unknowable god?

Be that as it may, Euthyphro's introduction of a standard for establishing the hierarchy within the Athenian pantheon has an implication of which the "expert on piety" is clearly unaware. Commenting on the "fundamental mistake" of the First Definition, Strauss, now, does not make any reference to the formal mistake Euthyphro made by failing the definitional requirements implied in Socrates's question "What is piety?" Instead, Strauss points to the grave theological consequence of Euthyphro's appeal to Zeus's justice: "It is only now that S. points out E.'s fundamental mistake. → E. has said 'Zeus is the justest of the gods' without raising the question 'what is justice?' There is a criterion higher than the gods for judging of the gods. And if we know this, we do not need stories about the gods" (pp. 30–31). Euthyphro's assertion that Zeus is "the justest of the gods" entails the radical claim that the gods are not absolutely supreme since "there is a criterion higher than the gods for judging of the gods." In the staccato style which is typical of the notebook, Strauss comments: "The ideas replace the gods. The new gods are the ideas" (p. 30; cf. pp. 35, 46, 88, 117, 124, and 127–28).

According to Strauss, Euthyphro fails to realize the far-reaching implication of his First Definition because he fails to ask the question "What is justice?" If he had raised this question, he would have been forced to acknowledge that according to his own claim, the gods are subject to an "idea" (ἰδέα or εἶδος, see 5d4, 6d11, and 6e3) or, in the language of Strauss's notebook, to a "criterion," "norm," "pattern," or "standard" that allows Euthyphro to rank the gods and identify Zeus as the "highest" deity.[19] If Euthyphro had raised, and answered, the question "What is justice?," he would have been compelled to admit that if there were an "idea" of justice, a just god or the just gods would have to comply with this "idea" and that, therefore, this "idea" would be "higher than the gods." Moreover, Euthyphro would then have to recognize that the guiding function of the myths is replaced by the knowledge of this higher "idea." Without realizing it, Euthyphro has thus not only made the gods "superfluous" but also, in a way, substituted philosophy for piety: "Quest for the ideas, or philosophy, replaces piety: the ideas are S.'s new gods" (p. 46).[20]

Now we are finally in a position to understand why Strauss ultimately refuses to call Euthyphro a "fool" and why he sees in Euthyphro's First Definition a "divination of the truth." The introduction of a standard that allows one to rationally articulate or assess divine perfection independently of the traditional myths represents a crucial step toward a philosophical response to the orthodox view of the gods. Deviating somewhat from Strauss's and Plato's way of speaking but—one could argue—keeping with their way of thinking, we shall call this alternative notion of the gods 'philosophical theology.'[21]

In his notebook, Strauss provides two shorthand accounts of the philosophical theology that Euthyphro inadvertently and halfheartedly endorsed. Strauss's first sketch barely covers one line and reads: "What about a theology in agreement with [the] doctrine of ideas? god = pure mind = mind that grasps the ideas which are independent of his will" (p. 36). According to this note, a theology that takes the "doctrine of the ideas" into account conceives of god as a "pure mind," that is, a mind that perfectly perceives or intuits the "ideas" without distorting them through an act of will or sense perception.[22] This notion of a god as a knowing being implies that the "ideas" or, more generally, the objects of knowledge have to be understood as "independent" of divine (or, for that matter, human) volition and arbitrariness. This is necessary because it is a condition for the possibility of knowledge that the objects of knowledge are not affected by the knower. As Strauss puts it in his later lecture on the *Euthyphro*, "That of which knowledge is knowledge, is prior. The ideas are prior to knowledge of the ideas. Therefore if one denies the primacy of the ideas, one denies the possibility of knowledge" (p. 89, cf. p. 46).

In short, as a direct consequence of the "heretical" principle underlying Euthyphro's First Definition, the gods worshipped by the city of Athens are stripped of the status traditional piety assigns to them, namely, that of the first things or highest beings. Instead, the gods are now conceived of as beings that are beholden to the "ideas." With his explicit appeal to Zeus's justice, Euthyphro implicitly and unknowingly introduces a version of the doctrine of "ideas" which effectively destroys the possibility of orthodox theology: "E.'s first, implicit definition amounts then to a silent rejection of the orthodox view," Strauss writes in his notebook (p. 45). In the notes for his first lecture on the *Euthyphro*, Strauss goes even further: "E.'s heresy, consistently followed up, will lead to S.'s heresy" (p. 117).

## THE ORTHODOX ALTERNATIVE TO A PHILOSOPHICAL THEOLOGY

Before I come to Strauss's second sketch of the philosophical theology that Euthyphro "unwittingly" and, we might add, somewhat unwillingly suggests in his first attempt to define piety, let me briefly outline the most demanding version of the orthodox alternative to which Euthyphro is still strongly attached. According to Strauss, any consistently orthodox theology rests upon the claim that the gods are absolutely supreme: "The common notion of piety is based on the premise that there is nothing higher than the gods—that in order to act well, the gods do not have to comply with a higher standard: the common notion of piety is based on the implicit denial of the existence of ideas" (p. 39).

By asserting that the gods are absolutely supreme, the defenders of the orthodox position are forced to deny the primacy of the "ideas." What the gods do, or don't do, is determined by nothing but their free or arbitrary will. The "ideas" and, for that matter, all criteria, norms, patterns, and standards are thus conceived of as ultimately irrelevant for, dependent on, or subject to the sovereign authority of the divine being or beings. As almost goes without saying, this claim has grave consequences. If, as Strauss suggests, the only knowledge possible is the knowledge of "ideas," then the gods cannot be conceived as knowing beings: "The tacit presupposition of the vulgar notion [of piety] is then that the gods are ignorant, ignorant especially as regarding justice → the gods fight with each other" (p. 39). The gods' fighting is, according to Strauss, a direct consequence of the claim that they, as opposed to the "ideas," are the highest beings simply.[23] The myths represent the gods as fighting gods precisely because the myths also claim that there is no "higher norm" for the gods, that they do not have "any standard independent of their arbitrariness," and that they are "not . . . guided by knowledge" (p. 35; cf. pp. 39, 98, and 118, see 7c10–d5). To illustrate this corollary, and to reveal its broader significance, Strauss in the notebook rephrases his argument in terms of a monotheistic theology:

"In the language of monotheism, if the divine will is not guided by divine intelligence, i.e. if all necessity rests on a basis of arbitrariness, everything is possible, everything is permissible → chaos and fight" (p. 39).

Against the backdrop of the distinction between a philosophical theology and its orthodox counterpart, we can begin to understand the real force of the dilemma Socrates famously confronts Euthyphro with in 10a1–3. At the same time, we are reminded that in following the interpretation Strauss develops in his notebook by paying unusually close attention to the dialogue's action, we have left the confines of the dialogue's speeches in the narrow sense. For while we as readers are now able to appreciate the implications of the dilemma, Euthyphro himself is utterly unable to understand what Socrates is talking about:

> Socrates: Consider the following: the pious, is it loved by the gods because it is pious, or because it is loved is it pious?
> Euthyphro: I do not know what you mean, Socrates. (10a1–4)

The dilemma that Socrates here confronts the puzzled Euthyphro with is, according to Strauss's notebook, equivalent to the question "Are the gods subject to a higher norm or are they <u>not</u> subject to it?" (p. 40). If, on the one hand, divine love itself were ruled by something that is independent of this love, the gods would not be the highest beings simply. If, on the other hand, the gods were the highest beings simply, it would have to be their love that makes the pious pious. Euthyphro's failure to understand this dilemma shows that he hopes to have it both ways: He opts for the dilemma's first horn by appealing to Zeus's justice while he also opts for the dilemma's second horn by appealing to Zeus—and not, for example, justice or the "idea" of justice—as the absolute authority.

However, such inclusiveness is not feasible. As Strauss makes clear by sharply distinguishing the two theologies, one is ultimately forced to take sides in order to remain consistent: Orthodox theology decides the dilemma in favor of the second horn and, therefore, radically denies the primacy of "ideas" and asserts that the gods' love—as well as all their actions, volitions, and thoughts—is absolutely free or arbitrary or not grounded in any knowledge. A philosophical theology, conversely, would either choose the dilemma's first horn or deny altogether that self-sufficient beings are able to love.

From the point of view that we have now reached we can schematically restate the alternative between the two theologies in the following way: For a philosophical theology, the all-important divine attribute is wisdom, while in the eyes of an orthodox theologian, the all-important divine attribute is power, or, spoken more precisely (if somewhat anachronistically), omnipotence. For this reason, even the biblical view of divine perfection (which seemingly lays claim to both attributes) is ultimately indicated by omnipotence or will, rather than by wisdom. Much like Euthyphro's theology, the theology implied in or suggested by the Bible can therefore be reduced to the simple if consequential claim that will is above wisdom.[24]

In his notebook, Strauss, however, does not leave the two different theologies simply at odds with each other. Instead, he begins—immediately after asserting that "the common notion of piety is based on the implicit denial of the existence of ideas" (p. 39, cf. p. 35)—to articulate the outlines of an internal critique of the claim made by orthodox theology: "But this is absurd: God could kill himself and decree that the world will last forever after his suicide and follow immutable laws. Not everything can be possible: there must be necessity at the bottom of arbitrariness: there must be ideas determining even the will of God" (p. 39, cf. p. 118).

In this way, Strauss counters the claim that "there is nothing higher than the gods" with a reduction-to-absurdity argument. If a god is conceived of as not being subject to, or dependent on, any "ideas," criteria, norms, patterns, or standards, there is literally no limit to what he could do or would refrain from doing. According to Strauss, this cannot be anyone's considered opinion: "Not everything can be possible."[25] Needless to say, this does not mean that a consistently orthodox position cannot be practically maintained. It means, however, that any defense of this position has to be grounded not in any justification, but in unquestioning obedience: "the pious has no other reason than the inscrutable will of the gods. . . . To obey means 'not to reason why?' Customary practice is to be divorced from alleged ἐπιστήμη [knowledge]" (pp. 58–59, cf. pp. 55 and 57).[26]

## THE PHILOSOPHER'S ANALOGICAL ARGUMENT

After I have outlined the orthodox view, let me briefly turn to Strauss's second sketch of the philosophical theology. In light of its alternative, the reach and the limits of the theology that Euthyphro has suggested "unwittingly" in his

First Definition of piety will come into sharper relief. A few pages after his first sketch—and with an explicit reference to this first sketch—Strauss writes, "What then is the right attitude to the gods? God = pure mind = mind that grasps the ideas perfectly (p. 12, l. 3 [here p. 36])). Philosophy = ὁμοίωσις θεῷ [assimilation to god]" (p. 40). Here, Strauss again explores the notion of god as a "perfectly" knowing or wise being. Now, however, he focuses on the "right attitude" of human beings to this god and comes to the surprising, or perhaps unsurprising, conclusion that philosophy itself is philosophical theology's equivalent of piety. "Philosophy = ὁμοίωσις θεῷ" is, we might say, the deepest meaning of Euthyphro's half-conscious "divination" that piety consists not in traditional worship but in imitation of the gods.

As the continuation of the second sketch shows, the equation of "assimilation to god" with philosophy allows Strauss to further articulate the argument on which the philosophical theology is based: "God : philosopher = actual philosopher : potential philosopher—but the actual philosopher loves the potential philosophers; ergo God loves the philosophers; the philosophers are θεοφιλεῖς [dear to the gods] → θεοφιλές [dear to the gods] ≠ ὅσιον [pious]. But: do the gods love?" (p. 40, cf. p. 41).

In this compressed and abbreviated line of argument, we see Strauss using the philosopher as the analogue for understanding the character of god as well as of god's relationship to human beings in general and to philosophers in particular: Strauss compares god's (yet to be understood) relationship with the philosopher to the (better understood) relationship between "actual philosophers" and "potential philosophers." On the basis of this analogy, Strauss concludes that gods, like philosophers, indeed prefer to be imitated rather than worshipped (cf. pp. 116, 118, 120, and 122). "The analogy of the σοφός [wise man]" shows, as Strauss writes in an outline for his 1950 lecture on the *Euthyphro*, that god, like the wise man, "likes more the people who do what he does than those who merely do what he tells them to do" (p. 124, cf. pp. 86–87). Thus, the principle underlying Euthyphro's First Definition as well as its "unforeseen and dangerous consequence" are, in a way, confirmed. If a god's or the gods' nature is to be understood along the lines of that of the philosophers, it follows that the "right attitude" toward the gods is not mimetic piety but piety in the traditional sense or, as Strauss laconically puts it here, it follows that "θεοφιλές ≠ ὅσιον."

To be sure, these conclusions are hypothetical. The "analogy of the wise man" draws on the fact that all, or almost all, people who speak of god imply that god is the highest or most perfect being and, therefore, attempt to articulate some features of this notion of god as the highest or most perfect being by extrapolating from human perfection.[27] In a note on the *Euthyphro*, Strauss shows by example how this extrapolation works: "How do we know that the gods are good? τί ἐστι θεός; [what is (a) god?] a superior being—we know something of superiority among human beings, the σοφός [wise man]—the σοφός [wise man] is not evil—ergo, the gods will be still less evil" (pp. 99–100). Here, Strauss infers a feature of divine perfection by extending a feature that characterizes the wise man, the allegedly most perfect specimen among human beings: Since the wise man is "not evil," the gods "will be still less evil." [28] Thus, the analogical argument helps to provide something like the minimum requirements of what divine perfection would look like if this perfection is to be understood in light of human perfection. As almost goes without saying, the articulation of this notion of the highest or most perfect being does not prove, and is not meant to prove, the existence of the being in question.[29] Similarly, it does not, and cannot, disprove the existence of a very powerful or omnipotent being which falls short of the standards set by the wise man. However, "the analogy of the σοφός" lays the ground for the rational refusal to recognize any being as the highest or most perfect being that fails to live up to the perfection of the wise man.[30]

With the reach as well as the limits of the "the analogy of the σοφός" in mind, we can now recognize that Strauss's last restatement of the notebook's opening lines takes for granted what he calls into question in his second sketch of the philosophical theology. The analogical argument suggests, but does not demonstrate, that "what the gods love" is indeed "that men imitate them" (p. 55). To the contrary, Strauss's second sketch explicitly calls into question whether the gods should really be conceived of as loving beings: "But: do the gods love?" (p. 40).[31] Don't we want to—or have to?—conceive of the most perfect being as truly self-sufficient? And, if that is the case, would a being that is not in need of anything be able to truly love?

However, especially here the forest should not be missed for the trees: Strauss's last restatement takes it for granted that the gods love because Euthyphro takes it for granted that the gods love. In Plato's dialogue Socrates goes out of his way to make sure that Euthyphro does not question his belief in divine philanthropy. As we saw, Socrates almost silently corrects the Second Definition by adding the word ἄνϑρωπος or "human being" in line 7a7 without giving Euthyphro much of a chance to see the importance, and questionable justification, of that addition (cf. p. 146 above). Similarly, both horns of the dilemma he confronts Euthyphro with in 10a1–3 presuppose, as a matter of course, that the gods love (cf. p. 151 above). In doing so, Socrates lets Euthyphro experience the critical power of philosophical theology without calling attention to its capacity for improving one's own self-reflection or one's understanding of the soul.[32]

From the notebook's last restatement, we learn why Socrates, according to Strauss, proceeds so carefully: He shields Euthyphro from grasping the most radical implication of his half-conscious insight into philosophical theology because Socrates wants to "lead [Euthyphro] back to the common view according to which it is precisely the ordinary worship that is pleasing to the gods" (pp. 55–56). The man Socrates meets in Plato's *Euthyphro* is not a "fool," but he is, as we saw, a "an expert on piety who is a man of questionable piety." Moreover, he is a man habitually incapable of facing up to the "unforeseen and dangerous consequence" of the insight he has stumbled upon.[33] Socrates, on the other hand, shows himself to be a man who not only knows how to radically pursue the problems "unwittingly" suggested by Euthyphro but also is capable of guiding Euthyphro's return to the safer grounds of the "common view." It is, then, not altogether surprising that Strauss concludes his last restatement with the confident claim: "S. is really pious."

**Notes**

1. Leo Strauss, *Thoughts on Machiavelli* (1958; Chicago: University of Chicago Press, 2006), 13.

2. Strauss probably used the restatements as the basis for his opening remarks in the sessions of his 1948 seminar on the *Euthyphro* and the *Crito*. See the introduction to this volume, p. 2.

3. See Seth Benardete, "Strauss on Plato," in *The Argument of the Action: Essays on Greek Poetry and Philosophy*, ed. Ronna Burger and Michael Davis (Chicago: University of Chicago Press, 2000), 409.

4. In the notebook, Strauss does not treat the *Euthyphro* as an aporetic dialogue—in fact, the word *aporia* does not occur. See, however, *The City and Man* (1964; Chicago: University of Chicago Press, 2007), 105–6.

5. I use Seth Benardete's translation of the *Euthyphro* (in this volume, pp. 187–217). In order to make it easier to follow the argument of Strauss's notebook, I have adapted the translation throughout to reflect the notebook's vocabulary. As a consequence, Socrates and Euthyphro use here Strauss's "pious" instead of Benardete's "holy." See n. 19 in the introduction to this volume.

6. According to Vasilis Politis, this interpretation of 5d7–e2 is "very common and apparently exceptionless" (*The Structure of Enquiry in Plato's Early Dialogues* [Cambridge: Cambridge University Press, 2015], 141, cf. 139–49 and 222–25).

7. On the so-called Priority of Definition Principle implied in the Socratic "What is?" question, see Hugh H. Benson, "The Priority of Definition and the Socratic Elenchus," *Oxford Studies in Ancient Philosophy* 8 (1990): 19–65.

8. Peter Geach not only strongly objects to the Priority of Definition Principle—which he

calls "the Socratic fallacy"—but also tries to rehabilitate the role of examples in elucidating terms. See "Plato's *Euthyphro*: An Analysis and Commentary," *The Monist* 50, no. 3 (1966): 369–82.

9. Among other things, Euthyphro has been referred to as a "complacent fanatic" who "for sheer sluggishness of intellect it would be hard to beat" (G. Vlastos), as "dogmatic" and "not very bright" (H. Teloh), a "spoiled child" (P. Shorey) and a "comic figure" who exhibits "pure imposture and alazony" (L. Versényi) and "combines within himself the worst features of a sciolist and a prig" (J. Adam). Cf. John Beversluis, *Cross-Examining Socrates: A Defense of the Interlocutors in Plato's Early Dialogues* (Cambridge: Cambridge University Press, 2000), 162–63.

10. See, among many others, S. Marc Cohen, "Socrates on the Definition of Piety: *Euthyphro* 10a–11b," *Journal of the History of Philosophy* 9, no. 1 (1971): 1–13.

11. See, for example, M. L. McPherran, "Socratic Piety in the *Euthyphro*," *Journal of the History of Philosophy* 23, no. 3 (1985): 283–309, and Gregory Vlastos, "Socratic Piety" (1989), in *Socrates: Ironist and Moral Philosopher* (Ithaca: Cornell University Press, 1991), 157–78.

12. As far as I can see, this is the major difference between Strauss's interpretation of the *Euthyphro* and those interpretations inspired or animated by his approach. See, for example, Christopher Bruell, *On the Socratic Education: An Introduction to the Shorter Platonic Dialogues* (Lanham, MD: Rowman & Littlefield, 1999), 117–33, or Ronna Burger, *On Plato's "Euthyphro"* (Munich: Carl Friedrich von Siemens Stiftung, 2015). While Lewis Fallis pays close attention to the First Definition, he, too, does not follow Strauss's interpretation in this regard (see *Socrates and Divine Revelation* [Rochester: University of Rochester Press, 2018], 51–52).

13. Among his contemporaries, Euthyphro is by no means alone in appealing to Zeus's treatment of Kronos—see, for example, Aeschylus's *Eumenides* (640–43) or Aristophanes's *Clouds* (904–6).

14. In the lecture "On Plato's *Euthyphron*," Strauss strongly underlines the fact that "only the first answer has a direct relation to Euthyphron's taste, to his action," and "only the first answer is a speech of Euthyphron in harmony with Euthyphron's deed, with his life, with the principle animating his life," and that it, therefore, is "the only answer given by Euthyphron which throws light on that view of piety which is characteristic of him" (p. 85).

15. Reginald E. Allen claims that "there is not a word in the *Euthyphro* to suggest that it is the moral duty of men to become like god, or gods" (*Plato's "Euthyphro" and the Earlier Theory of Forms* [London: Routledge, 1970], 8).

16. In the secondary literature, Euthyphro is frequently represented as "an earnest and simple believer in the old traditional religion of the Hellenes" (Geach, "Plato's *Euthyphro*," 370; cf. 373). Strauss, on the other hand, situates him between orthodoxy and heterodoxy: "Euthyphro occupies a middle position between Socrates and Meletus" (p. 82; cf. pp. 26, 28, 43, 47, 49–50, 81, 83, 85, 87–89, 116–17, 124, 127, and 130).

17. Strauss discusses the unfounded character of the knowledge claim "that the gods are pleased by the customary worship" at various points in the notebook (see pp. 45–46, 57, 116, and 122).

18. In the notebook, Strauss shows that "E[uthyphro] questions the root of ἀγαθόν [good] = πάτριον [ancestral]" (p. 25) not only by accusing his father, but also by choosing Zeus as his model: "If it is pious to imitate the old gods, the safest course in case of conflict among the gods is to imitate the oldest god. The justest god whom E[uthyphro] selects, is not the oldest god—he selects the highest god among the present gods" (p. 47, cf. pp. 89, 117, and 123). Denying the primeval identification of the "good" and the "ancestral" uproots piety, as Strauss notes in a different context: "Piety is replaced by philosophy" (*City and Man*, 65).

19. In the notebook, Strauss uses all four terms as synonyms for "idea" (pp. 29, 31, 34–35, 38–40, 42, 46, 48, 90, and 118). Because several features of the so-called Platonic Doctrine of Ideas are not found in the *Euthyphro*, scholars are divided over the question whether or not the occurrences of ἰδέα or εἶδος should be read in light of this doctrine. Strauss's main point is, to begin with, neutral with regard to this scholarly discussion. The term "idea" refers

in the notebook not to a transcendent reality of some sort but to an "intelligible necessity" (p. 36; cf. pp. 89–90, 118, and 127).

20. Cf. "Jerusalem and Athens" (1967), in *Studies in Platonic Political Philosophy* (Chicago: University of Chicago Press, 1983), 166. See n. 18 above.

21. In the notebook, as well as elsewhere, Strauss himself speaks of "natural theology" (p. 30, see p. 11n13) to describe the alternative. This term, however, comes with considerable historical baggage that invites grave misunderstandings. See Heinrich Meier, *Political Philosophy and the Challenge of Revealed Religion* (Chicago: University of Chicago Press, 2017), 61.

22. For Strauss's use of this notion of "pure mind," cf. *Leo Strauss on Hegel*, ed. Paul Franco (Chicago: University of Chicago Press, 2019), 35.

23. In the case of Euthyphro, it is, of course, the other way around: "Euthyphron's premises (= the mythical notion of the gods as fighting gods)," Strauss writes in the notebook, are "decisive for the implicit denial of the ideas" (p. 35).

24. In the eight session of his 1957 seminar on Plato's *Gorgias*, Strauss explicitly makes this point with regard to the *Euthyphro*: "[Euthyphro] also develops a certain theology whose thesis can be reduced to one simple proposition: will is above reason. But that means, since will is above reason, prior to when reason had its say, it cannot be will, rational desire—it can only be desire. It is essential to this view that these gods—however modest [Euthyphro] may be—these gods are desire incarnate."

25. At a different point in the notebook, Strauss illustrates the "absurd" consequences of the theological claim that the gods' volition and action are not subject to, or dependent on, anything other than the gods' arbitrariness by using the example of William of Occam's notorious nominalism: "Nominalism (Occam): radical denial of essences and universal archetypes → murder etc. is bad, because it is prohibited by God, and it is not prohibited by God because it is intrinsically bad. God could command murder—even that men shall hate Him; God could have been incarnated in a donkey as well as in man, or take on the nature of wood or stone (→ he could have created other gods → polytheism → fights)" (pp. 35–36). See also a similar, if somewhat more restrained, passage in the 1952 lecture, p. 90.

26. In an outline for his 1950 lecture on the *Euthyphro*, Strauss explains this point further: "To worship the gods in the customary manner with sacrifices and prayers is pleasing to them—why?—we do not know—they are pleased by it because they are pleased by it (cf. 15c5–6 with 10d)—no λόγος [argument/account] is possible" (p. 122). See also n. 12, p. 104.

27. On Strauss's use of the analogy of the wise man, see Marco Menon, "Leo Strauss and the Argument of Natural Theology," *Etica & Politica* 38 (2016): 572–89. Cf., again, Meier, *Political Philosophy and the Challenge of Revealed Religion*, 61.

28. In various lectures from the late 1940s and early 1950s, Strauss uses "the analogy of the σοφός" to argue, for example, that a god would not condemn erring human beings to eternal damnation since even a wise man merely pities fools and would not react with indignation toward their foolery. See "Reason and Revelation" (1948), in Heinrich Meier, *Leo Strauss and the Theologico-Political Problem* (Cambridge: Cambridge University Press, 2006), 153–54. and 162; "Leo Strauss's *Jerusalem and Athens* (1950): Three Lectures at Hillel House, Chicago," *Journal for the History of Modern Theology / Zeitschrift für Neuere Theologiegeschichte* 29, no. 1 (2022): 170; "Progress or Return? The Contemporary Crisis in Western Civilization" (1952), in *Jewish Philosophy and the Crisis of Modernity: Essays and Lectures in Modern Jewish Thought* (Albany: State University of New York Press, 1997), 129; and "The Mutual Influence of Theology and Philosophy" (1952/54), *Independent Journal of Philosophy* 3 (1979): 116–17.

29. Strauss's most outspoken statement on the function as well as the limits of the analogy of the wise man can be found in his "Notes on Lucretius," in *Liberalism Ancient and Modern* (1968; Chicago: University of Chicago Press, 1995), 130: "The fundamental theologumenon is meant to articulate in the most adequate manner our notion of the gods as *entia perfectissima* . . . ; the fundamental theologumenon is not meant to prove the existence of gods; their existence is not known."

30. In his interpretation of the *Clouds,* Strauss shows the practical implication of this refusal: While Socrates is of the opinion that Zeus and the other traditional gods "do not even exist," he knows that "even if they did exist, he would not have taken them as his model because of their childishness as shown by their indifference to learning" (*Socrates and Aristophanes* [1966; Chicago: University of Chicago Press, 1996], 33).

31. While Strauss asserts in the notebook that "the experience of the philosopher" shows "that the higher would care for the lower" (p. 42), in his contemporary lecture "Reason and Revelation," he claims that a "wise man . . . would not care particularly for anyone except his friends, i.e. those who are actually or potentially wise" and that, "accordingly, God . . . cannot be conceived as *loving* men, i.e. beings who are infinitely inferior to him in wisdom" ("Reason and Revelation," 153f.; cf. "Leo Strauss's *Jerusalem and Athens* [1950]," 170).

32. In his notebook on the *Euthyphro*—as opposed to his lectures on the dialogue (see pp. 93 and 113; cf. p. 125)—Strauss does not explicitly state that "the argument is characterized by the abstraction from the soul; the phenomenon of the soul is deliberately disregarded" (*Plato's "Gorgias"* (1957), ed. Devin Stauffer [Leo Strauss Transcripts], Session 12, February 26, 1957). See also Strauss's remarks on the silence regarding the soul in the *Euthyphro* at the beginning of the thirteenth session of his 1959 seminar on Plato's *Laws* (*Plato's "Laws"* (1959), ed. Lorraine Pangle [Leo Strauss Transcripts], Session 13, February 26, 1959).

33. In his 1966 seminar on Plato's *Apology of Socrates* and *Crito,* Strauss spells out the consequences Euthyphro's character has for his conversation with Socrates: In the *Euthyphro,* "Socrates first tries to go deeper into the question of piety but then, precisely because this man Euthyphron is not able to bear that and it would only harm him, he leads him back to the simple view: prayer and sacrifices, that's all, as prescribed by law" (*Plato's "Apology of Socrates" and "Crito"* (1966), ed. David Janssens [Leo Strauss Transcripts], Session 6, November 3, 1966).

CHAPTER 2

# Comments on Strauss's Notes on the *Crito*

SVETOZAR Y. MINKOV

Strauss's interpretation of the *Euthyphro* is the core of our volume. Strauss's brief but incisive commentary on the *Crito*, however, belongs to and completes Strauss's course notebook from the spring of 1948 and is an illuminating complement to his analysis of the *Euthyphro*. In commenting on the *Crito*, Strauss himself refers, on a number of occasions, back to the results of his commentary on the *Euthyphro*. Strauss's commentary on both dialogues amounts to an analysis of Socrates's attitude to the law and obedience—obedience to what he shows are the kindred authorities of the gods and the *polis*. By turning to the *Crito*, Strauss enriches his commentary on *Euthyphro* in the following ways:

1. Both commentaries have as their running themes the problem of piety and the problem of justice and therewith Socrates's piety and justice. Having shown the priority of justice (or the philosophical understanding of justice) to piety in his analysis of the *Euthyphro*, Strauss turns to the question of justice in his analysis of the *Crito*. Put another way, the *Crito* allows Strauss to examine the political underpinnings of the theological claims made in the *Euthyphro*.

2. In the course of commenting on the *Crito*, Strauss points back to his analysis of the *Euthyphro* and states this result of the analysis: "it is impossible to cater to the <u>whims</u> of the many—but this does not mean that <u>all</u> their opinions have to be discarded" (p. 65). Similarly, the opinions about

the gods should not be wholly discarded, but instead should be examined, first, in light of justice and, second and more important, in light of the useful or good as discovered by the knower or expert.

3. Both commentaries underscore and then undermine the claims of Euthyphro and Crito to be an expert in piety and an expert in justice respectively. One could unify the two claimed competencies and speak, as Strauss does, of an "expert regarding the soul." The apparent unavailability of such an expert—or the rational character of the philosopher's knowledge of ignorance—leads to the conclusion that philosophy, rather than justice or piety, is "the one thing needful," a conclusion reached in the *Euthyphro* commentary and one with which the *Crito* commentary begins and which it proceeds to clarify.

4. The problem of the absence of "soul" from both dialogues and the ambiguity regarding "soul" in the *Crito* may be resolved through Strauss's notebook commentary. In *Studies in Platonic Political Philosophy,* Strauss remarks that Socrates "uses instead [of 'soul'] periphrastic expressions like 'whatever it is of the things belonging to us with which justice and injustice are concerned' and which deserves higher honor than the body."[1] Christopher Bruell seems quietly to critique Burnet in remarking, "The same commentators who take it for granted that the unnamed object of this reflection is the soul, take it for granted also that the address of 'the laws' expresses Socrates's own view."[2] Strauss might not take either position for granted, and he may not take "the Laws" in the *Crito* to speak for Socrates,[3] but there is indeed an ambiguity concerning the superiority of soul to body which could lead to the assimilation of noble patriotism or high religiosity to philosophy (see also *Studies in Platonic Political Philosophy,* where Strauss says that the *Crito* "does not force us to wonder whether or not the soul is more venerable than the fatherland [cf. *Laws* 724a1–727a2]" and *Thoughts on Machiavelli,* 10, 175).[4] Or to put it another way, if soul is superior to body,[5] why does Socrates favor bodily considerations of safety (as Strauss shows: "a beautiful woman in white dress suggests that 'security,' not 'fame,' should be considered. This is unambiguous") over the more "spiritual" or soul-like considerations of fame or honor? The *Crito* section of the notebook points to the following solution. The ultimate evil is a diseased soul, or a "mental perturbation or sickness." But is health of soul found in patriotism and religion or in the pursuit of clarity and the giving of reasonable accounts? Strauss writes, "S. is not an expert—he seeks for

justice = philosopher. S. knows that he knows <u>nothing</u>: he <u>knows</u> that he knows nothing. He knows what is <u>implied</u> in <u>quest</u> for truth. Quest for truth is most important → the soul is higher than the body (confirmed by absurdity of opposite view)." Yet, as Strauss notes later, in the Laws' address, "ψυχή [soul] is replaced by πατρίς [fatherland]." Is the salvation of one's fatherland higher than the salvation of one's soul? Strauss continues the reflection on the relation of philosophy to justice: "Quest for truth → indifference to bodily goods → no <u>motive</u> for hurting others = for being unjust." While the primary motive of Socrates is beyond justice, the strength of his philosophic concern deprives him of a motive for being unjust. With some exaggeration, one can say that "all 'aggressiveness' proceeds from weakness of soul." Strauss adds two more considerations in defense of the philosopher's transcendence of justice: (a) "Moreover: quest for truth → society → beliefs required for society = justice," that is, for the sake of the social conditions of his own activity, the philosopher would support the cause of justice; (b) "Moreover: fundamental difference between nonphilosopher and philosopher → justice ≠ equality," that is, the philosopher's superiority to society is itself a case of hierarchical justice.

5. The question in the *Crito* of whether the *polis* or "the many" (personified—parent-like or godlike) can bring the greatest good or cause the greatest harm to a human being (body and soul together) is correlative to the question Strauss highlights in commenting on the *Euthyphro*: can the gods cause the greatest good or inflict the greatest harm to one (and out of what motive or motives)? This parallel of the many, or of parents/ancestors, to the gods becomes prominent by virtue of Strauss's pairing of the *Euthyphro* with the *Crito,* whereas the theological question is more subdued in Strauss's later pairing of the *Crito* with the *Apology of Socrates* (in *Studies in Platonic Political Philosophy*). Similarly, in the *Crito* "the τύχη [chance] is now replaced by the power of the multitude," whereas in the *Euthyphro* piety is connected with "an attempt to control τύχη [chance]" via the gods (pp. 53, 91, and 114). In both cases, however, Strauss indicates that the philosopher ultimately "obeys" only (his own) reason in light of the question "what is the good?" or "what can hurt or benefit me or my body and soul (the most)?" (His approach is that of "imitating" what is most reasonable, rather than obeying whatever or whoever promises most beguilingly or threatens most angrily.) This "utilitarian" consideration had been suggested by Socrates but found outrageous by Euthyphro at the

end of the *Euthyphro*: the commercial exchange between men and gods. In contrast to Socrates's own approach, Crito, Socrates's old friend, or rather "a fool benevolent to Socrates," recommends that Socrates break out of prison not for the sake of utility or safety, but in order to avoid disgrace or violating the duty of gratitude.[6] Strauss thus shows the psychological roots of the inclination to unqualified obedience to God and country.

6. In drawing the contrast between Socrates and Crito (adding it to the contrast of Socrates with another "fool," Euthyphro), the commentary on the *Crito* allows Strauss to adumbrate the natural inequality of men and to indicate the prudential (and qualified) basis of Socrates's obedience to the law and to moral and religious duty: "No knowledge of δίκαια [just things] → quest for such knowledge = philosophy → philosophy needs πόλις [city] and πόλις [city] needs laws" (p. 69).

**Notes**

1. Leo Strauss, *Studies in Platonic Political Philosophy* (Chicago: University of Chicago Press, 1983), 58.

2. Christopher Bruell, *On the Socratic Education* (Lanham, MD: Rowman and Littlefield, 1999), 217.

3. Strauss, *Studies in Platonic Political Philosophy*, 60–66.

4. Strauss, *Studies in Platonic Political Philosophy*, 62; Strauss, *Thoughts on Machiavelli* (Chicago: University of Chicago Press, 1968), 10, 175. That "honoring the soul" does not consist (solely) in obeying the laws is also indicated in *The Argument and the Action of Plato's "Laws"* (Chicago: University of Chicago Press, 1975), 66, as well as near the beginning of session 14 in the 1971–72 course on the *Laws* Strauss taught at St. John's College in Annapolis, MD: https://wslamp70.s3.amazonaws.com/leostrauss/s3fs-public/Laws%201971-72.pdf. See also session 21: "But in this very dialogue with Crito, he avoids and underlines this avoidance of the word soul. That is, the soul is the reservation—and the goodness of the soul is the reservation against the laws of the city" (466). But this "question, of course, in the *Crito* could not with propriety be raised because it would complicate matters much beyond Crito's interest" (session 14, p. 316).

5. Leo Strauss, *The City and Man* (Chicago: Rand McNally, 1964), 15–16.

6. In referring to *Crito* 53a8ff., Strauss mention an "argument" instead of "the laws" (cf. *Studies in Platonic Political Philosophy*, 64: "profitable crime") in noting the turn from considerations of justice to considerations of the good (p. 73).

CHAPTER 3

# An Introduction to Strauss's "On Plato's *Euthyphron*"

WAYNE AMBLER

Plato's *Euthyphro* takes its title from Socrates's one and only interlocutor in the dialogue. It might seem that his limitations would keep us from learning much from the conversation, for this ridiculous man thinks he possesses divine wisdom and knows what piety is, but he also contradicts himself readily, cannot always understand Socrates's basic questions (much less answer them adequately), sometimes forgets what has been established, and seems unfazed by his incoherence. Utterly in the dark about the extraordinary man with whom he converses, he enters the conversation imagining that he and Socrates are kindred spirits, for he thinks they both are set apart from ordinary folk by their close ties to divine beings.[1] The ensuing conversation leads him to lower his estimation of Socrates, while he blames himself not at all for his demonstrated inability to hold himself to a consistent definition of piety.

One of the most striking features of Strauss's lecture is that it gives Euthyphro a good share of the credit for making the dialogue as rich as it is. Not only does his personal situation invite instructive and dramatic contrasts with that of Socrates, but—as we shall see—Euthyphro introduces

This chapter was originally published as "An Introduction to Strauss' 'An Untitled Lecture on Plato's *Euthyphron*,'" in *Brill's Companion to Leo Strauss' Writings on Classical Political Thought*, ed. Timothy W. Burns (Leiden: Brill, 2015), 361–78. I am grateful to Eric Buzzetti, David Levy (of Rome), and the editors of this volume for their thoughtful suggestions on earlier versions of this paper.

the movement that leads to what Strauss calls "the most uncompromising formulation of the problem of piety" (¶19, p. 92; ¶1).[2] He does so when he proposes his first definition of piety, which Strauss takes to summon us to imitate the gods, not necessarily to obey them. Since the gods themselves do not pray and sacrifice, imitating them requires that we cease to be pious in any familiar sense. Notwithstanding his limitations, it is the seemingly ultra-pious Euthyphro who, in Strauss's view, leads us to a radical and unsettling critique of conventional piety and perhaps of piety altogether (¶¶12–14, 19).

Euthyphro is not capable of consistency, least of all when confronted by Socrates's questions, and Strauss discusses his subsequent definitions of piety as retreating in the direction of a more conventional view (¶¶19, 12). But before he analyzes the shifts in Euthyphro's definitions of piety, Strauss tracks the encounter of the two men in front of the office of the Athenian judicial authorities, where they explain their respective and very different cases to one another. Strauss considers the dramatic details of their meeting to be deeply important for their conversation, and this is a second striking characteristic of his lecture. As he puts it, "The discussion, the speech, the *logos*, is one part [of a Platonic dialogue]; the other part is the *ergon*, the deeds, the action, what is happening in the dialogue." The action of the dialogue begins with Socrates explaining that he would soon be brought to trial, so the questions naturally arise whether he was guilty of impiety as charged and, more generally, why he got into such trouble with Athens. But Socrates was a philosopher, so the very setting of the conversation invites the more general question of the relationships between philosophy and piety, and philosophy and the city (¶2).

The most abiding question of the dialogue is "What is piety?" and it does not include even a single word related to "philosophy." Strauss, on the other hand, uses such words twenty-one times in his lecture,[3] and his emphasis on philosophy grows out of the seriousness with which he takes the opening drama, which is so closely tied to Socrates's life and death. Memorable evidence of the importance of this theme is supplied also by the following declaration, with which Strauss brings his lecture to a close: "Whether the Bible is right or philosophy is [is] of course the only question which ultimately matters" (¶21).

Another theme of the lecture, which is also a characteristic of it illustrated in the passage just quoted, is the importance of questions. Strauss provokes us to ask about the relationship between the Bible and philosophy, but he does not lay out an answer. Indeed, the lecture as a whole has a questioning character. This is indicated nicely by the statement "no solution to the problem of piety shall be given lest the reader be prevented from seeking the solution for himself" (¶12). He attributes this view to Plato, but it applies to himself as well, as we can see by his opening and closing paragraphs, which include tributes to thinking and wakefulness, not to conclusions or doctrines.

One way to stimulate readers' thinking, then, is to avoid answering questions openly. Another is to answer them more than once, so readers are left to ponder whether and how they relate to one another. Strauss does this by advancing several different answers to the question of the relationship between piety and philosophy, all in need of careful testing. One "answer" sees them as opposed alternatives, with no clear way of deciding between them (¶21, p. 94; ¶¶14–17).[4] Another reconciles them by considering an unconventional sort of piety, one represented not by Euthyphro or Meletus but by the philosopher himself (¶¶10, 13). A third neither reconciles philosophy with piety nor leaves them as incommensurable alternatives: it sees philosophy as replacing or obliterating piety (¶¶12–14, 20). These alternatives do not correlate neatly with Euthyphro's three definitions of piety, but as the dialogue takes up different understandings of piety, it is natural for it also to consider different possibilities for the relationship between piety and Socrates's defining activity.

It is tempting to say that the confusing variety of Strauss's suggestions are meant to tease us a bit, in keeping with what the lecture's very last paragraph calls "the somewhat jocular character" of the *Euthyphro* and of philosophy more generally. He may mean to contribute to this jocularity when, in the previous paragraph, he identifies what he called "an irritating half-truth" way back at the very beginning of the lecture. It is that "piety is superfluous and that the gods are superfluous except for the many" (¶20). The reasons for this strikingly impious conclusion were set forth especially in paragraphs 14 and 17–18, but only now do we hear why they establish only a half-truth. It is that "we know that the gods exist. Not indeed the gods of the city of Athens, but the living gods." So some gods having been dismissed as superfluous except for the many, other gods—living gods—now appear as deserving of our most serious attention. Unsurprisingly, Strauss leaves us with only a few hints about how these gods might alter the reflections of the preceding pages.

I have thus far tried to make three suggestions to identify the most prominent characteristics of Strauss's lecture. One is that he stresses Euthyphro's first definition as making the radical suggestion that piety is imitation of god, not obedience to him. Another is that he makes the relationship between philosophy and piety one of his major themes and offers different and conflicting suggestions about this relationship, just as he entertains different ways of identifying piety. A third, which is illustrated by the first two, is that the lecture is purposefully designed to stimulate its readers' and listeners' thinking, an activity Strauss associates with philosophy and Socrates, not with piety. To understand each point better, we need to undertake a more patient look at the lecture. Those interested in such a patient look will find the notebook to be especially useful, for it stays closer to Plato's text and hence helps us see better the textual foundation for the lecture.

I divide the lecture into five sections whose boundaries are often blurry. These are as follows: Introduction (¶1), Socrates's impiety and the political community (¶¶2–8), the larger "cosmos" of the Platonic dialogues (¶¶9–10), the different views on piety of Meletus, Euthyphro, and Socrates (¶¶11–18), and an overview and conclusion on philosophy and piety (¶¶19–21). I will omit much in order to keep an eye out especially for Strauss's consideration of the major themes as identified above.

## INTRODUCTION: PARAGRAPH 1

Strauss stresses the limits of the *Euthyphro*'s teaching before he even begins to explicate it: its subject is piety, but Strauss affirms that it is only a part of Plato's teaching on this subject, an unusually radical and even "irritating" part (¶¶1, 19–20).[5] By stressing its limits he cautions us against accepting the radical suggestions it makes or irritating alternatives it poses. Seeing less irritating conclusions and even "comforts" that lie beyond the limits of the *Euthyphro,* Strauss assuages the irritation he finds in the *Euthyphro* itself (¶¶1; 20; 5, p. 78).[6] He goes out of his way to indicate that the *Euthyphro* is part of a Platonic "cosmos" that shows signs of suggesting a perhaps less radical and less uncomfortable teaching on piety (¶¶9–10). Even more directly, he mentions at the outset two kinds of "comfort" that Plato supplies (¶1). The first is "thinking itself," for it "may be said to be the most satisfying activity regardless of the character of the result."[7] The second is necessary only for those who believe that "the result is more important than the way to the result" (¶1). Strauss supplies evidence for the former of these "comforts" in his thought-provoking manner of writing and by his beautiful invocation of Socratic wakefulness in his very last lines. One way he will support the latter, which he says depends on "Plato's moral character," is by his description of the cosmos just mentioned, a cosmos that may suggest that philosophy does not reject piety but culminates in it (¶10; *Theaetetus* 176a5–b3). But he clearly writes not to offer comfort but to warn us that the *Euthyphro*'s teaching on piety may be disconcerting.

As Strauss sees it, courage is a necessary requirement of thinking consistently about piety (¶14, p. 87); we must "digest" certain truths, not merely grasp them (¶1, p. 75); we must not "shrink" from their implications (¶12, p. 86); and in his final paragraph he identifies the spirit of philosophy as "serenity on the basis of resignation," not hope or fear (¶21). Strauss will soon raise the uncomfortable possibility that there are no truths to ascertain, or that knowledge is simply impossible; and, however this may be, it is unlikely that the philosopher finds things to be exactly as might be wished.

Half-truths abound, but at least irritating half-truths come with an advantage. Popular half-truths are so familiar we readily accept them as if they were the whole truth, but, Strauss notes, we can reach irritating half-truths only if we think. Thinking successfully is more important than avoiding irritation. I am tempted to infer that irritating half-truths bring an advantage like the sting of Socrates's famous gadfly, but Strauss's stated point is that we must think to reach the irritating half-truths of the *Euthyphro*, not that their irritating quality is what drives us to think further. If "thinking may be said to be the most satisfying activity" (¶1), we have a motive to think our way even to irritating half-truths, not only a motive to think our way beyond them. But as Strauss's essay as a whole will suggest, this all requires that knowledge be possible, and this very fundamental question is at issue in the *Euthyphro*.

When Strauss says that the *Euthyphro* is paradoxical, he adds that this is also true of the other dialogues (¶19), but when he calls its teaching "irritating," he implies it is in a class by itself. Strauss may thus suggest that some of Plato's other texts, if only in some respects, offer resting places for weary thinkers in a way the uniquely irritating *Euthyphro* does not.[8]

Strauss's emphasis on the importance of rigorous thinking is conveyed also by what he indicates about the way the *Euthyphro* is written. Good writing requires readers to think for themselves, at least partly because thinking itself may be the most satisfying activity. As noted above, the *Euthyphro* never comes to a clear conclusion about what piety is. Either the hunt is more important than the game it seeks, or the hunt can never succeed if the hunter expects the game to be handed to him on a silver platter. We must earn for ourselves the greatest benefit or satisfaction from our reading of Plato and perhaps from Strauss as well. So, Strauss's lecture on the dialogue on piety includes several beautiful tributes to the life of thought.

## SOCRATES'S IMPIETY AND THE POLITICAL COMMUNITY: PARAGRAPHS 2–8

Paragraphs 2–8 contain three points worthy of special note. One is that Strauss invites us to assess piety by considering whether Socrates possessed it. Athens will soon try Socrates by the standards of orthodoxy; are we here summoned to the trial of orthodox piety by the standards of Socratic philosophy (¶2, p. 76)? Second, Strauss concludes with unusual clarity that Socrates was indeed impious when judged by the standards of orthodox piety (which of course leaves open the possibility that Socrates was pious if, for example, philosophy is piety properly understood).[9] Third, Socrates's impiety is not a sufficient explanation of the Athenians' actions against him: it is possible to be impious and still go through the motions necessary to escape attention (¶4). If Socrates's impiety did not lead directly to his trial and execution, what did?

The *Euthyphro* never establishes what piety is, but Strauss finds that general opinion and the trial of Socrates imply a provisional definition: "piety consists in worshipping the ancestral gods, but according to ancestral custom" (¶2). He then asks whether piety so understood is good (or is a virtue) and, on the grounds that Socrates sets the standard for virtue and yet was impious, infers that piety is not good. To reach this conclusion he rejects firsthand and friendly testimony in support of Socrates's innocence, for Euthyphro, a self-proclaimed expert, thinks it ridiculous that the Athenians have brought Socrates to trial on such a charge (¶3).[10] Strauss establishes Socrates's impiety in two ways: first, Socrates professes not to know what one must know to be pious (¶4), and second, he claims to know things that run counter to what the city believes about the gods (¶5). Both his ignorance and his knowledge convict him. Rather, they convict piety and Athens, for philosophy or Socrates himself is here the standard by which the goodness of piety is judged.

Socrates himself stresses that he has for a long time thought it important to know the divine things (¶4; *Euthyphro* 5a5–8), but he also holds that, in spite of his efforts, he remains ignorant of them (*Euthyphro* 6b2–3).[11] Socrates lives without having yet gained the knowledge he values so highly, but he continues to seek it. He certainly does not confuse belief in the tales of the Athenians with the knowledge he seeks, and he may not see any reason to believe that the gods of the Athenians exist at all. How can one who knows that he does not know the divine things be an honest worshipper of gods whose existence he seeks to investigate? Socrates is thus not pious in the orthodox sense. Knowledge requires careful examination of all important claims (¶4, p. 77; see *Euthyphro* 9e4–7); orthodoxy resists examination.

After finding him guilty for his ignorance, Strauss indicates that Socrates sometimes drops his claim of ignorance and "seems to believe to know" something about the gods. He seems to believe he knows that the orthodox tales are wrong (*Euthyphro* 6a6–9; *Republic* II) and that the gods are "good and just and, therefore, both the givers of all good things and only of good things to man and incapable of fighting with each other" (¶5, p. 7b).[12] On such grounds, Socrates becomes as guilty of impiety for his knowledge as he is for his ignorance.

Strauss interrupts his demonstration of Socrates's impiety to stress that his guilt alone does not explain why the Athenians brought him to trial: it is easy to feign conventional belief, so if Socrates's impiety alone was not sufficient to get him into trouble, what provoked the charges brought against him? If, in other words, there is an essential conflict between philosophy and the political community, of what elements does it consist? Strauss takes up this question, while continuing to assess Socrates's piety from different points of view (¶¶4–7).

To explain why Euthyphro's bold claims about his knowledge of the gods only got him laughed at, whereas the Athenians will put Socrates on trial for a capital offense, Socrates answers that the Athenians do not care much if someone is clever, but they get angry if they think he teaches his wisdom to others.[13] Their concern is less with the beliefs themselves than with their diffusion and possible political impact. Here is how Socrates puts it to Euthyphro in a passage Strauss looks at closely: "Perhaps you're thought to offer yourself rarely and to be unwilling to teach your wisdom: but I'm afraid that they might think that out of my philanthropy I speak unreservedly to every man, and even that I would pay gladly in addition if anyone's willing to listen to me."[14] Since neither Socrates's cleverness (*Euthyphro* 3c6–9: *deinon*) nor even his impiety is sufficient to explain the trouble he got into at Athens, Strauss tests Socrates's own claim that his problem with Athens grew out of an odd sort of philanthropy.

Instead of referring to Socrates's philanthropy, Strauss calls it his "*apparent* philanthropy," and in fact the passage just quoted points to Socrates's possible reputation for a philanthropic willingness to speak openly to the Athenians, not to the fact that he does so.

Strauss actively doubts the accuracy of Socrates's qualified claim to philanthropy first by noting that his conversation with Euthyphro does not begin with the slightest sign that Socrates tries to spread his wisdom to this odd young man; rather, Euthyphro buttonholes him, and only Socrates's politeness allows the conversation to continue (¶6). Socrates is also relatively circumspect about what he says to Euthyphro. He does acknowledge his vexation at the wild stories told about the pagan gods, but even here, while admitting vexation, he stops short of claiming to know that they are false, and nowhere does he try to raise Euthyphro to a philosophic understanding of the gods.

Strauss also tests Socrates's apparent claim to share his thoughts generously by the evidence of the *Republic*, the *Charmides*, and the *Lysis* (¶7). In book 2 of the *Republic*, Socrates lays out a theological teaching that is in clear conflict with Athenian orthodoxy. This might suggest a certain risky "philanthropy," but his interlocutors here are more likely than Euthyphro to profit from any such risk and are probably less likely to report any radicalism to the authorities, especially since the dialogue silences Thrasymachus and defends justice. The other two dialogues show Socrates's enthusiasm for the conversations they report, but his conversation with Euthyphro would never have occurred if Socrates had not been obliged to visit the legal authorities. The differences among these four dialogues demonstrate that Socrates is discriminating in what he says to whom, and in fact we never see Socrates simply pour forth his opinions "unreservedly."

Another reason to question his possible reputation for philanthropy is that Socrates says he might seem to be happy to pay those willing to listen to him, of which behavior there is no report. Still, Strauss dismisses Socrates's odd claim only provisionally, and the reason for his hesitation seems to be that Socrates was sometimes openly eager to talk with some of the Athenian youth. Perhaps the *Charmides* and the *Lysis*—in contrast to the *Euthyphro*—offer better examples of what Socrates had in mind by his claim that he speaks "unreservedly" to others. Strauss here finds it doubtful that Socrates had any lasting effect on Euthyphro (¶11, p. 84), to whom he never even mentioned the word "philosophy," but was the same true of young men like Lysis and Charmides, with whom he seemed eager to speak?

Consider Charmides's notorious career at Athens and the conclusion of the *Lysis*: by the end of his conversation with Socrates, the model son Lysis is "seen engaging in a minor rebellion against his family's authority."[15] Although Strauss indicates that Socrates was not indiscriminate in what he had to say when in the hearing of the general public, he also calls attention to the range of attitudes with which Socrates entered different conversations and to the range of effects he had on those with whom he conversed. The question of Socrates's influence on the young raises practical or political problems in a way the mere fact of impiety, if uncommunicated, does not. Hence, Strauss can refer to Socrates's "apparent philanthropy" as "corrupting the young" (¶4, p. 78), though he does not yet mention the motives that may have been behind this possible philanthropy.

After finding that philanthropy does not explain Socrates's conversation with Euthyphro, Strauss suggests it is "an act of justice" (¶7). If Socrates can show Euthyphro that he is not wise, he may induce him to suspend his prosecution of his father. He would at the same time make Euthyphro better, and it is prudent as well as just to make those with whom we live less harmful to ourselves.[16] But this particular substitution of prudence for justice is beset by the problem that it can also be dangerous to try to improve others; it can provoke resentment and retaliation. Whether prudent or not, and whether initiated by justice or not, Socrates's conversations were in Strauss's view beneficial to him and to his friends, and they remain beneficial to us, for it was from them that Socrates learned about human nature and through him that we might (¶7, p. 80).

In this quick survey of the problem between Socrates and Athens, Strauss considers Socrates's impiety, his philanthropy, his justice, his prudent effort to make others better, and his effort to learn about human nature. I presume this declension of possible motives is intended to help us understand Socrates and, hence, philosophy itself (see the enjoinder to "see philosophy as it is" at the very end of the lecture). In the end, Socrates's quest for knowledge explains his other apparent concerns, including justice, at least in this paragraph.

Strauss returns in paragraph 8 to what he calls "the main issue, Socrates's impiety." His summary reconciles what might look like Socrates's belief that he knows the ancestral tales of the gods to be wrong with his professed ignorance of the divine things: Socratic ignorance is compatible with considerable knowledge. Knowledge that is insufficient for some purposes may be sufficient for others, as was already implied in the conclusion that Socrates is impious both in what he knows and in what he does not know.

After having stressed Socrates's impiety, however, Strauss now speaks for the first time of "true piety": if we knew what true piety was, we might well find Socrates to have been not less pious than others but more pious. At a minimum, if a Socrates thinks he knows that the ancestral tales are wrong, how reasonable is it to accept these same tales as a basis for declaring him to be impious? By bringing "true piety" into the discussion, Strauss turns Socrates's relation to piety upside down. If true piety requires one to know the divine things, who is more likely to meet this requirement than Socrates himself (¶8, p. 80)? The philosopher is once again the standard by which the city and its orthodoxy are judged, and the judgment is unfavorable.

If the law could be based on true piety, it would make sense to say that Socrates ought not to have been punished for impiety. This is not because we know that he was truly pious, but because only one as wise as he could know whether he was or not. Who can really claim to know the truth about the divine things? Strauss draws the apparent practical conclusion with an uncharacteristic statement: "I personally believe that [not punishing Socrates for impiety] would have been a wise decision," and he adds, "the most obvious message of the *Euthyphron*" is that "it would be wonderful if the crime of impiety could be wiped off the statute books" (¶8). Yet no sooner does he say this than he invokes Plato's own authority to resist this now-familiar way of exonerating Socrates. According to Strauss, Plato himself would reject this "most obvious message" of the *Euthyphro* on the grounds that cities must treat impiety as a crime. He gives no explicit defense of this conclusion. Later, however, he makes a similar point and indicates that justice is often perceived as lacking a sanction sufficient to secure its widespread practice; piety and the gods are invoked to remedy this perceived insufficiency (¶18, p. 91). This political need for piety appears to hold even though one cannot expect cities to know what true piety is. The requirements of the city and of philosophy are fundamentally at odds.

## THE LARGER COSMOS OF THE PLATONIC DIALOGUES: PARAGRAPHS 9–10

Paragraphs 9 and 10 do not take up the question just raised, of precisely why cities must treat impiety as a crime. Rather, they make a new beginning, one that promises a "more exact analysis" of the dialogue and one that tries first to see how the *Euthyphro* fits in the "cosmos" of all the dialogues. Perhaps doing so will point the way from the "irritating half-truth" of the *Euthyphro* to a more satisfying whole truth taught by the dialogues all together.

The cosmos of the dialogues might show piety to be a virtue even if the *Euthyphro* does not. There are dialogues on moderation, justice, and courage. If one rejects the authenticity of the *Theages*, which is on wisdom, then one might see the *Euthyphro* as Plato's way of substituting a treatment of piety for one of wisdom, thus promoting piety to the rank of the four cardinal virtues. Strauss's suggestion of this very indirect way of defending piety as a virtue must face the obstacles that the *Theages* does not appear to be spurious and the *Republic* treats the four cardinal virtues, as well as the virtues of the philosopher, without mentioning piety as one of them. Moreover, the *Theaetetus* is devoted to science, to which wisdom is related, and Strauss sees this too as discouraging the attempt to substitute piety for wisdom as a cardinal virtue. If the *Euthyphro* itself does not treat piety as a virtue, it does not seem that other dialogues do so either. This partly playful attempt to see Plato as promoting piety to the ranks of the cardinal virtues ends in failure.

But if the overall cosmos of the Platonic dialogues does not supply strong reasons for thinking that piety is a virtue, the *Theaetetus* might do so on its own (¶10). Instead of contrasting the philosophic and the pious life, the *Theaetetus* even calls upon the philosopher "to flee from here thither" and for assimilation to god (¶10, *Theaetetus* 176a5–b3). Here, then, is a solemn text that gives us reason to see piety as a virtue and even a philosophic virtue. But no single Platonic text is determining, Strauss promptly notes, and he cautions the reader to consider the context here. He appears not to see this important passage in the *Theaetetus* as rescuing piety from the often critical treatment it receives in the *Euthyphro*.

If Strauss is not prepared on the basis of the *Theaetetus* to declare that science or philosophy culminates in piety, his mention of this other dialogue helps at least to emphasize the important relationship between science or philosophy and piety (¶10, first two sentences). As we have seen before and will see again, Strauss's discussion of piety examines especially its relationship to philosophy and the possibility of knowledge. Calling attention to the links between the *Theaetetus* and the *Euthyphro* helps to focus attention on this relationship (¶9, p. 81).

## DISTINGUISHING THE VIEWS OF MELETUS, EUTHYPHRO, AND SOCRATES: PARAGRAPHS 11–17

Strauss again registers a sharp change in his immediate subject, which he now announces to be the setting of the dialogue. It would appear, however, that his focus is now on the main positions expressed or implied by the two interlocutors, with frequent references to Socrates's accuser Meletus as well.

Strauss's reading is distinguished above all by his detection of two radical theses latent in what Euthyphro said but of which he was largely unaware. The first of these is that piety is imitation of the gods, not obedience to them (¶¶12–13). The second is that the ideas are prior to the gods (¶¶14–17). Strauss sees these theses as being opposed to piety as ordinarily understood and perhaps to piety altogether. Understanding these critiques of orthodox piety, which the boaster Euthyphro implies but does not understand, seems to me to pose the greatest challenge of Strauss's lecture.

In the first of his three definitions, which Strauss clearly considers to be his most important one (¶12, p. 86; ¶19, p. 92), Euthyphro remarks that piety is "the very thing that I am now doing." He here refers to his prosecution of his father for murder (*Euthyphro* 5d8–9), which he understands to receive some of its justification from Zeus's harsh treatment of his father, Kronos. Strauss seizes upon this first part of Euthyphro's definition for its implication that piety is imitation of the gods, not obedience to them. Whether he knows it or not, Euthyphro implies a radical rejection of orthodox piety, as Strauss explains. If to be pious is to imitate the gods, then piety would no longer require the offering of sacrifices or the saying of prayers, for surely the gods themselves do not sacrifice or pray. Since the gods themselves do not have other gods before whom to be pious, to imitate them would require that we too cease to be pious in any familiar sense. Strauss concludes that to imitate the gods in their lack of piety requires that we become heretical or "deviationist" with regard to the beliefs and practices of ordinary Athenians (¶12, p. 86). To follow this thought consistently, as Euthyphro does not, requires courage as well as insight.

To imitate the gods, however, one must know what the gods do, and Euthyphro's only idea of what they do comes from the common tales. These tales, however, are the same authority that insists we should obey the gods, not imitate them,[17] and Euthyphro has already broken away from their teaching in this regard. Since he proves unable to abandon ancestral authority consistently, Strauss concludes bluntly, "He ought to return to orthodoxy" (¶12). This "ought" is based on Euthyphro's personal limitations, not on the soundness of orthodox piety. Among other things, orthodoxy is represented by Meletus, the man who brought Socrates to trial.

While denying that Euthyphro makes more than a confused effort to escape an orthodoxy based on mere tales, Strauss takes seriously Euthyphro's implied redefinition of piety as imitation of the gods, and he supplies a reasoned foundation for it (¶13, pp. 86–87). Euthyphro—or some part of him—seems to have stumbled on the radical view that one must imitate the gods in order to please them, even though imitation would be impious in the conventional understanding (¶14, p. 87). To add weight to the case for imitating the gods, Strauss presents a more coherent version of it, one based on the example of the wise man, whom he unhesitatingly declares to be "the highest human type" and, "therefore," "our only guide to knowledge of the gods or of what would please the gods." If the gods are like the wise, they will prefer imitators to the blindly obedient (¶13). This analogy supplies an attractive case for piety as imitation, as well as an insight into the way the wise are likely to judge those who are not similar to them, regardless of whether they are obeyed or admired or not. Still, it rests on an unconfirmed view of the gods, though one Strauss advances with surprising emphasis.[18]

Having contradicted himself one way, Euthyphro next does so in another. His effort to resolve this second contradiction captures Strauss's greatest interest and leads to his focus on the ideas, which dominate paragraphs 14–17.[19] Like piety as imitation of the gods, the ideas crowd out such traditional pious practices as praying and sacrificing.

Euthyphro implied that piety requires us to imitate the gods. He also says the gods are in radical disagreement with one another, even to the point that they fight one another. It is thus impossible to imitate all the gods.

To imitate one is to offend another. Euthyphro senses this difficulty and supplies this solution: he chooses to imitate Zeus, the most just and best of the gods (*Euthyphro* 5e5–6a3). To make this choice among the warring gods, however, Euthyphro must know what is good and just: he cannot know Zeus is most just if he does not know justice. But if he already knows what justice is, why does he need the example of Zeus at all? Zeus's justice is only a pattern of a more fundamental pattern. What Euthyphro really seeks is to be just, a goal he could achieve by guiding his actions directly by the idea of justice. Although he does not realize it, Euthyphro has just implied that Zeus and piety in general are superfluous: what we need is knowledge of goodness and justice, not gods who themselves need this knowledge and must be judged by it. Hence, "The ideas replace the gods" (¶14, p. 88).

Paragraphs 15–17 stress the starkness of the alternatives, gods or ideas (¶15), consider whether there is a way to avoid or mitigate the opposition between them (¶16), and reflect on their implications regarding the possibility of knowledge (¶17). Euthyphro implied that an idea of justice guided his choice of Zeus as the god to imitate; however, it is Socrates who brings this out, and Strauss now focuses on him as the champion of the ideas (¶15, p. 88, and see *Euthyphro* 5c8–d6).

Seeing Socrates as the champion of the ideas does not defend him against the charge of impiety, Strauss notes, but it relocates his guilt. Socrates says he was charged with "making new gods and not believing in the old ones" (*Euthyphro* 3b1–4), but Strauss now has him introducing the ideas, not gods or divine things, into Athens. Nor are the ideas new (*Euthyphro* 3b2, 5a5–8), for they are "the first things, the oldest things" (¶15), and Socrates did not "make" them, as had been claimed in the charge that he was guilty of being a "poet" or "maker" of gods (*Euthyphro* 3b2). But the ideas are not made, and neither do they make (or do anything at all). Socrates's accuser Meletus was a poet, but Socrates's view is "the radically unpoetic view" (¶15).[20]

Strauss seems more concerned at this point to stress that there is an issue between piety[21] and philosophy than to resolve it. He experiments with a way of avoiding the issue, but he appears to find the results more amusing than satisfying (¶16). He thus devotes himself to sketching the implications of these stark alternatives, especially as they regard knowledge.

If knowledge is possible, there must be something for us to know, something prior to our knowing. If "genuine knowledge" is knowledge of something unchanging, of intelligible necessity, it may make sense to speak of the ideas as the primary beings. If one sees the gods as the primary beings, however, there would be nothing prior to the gods for them to know. Their action could not be guided, for example, by their knowledge of justice; it must be "blind" (¶17, pp. 89–90). It thus makes sense to think of such blind gods as being at war with one another; and if anything were to be deemed "just," it would be so only because some god happened to deem it just at some moment, not because of its intrinsic merits.

Monotheism might seem to solve the problem that action becomes arbitrary in the absence of knowable ideas, for it eliminates the possibility of fighting gods; but Strauss declares flatly that the *Euthyphro* does not settle this question (¶17). He nevertheless goes on to say that even a single god would have to be understood as being "good or just or wise," in which case He would be limited by these ideas; or, alternatively, if He is not subject to preexisting ideas, He cannot possess knowledge, for there is nothing fixed for Him to know. He could perhaps create anything, but there would be nothing fixed for Him to use as a pattern or guide for His creation. Since they would be subject to infinite and arbitrary change, necessity and nature as we understand them would not exist. A god prior to the ideas would be a god who could permit or effect continual and unpredictable changes in what is good or just.[22] Even if there were only one divine will at every particular moment, I infer that it would be as if there were many gods over time. Perhaps monotheism in some other way can solve the problems raised by the *Euthyphro*, but Strauss stresses rather the difficulties that it would face.

## IS PIETY NECESSARY? PARAGRAPH 18

If Zeus patterned his actions on ideas more fundamental than he, he would be superfluous. He would be superfluous at least for those seeking and able to understand the ideas on whose basis he acted, but do most of us look to the gods only to understand? Men in general do not find the gods superfluous, even when they think they know what is just without a god's instruction. Would we not be happy with a god who used his powers to help see that justice is achieved, even if philosophers do not need him as a model to identify what justice is? When Abraham boldly appealed to God not to punish the righteous along with the guilty of Sodom and Gomorrah (*Genesis* 18:20–32), for example, he was seeking not to learn the idea of justice but to hold God to the standard of his own understanding.

In acknowledgment of our powerful need for piety, Strauss turns, if for only one paragraph, from the effort to identify piety to the distinct question of why human beings continue to believe in gods and promote piety as much as they do (¶18). He finds the dialogue's answer to this question in Euthyphro's third definition. Reflecting on this definition and the cross-examination it prompts, Strauss proposes two distinct reasons that we need gods. One is the power of chance; the other is the weakness of justice.

Strauss already indicated that a certain courage is required to be impious (¶14): now he notes how difficult it is for us to accept the vast extent to which what we treasure is vulnerable to chance (¶18, p. 91). It is not easy to fully digest the fact that much of what we care about most can vanish in an instant, so perhaps it is not surprising if we comfort ourselves by thinking that we have great resources with which to keep chance from destroying our lives. When we serve the gods, we believe we might secure their assistance where we need it deeply.

The legislative art is concerned with subjects about which genuine knowledge is especially difficult and disagreement is especially likely; its primary goal is justice. Euthyphro divides justice into a part regarding men and a part regarding gods, the latter of which is piety (*Euthyphro* 12e5–8). Justice toward men is weak, unfortunately, for irrational men do not see clearly why they should be just when their interest tempts them in another direction. We need the powerful sanctions supplied by piety and the gods, Strauss suggests, to remedy the weakness of justice among men (¶18, p. 91). The practical needs of political life tie piety to the law, which is rooted in ancestral custom. Strauss thus links this case for piety to the case for law and custom.

The ideas may replace the gods when it comes to guiding the philosopher's understanding, but there is no reason to pray or sacrifice to them: they offer cold comfort as we face the power of chance and the weakness of justice. This is why, I think, Strauss sees the *Euthyphro* as teaching that if there are ideas or some sort of intelligible necessity, piety is superfluous "except for the many" (¶20). If the absence of gods is a threat to cities and to our hopes for a secure happiness, the presence of omnipotent gods is a threat to philosophy, for then there are no stable ideas for the philosopher to understand.

From such thoughts on the psychological and civic necessity of piety, Strauss returns to Socrates's effort to dissuade Euthyphro from prosecuting his father. The link, I think, is that if piety as understood in this third definition is ultimately in defense of custom and the law, then the pious Euthyphro should adhere more closely to prevailing customs and abandon the prosecution of his father, which violates them. The philosopher Socrates is here the defender or ally of orthodoxy; and in what the last sentence of paragraph 18 implies is a digression, Strauss affirms that "society is not possible if ancestral custom is not regarded as sacred as far as practice is concerned," so laws punishing impiety are necessary (p. 92). In articulating this general principle, Strauss treats Euthyphro as the one who must be muscled back to orthodoxy (¶18, last sentence), even though Socrates represents a bigger threat to it by far (¶8, p. 80). Socrates is more aware than Euthyphro of the political need for orthodoxy and hence can defend it in some cases.

## OVERVIEW AND CONCLUSION: PARAGRAPHS 19–21

Paragraph 19 offers a general look back over the *Euthyphro* and has two subjects: the first is its unusual movement from higher to lower, from "A) exposition of the truth; [to] B) explanation of the basic error." The second is Socrates's comparison of Euthyphro to Proteus. With regard to the first, Strauss offers two ways of explaining this movement. One pertains to the drama: Euthyphro's "heresy" becomes evident in his first definition, and then Socrates struggles mightily to bring him back to orthodoxy. The second explanation is more theoretical: the (heretical) truth comes early in the dialogue, in Euthyphro's first definition, while "the basic error" is explained later. Rather than encouraging Euthyphro by helping him to see that his first definition contains the seeds of a powerful critique of orthodoxy, Socrates tries to show him that ordinary orthodoxy suits him better than incoherent radicalism.

Strauss stressed the importance and radicalism of Euthyphro's first definition some time ago (¶12): piety is imitating the gods, not obeying them. But since the gods disagree with one another, this radical view led Strauss to link it with Euthyphro's implicit appeal to an idea of justice as a way of defending his selection of Zeus as the god to be imitated (¶¶14–15). I take "the truth," then, to refer to piety as imitation, not obedience, and to ideas as patterns for us to imitate. Strauss states the radical result in the next paragraph: the *Euthyphro*'s "irritating half-truth" is that piety and the gods are "superfluous" (¶20).[23]

It is more difficult to say what Strauss means by the "explanation of the basic error." If the basic error is conventional piety, which the radical

Euthyphro failed to escape, what is its "explanation"? Strauss explains the power and persistence of conventional piety most directly in his account of the human need to deny the power of chance and the political need to strengthen the sanction for injustice; both the power of chance and the weakness of justice help explain the prevalence of a kind of piety that even Euthyphro can see to be inadequate (¶18; *Euthyphro* 14e6–8). Perhaps a second and more general reason for Euthyphro's mistakes also supports this general explanation: Euthyphro somehow stumbles on the core of a radical critique of conventional piety, but he lacks what it takes to grasp or "digest" its full power (¶¶12, 21).

When Socrates refers to Euthyphro as Proteus, it would be natural to note the irony: Euthyphro's claim to divine wisdom is dubious, and he changes "shapes" because he is confused, not because he is a divinely gifted escape artist like Proteus (*Euthyphro* 15d2–3; *Odyssey* 4.382–570). Strauss stresses instead the differences between Socrates and Menelaus, the questioner of the original Proteus. Unlike Menelaus's, Socrates's problems arose out of his ill-disguised lapse from conventional piety; and even at this late moment, just before his arraignment on charges of impiety, he does not ask how he could better conform to the prevailing customs for offering sacrifice (¶19, p. 93). His stated and, I think, actual goal in this conversation is to understand piety, not to become pious. Strauss's comments on Proteus underscore Socrates's probing unconventionality rather than Euthyphro's all-too-human incompetence.

Paragraph 20 returns to Strauss's opening statement that the *Euthyphro* conveys an irritating half-truth and now identifies it: it is "that piety is superfluous and that the gods are superfluous except for the many." As he did before, Strauss assuages the irritation provoked by this half-truth by looking beyond the *Euthyphro*. Whereas he before looked to the larger cosmos of other Platonic dialogues (¶¶9–10, pp. 80–81), he might now appear to look even beyond the Platonic cosmos altogether. He flatly declares, "We know that the gods exist. Not indeed the gods of the city of Athens, but the living gods." He traces this knowledge to "demonstration," to demonstration starting from "the phenomena of motion, of self-motion, life, of the soul." So, as the lecture concludes, Strauss makes an exceedingly brief case for gods to which he has not previously referred.

The argument that motion, self-motion, life, and soul are the foundation of a demonstration that gods exist also turns out to belong to the cosmos of Plato's dialogues (see *Laws* 894b–899d). Indeed, the Stranger argues there that misunderstanding "soul" is the key mistake of the atheists against whom he is arguing (892a).[24] This more pious argument of the *Laws*, which is rooted in soul, is silent about the ideas. The argument of the *Euthyphro*, which Strauss finds "irritating" and from which he concludes that piety is superfluous, is rooted in the ideas and is silent about soul.

Strauss's dramatic affirmation of the living gods' existence occupies just a few short sentences. Like his earlier appeal to the "cosmos" of the other dialogues (¶¶9–10), it seeks in short order to put the more radical teachings of the *Euthyphro* in a more comprehensive and more moderate context. But both passages also end with Strauss pulling his punches: in this later passage, he introduces soul as something that might temper the irritating teaching of the *Euthyphro*, and yet it concludes by suggesting that Plato might defend the *Euthyphro*'s impious half-truth by teaching that the ideas are higher than the soul (¶20, last sentence).

Thus, Strauss leaves it to us to test the adequacy of the arguments in the *Laws* that establish the existence of gods on the basis of self-motion and soul, just as he earlier invited us to test the depth of the piety at the center of the *Theaetetus* (¶10). Surely we are no less obliged to test the arguments that seem to imply the existence of the ideas and of intelligible necessity, whether they occur in the *Euthyphro* or elsewhere.

The core of Strauss's conclusion is an explanation of why his interpretation and Plato's text are occasionally a little jocular, notwithstanding the seriousness of the issues they treat and the risk that some might find this jocularity offensive. He makes his case by citing an important passage from Plato's *Symposium* and quoting a comment by Sir Thomas More. He concludes, "The beginning of philosophy . . . is not the fear of the Lord, but wonder. Its spirit is not hope and fear and trembling, but serenity on the basis of resignation" (¶21). His very last words express a beautiful call to Socratic wakefulness. I infer that the most important part of the whole truth that assuages the irritation accompanying the *Euthyphro*'s critique of piety is that philosophic thinking is possible, satisfying, and vouched for by Plato's example (¶¶21, 1).

## CONCLUDING QUESTIONS

I have meant to raise a major question I cannot answer. It concerns the extent to which Strauss understands the *Euthyphro* as teaching not only that piety and philosophy represent mutually exclusive alternatives but also as defending a judgment in favor of one of them. As noted above, his lecture sometimes seems to take the matter to be settled in favor of philosophy or the ideas, which render the gods superfluous (¶¶2, 13–14), but he elsewhere stresses the alternatives and the need to choose between them, not a settled judgment in favor of one or the other (¶¶15, 17, 21, 7–8). In any event, I do not see him attempting to establish that Socrates has proven that the ideas exist or that Euthyphro's claim to divine wisdom is groundless.[25] I conclude that one must look for these arguments and their examination further afield, if one is to seek the whole truth that lies beyond the "irritating half-truth" presented in the *Euthyphro*.

Let me repeat one of the several dramatic affirmations of Strauss's lecture that also supports this conclusion. It declares, at least partly in Plato's name, that "no solution to the problem of piety shall be given lest the reader be prevented from seeking the solution for himself." I see no reason to doubt that Strauss writes to entice us, and to give us hints and pointers, not to establish methodically that Socrates's philosophizing is superior to Euthyphro's belief in his close connection to the gods. We must thus test every one of Strauss's formulations and never take one alone to be sufficient to solve the complex problem at hand.

Called for by the lecture, such caution is further recommended by the notebook, published for the first time in this volume, for it casts a skeptical glance not only at Euthyphro's gods but also at the "ideas," which Socrates seems to champion. It refers to them as a "doctrine" four times (pp. 35–36), whereas the lecture never does, and it once calls this doctrine "an assumption" and puts "ideas" in scare quotes (p. 33). The Strauss of the notebook also asks directly, "Why is Plato so certain that there are ideas?" (p. 36).

Although the lecture links the case for philosophy with the ideas, the notebook makes it easier for us to wonder whether it is so clear that the case for philosophy depends on the existence of ideas. What, after all, do Socrates and Strauss mean by "the ideas"? The notebook uses the phrase "class-character" six times (pp. 34–35): Is it a strict synonym for "idea," or might some things have a class character, graspable by philosophy, without there being ideas in some independent sense? Could something similar be true of "intelligible necessity," which the lecture uses six times, all in ¶17? I would be very surprised if Strauss did not want us to demand of ourselves a more probing look at the ideas than the lecture offers, and the notebook helps to strengthen this point. It does so also by calling attention to other Platonic works in which Socrates takes up the ideas as a major theme, such as the *Phaedo* and the *Republic.* The question cannot be left to the *Euthyphro,* which uses the word "idea" (*idea*) only three times (5d, 6d–e), and the closely related word "form" (*eidos*) only once (6d), always in the singular and always referring to piety. Genuine piety requires gods, but it is not so clear to me either that philosophy requires ideas or that Strauss thinks it does.

**Notes**

1. Consider among other passages *Euthyphro* 4e1–5a2, 4a11–b3, 4d5–5a2, 11b6–d2, and 3b5–c4.

2. Parenthetical references are first to paragraphs of Strauss's lecture, of which there are twenty-one. I will add page numbers when it helps to do so.

3. He also begins his notebook with the question "Why philosophy?" See I.1 in this volume.

4. Dichotomies can provoke thought, and the lecture gives us these: philosophy and piety (¶¶2–7, 19, 21), ideas and gods (¶¶14–17), the philosopher and the city (¶¶8 and 18), philosophy and poetry (¶15).

5. Its teaching is irritating because it is unpopular (¶1). Paragraph 18 explains the ineradicable roots of this unpopularity.

6. Strauss elsewhere asks whether speaking in order to comfort others does not require one to speak less sincerely. *On Tyranny: Including the Strauss-Kojève Correspondence*, ed. Victor Gourevitch and Michael S. Roth (Chicago: University of Chicago Press, 2013), 30.

7. Contrast the case of the arts, such as those he discusses in ¶18, whose benefits depend upon particular outcomes that are outside of their power.

8. Strauss addresses a related point in his other bookend paragraph, 21, where he stresses the importance of recognizing the comic element in Plato. The taste for the tragic, which scholars possess to a greater degree, distorts the spirit of philosophy, according to Strauss. Among the "many reasons" for this scholarly failure, would he include Plato's own intention? Consider the solemn myths that populate a surprising number of dialogues, the declarations that were so moving to representatives of the Stoic and Neoplatonist traditions, and his famous statement about having made Socrates young and noble (*Second Letter* 314c). Such considerations may help explain Strauss's Delphic reference to "Plato's moral character" (¶1).

9. This possibility is considered in the notebook, pp. 32–33, 38–39, 46–47. Since Strauss has denied that the *Euthyphro* presents a final understanding of what piety is, he cannot give a final answer to the question of whether Socrates is pious.

10. The lecture's conclusion is similarly hesitant to offer a categorical judgment in favor of philosophy. Like Socrates's piety, it must be well understood before being defended (¶21). He thus appeals to philosophical thinking to determine what the philosophical life really entails.

11. Strauss's lecture does not include references to the pages of Plato's dialogue; I cite the passages that seem to me to offer the most likely basis of Strauss's comments. One of the great advantages of the notebook is that it makes frequent and explicit reference to passages in the *Euthyphro*, other Platonic dialogues, and other sources.

12. I doubt Strauss is in earnest in attributing this view of the gods to Socrates. He makes a slight modification of the text to which I think he refers, *Euthyphro* 15a1–2, and when he returns to summarize his discussion, he stresses Socrates's rejection of the orthodox

cult but does not say again that he holds the positive view that the gods are good (¶8, p. 80). A possibly attractive and perhaps pious view of the gods is also implied in the penultimate paragraph of the lecture, but it stops well short of declaring that these "living gods" are beneficent to human beings in general or to virtuous ones in particular. Nor does Strauss attribute this attractive view to Socrates. Strauss also denies that quoting Plato can resolve complicated questions p. 81), but the flattering view he attributes to Socrates rests on only a single line. Finally, on flattering views of the gods, consider Strauss, "Xenophon's *Anabasis*," in *Studies in Platonic Political Philosophy*, ed. Thomas L. Pangle (Chicago: University of Chicago Press, 1986), 122.

13. For a related but different explanation of how an innocent Socrates got into trouble in Athens, see *Apology of Socrates* 20c4ff., where Socrates tells the story of his examination of the Oracle at Delphi.

14. For a similar claim that he shared his opinions with one and all, see *Apology of Socrates* 33a5–b3. Adam concludes from it that Socrates "believed himself commissioned by God to preach to all who would listen." J. Adam, *Platonis Euthyphro* (Cambridge: Cambridge University Press, 1890). Such a reaction further justifies Strauss's open doubting that Socrates was really driven by "missionary zeal" to share his views.

15. David Bolotin, *Plato's Dialogue on Friendship: An Interpretation of the Lysis, with a New Translation* (Ithaca, NY: Cornell University Press, 1989), 65–66; *Lysis* 223a–b.

16. See also Plato, *Apology of Socrates* 25c–e.

17. The view that the gods seek obedience, not imitation, is nicely expressed in the passage about Proteus to which Strauss alludes later in the lecture. See Homer, *Odyssey* 4.353.

18. His emphasis is surprising at least when we think only of the *Euthyphro*, but in the passage of the *Theaetetus* to which he refers in ¶10, we see Socrates recommending that we seek a likeness to god as much as possible. In the notebook, Strauss uses the Greek, ὁμοίωσις θεῷ, to refer to this recommendation on four occasions, on which he explains how likening oneself to god would require a transcendence of piety (p. 31), would entail a likening of oneself to pure mind (p. 36), would amount to a redefinition of virtue (p. 36), and would suggest that God loves those who philosophize (p. 40). Unsurprisingly, he ends with a question that doubts the adequacy of the suggestions he has just made ("Do the gods love?" p. 40).

19. Strauss uses the word "idea" twenty-eight times in these four paragraphs. His only other uses are the two in paragraph 20.

20. See Strauss, *Socrates and Aristophanes* (New York: Basic Books, 1966), 311, for another strong statement of the opposition between poetry and philosophy, though it is silent about their possible disagreement over the primary beings.

21. Strauss does not mention the word "piety" in paragraph 15, but he takes "poetry" to be especially the making of gods.

22. In the notebook, when Strauss discusses what it would be like to have a god prior to the ideas, he further clarifies his point by citing the medieval Nominalism of Occam, which he explicates with a reference to a statement by Étienne Gilson, p. 36.

23. Identifying "the truth" with a "half-truth" would seem either to promote the latter or to demote the former. This too helps us wonder again what precise error keeps the half-truth of the *Euthyphro* from being the whole truth.

24. For further evidence that Strauss had the *Laws* in mind when he wrote of the demonstration of the gods in paragraph 20, consider that he elsewhere says the gods defended by the Athenian Stranger are subject to demonstration (*What Is Political Philosophy?* [Glencoe, IL: Free Press, 1959], 32–33). This very passage also speaks of the Stranger's "philanthropy," as the *Euthyphro* and Strauss's essay on it also refer to Socrates's "philanthropy" (¶¶4–7).

25. This statement from ¶8 is illustrative: "Socrates was impious because he knew, or believed to know, that the ancestral reports about the ancestral gods which were underlying ancestral custom are wrong." To "believe to know" is not yet to establish by rigorous proof.

# PART III
# Translation

# Translation of Plato's *Euthyphro*

SETH BENARDETE

[**2a**] Εὐθύφρων [Euthyphro]: τί νεώτερον, ὦ Σώκρατες, γέγονεν, ὅτι σὺ τὰς ἐν Λυκείῳ καταλιπὼν διατριβὰς ἐνθάδε νῦν διατρίβεις περὶ τὴν τοῦ βασιλέως στοάν. [What's new, Socrates, that you've abandoned your haunts at the Lyceum and now loiter here at the Stoa of the king (Archon)?] οὐ γάρ που καὶ σοί γε δίκη τις οὖσα τυγχάνει πρὸς τὸν βασιλέα ὥσπερ ἐμοί. [Surely you too don't happen to have any kind of suit before the king as I do.]

Σωκράτης [Socrates]: οὔτοι δὴ Ἀθηναῖοί γε, ὦ Εὐθύφρων, δίκην αὐτὴν καλοῦσιν ἀλλὰ γραφήν. [The Athenians, you know, Euthyphro, don't call it a suit but an indictment.] [**2b**]

Εὐθύφρων: τί φῄς; [What's that you say?] γραφὴν σέ τις, ὡς ἔοικε, γέγραπται· οὐ γὰρ ἐκεῖνό γε καταγνώσομαι, ὡς σὺ ἕτερον. [Someone has brought an indictment against you, it seems; for I shan't charge you with that, your indicting another.]

Σωκράτης: οὐ γὰρ οὖν. [No, of course not.]

Εὐθύφρων: ἀλλὰ σὲ ἄλλος; [Then another's indicted you?]

Σωκράτης: πάνυ γε. [Just so.]

Εὐθύφρων: τίς οὗτος; [Who is he?]

Σωκράτης: οὐδ' αὐτὸς πάνυ τι γιγνώσκω, ὦ Εὐθύφρων, τὸν ἄνδρα, νέος γάρ τίς μοι φαίνεται καὶ ἀγνώς· ὀνομάζουσι μέντοι αὐτόν, ὡς ἐγᾦμαι, Μέλητον. [I myself, Euthyphro, don't even know the man at all, so he's apparently quite young and unknown; but they give him the name, I believe, of Meletus.] ἔστι δὲ τῶν δήμων Πιτθεύς, εἴ τινα νῷ ἔχεις

Πιτθέα Μέλητον οἷον τετανότριχα καὶ οὐ πάνυ εὐγένειον, ἐπίγρυπον δέ. [He belongs to the Pithean deme, if you can recall a Pithean with long stringy hair and without a full beard, but a hooked nose.]

Εὐθύφρων: οὐκ ἐννοῶ, ὦ Σώκρατες· ἀλλὰ δὴ τίνα γραφήν [**2c**] σε γέγραπται; [No, I cannot recall, Socrates; but on what charge has he indicted you?]

Σωκράτης: ἥντινα; [What charge?] οὐκ ἀγεννῆ, ἔμοιγε δοκεῖ· τὸ γὰρ νέον ὄντα τοσοῦτον πρᾶγμα ἐγνωκέναι οὐ φαῦλόν ἐστιν. [Not an ignoble one, I think; for it's not contemptible to be as young as he is and understand so important a matter.] ἐκεῖνος γάρ, ὥς φησιν, οἶδε τίνα τρόπον οἱ νέοι διαφθείρονται καὶ τίνες οἱ διαφθείροντες αὐτούς. [He, as he says, knows how the young are corrupted and who corrupts them.] καὶ κινδυνεύει σοφός τις εἶναι, καὶ τὴν ἐμὴν ἀμαθίαν κατιδὼν ὡς διαφθείροντος τοὺς ἡλικιώτας αὐτοῦ, ἔρχεται κατηγορήσων μου ὥσπερ πρὸς μητέρα πρὸς τὴν πόλιν. [So he is likely to be rather wise, and having spied out my ignorance, he's gone before the city as before his mother to charge me with corrupting his contemporaries.] καὶ φαίνεταί μοι τῶν πολιτικῶν [**2d**] μόνος ἄρχεσθαι ὀρθῶς· ὀρθῶς γάρ ἐστι τῶν νέων πρῶτον ἐπιμεληθῆναι ὅπως ἔσονται ὅτι ἄριστοι, ὥσπερ γεωργὸν ἀγαθὸν τῶν νέων φυτῶν εἰκὸς πρῶτον ἐπιμεληθῆναι, μετὰ δὲ τοῦτο καὶ τῶν ἄλλων. [And he alone of the statesmen, it appears to me, begins correctly: for "correctly" it is to take care of the young first, so that they will become as good as possible, just as a good farmer properly takes care of the young plants first, and after them of the others.] καὶ δὴ καὶ Μέλητος ἴσως πρῶτον [**3a**] μὲν ἡμᾶς ἐκκαθαίρει τοὺς τῶν νέων τὰς βλάστας διαφθείροντας, ὥς φησιν· ἔπειτα μετὰ τοῦτο δῆλον ὅτι τῶν πρεσβυτέρων ἐπιμεληθεὶς πλείστων καὶ μεγίστων ἀγαθῶν αἴτιος τῇ πόλει γενήσεται, ὥς γε τὸ εἰκὸς συμβῆναι ἐκ τοιαύτης ἀρχῆς ἀρξαμένῳ. [So Meletus perhaps first of all cleans us out who corrupt the growth of the young, and when he has later taken care of the elders, he'll obviously be responsible for the largest and most important goods to his city, since that is likely to happen when he has made such a start.]

Εὐθύφρων: βουλοίμην ἄν, ὦ Σώκρατες, ἀλλ᾽ ὀρρωδῶ μὴ τοὐναντίον γένηται· ἀτεχνῶς γάρ μοι δοκεῖ ἀφ᾽ ἑστίας ἄρχεσθαι κακουργεῖν τὴν πόλιν, ἐπιχειρῶν ἀδικεῖν σέ. [I would wish it were so, Socrates, but I fear that the opposite might happen; for I think he is simply "starting from the hearth" and doing damage to the city in trying to wrong you.] καί μοι λέγε, τί καὶ ποιοῦντά σέ φησι διαφθείρειν τοὺς νέους; [Now, tell me in doing (making) what does he say you corrupt the young?]

**[3b]**

Σωκράτης: ἄτοπα, ὦ θαυμάσιε, ὡς οὕτω γ' ἀκοῦσαι. [Strange things, my wonder, to hear them spoken of so.][1] φησὶ γάρ με ποιητὴν εἶναι θεῶν, καὶ ὡς καινοὺς ποιοῦντα θεοὺς τοὺς δ' ἀρχαίους οὐ νομίζοντα ἐγράψατο τούτων αὐτῶν ἕνεκα, ὥς φησιν. [He says I am a maker of gods, and on this count, as he says, for making new gods and not believing in the old ones, he has indicted me.]

Εὐθύφρων: μανθάνω, ὦ Σώκρατες· ὅτι δὴ σὺ τὸ δαιμόνιον φῂς σαυτῷ ἑκάστοτε γίγνεσθαι. [I understand, Socrates, it's because you say that the daimonion comes to you occasionally.] ὡς οὖν καινοτομοῦντός σου περὶ τὰ θεῖα γέγραπται ταύτην τὴν γραφήν, καὶ ὡς διαβαλῶν δὴ ἔρχεται εἰς τὸ δικαστήριον, εἰδὼς ὅτι εὐδιάβολα τὰ τοιαῦτα πρὸς τοὺς πολλούς. [Hence he's drawn up this indictment on the ground that you are making innovations in divine things, and he goes to court to utter slander, knowing that slanders like that are easily addressed to the multitude.] καὶ ἐμοῦ γάρ τοι, **[3c]** ὅταν τι λέγω ἐν τῇ ἐκκλησίᾳ περὶ τῶν θείων, προλέγων αὐτοῖς τὰ μέλλοντα, καταγελῶσιν ὡς μαινομένου· καίτοι οὐδὲν ὅτι οὐκ ἀληθὲς εἴρηκα ὧν προεῖπον, ἀλλ' ὅμως φθονοῦσιν ἡμῖν πᾶσι τοῖς τοιούτοις. [So too, in my case, you know, whenever I say anything about the divine things in the assembly, predicting the future to them, they laugh at me as though I were mad; and yet there's nothing I've predicted that wasn't true, but in spite of that they envy all who are like ourselves.] ἀλλ' οὐδὲν αὐτῶν χρὴ φροντίζειν, ἀλλ' ὁμόσε ἰέναι. [But we mustn't pay any attention to them, but close our ranks.]

Σωκράτης: ὦ φίλε Εὐθύφρων, ἀλλὰ τὸ μὲν καταγελασθῆναι ἴσως οὐδὲν πρᾶγμα. [Now to be laughed at, my dear Euthyphro, is perhaps no matter.] Ἀθηναίοις γάρ τοι, ὡς ἐμοὶ δοκεῖ, οὐ σφόδρα μέλει ἄν τινα δεινὸν οἴωνται εἶναι, μὴ μέντοι διδασκαλικὸν τῆς αὑτοῦ σοφίας· ὃν δ' ἂν καὶ ἄλλους οἴωνται **[3d]** ποιεῖν τοιούτους, θυμοῦνται, εἴτ' οὖν φθόνῳ ὡς σὺ λέγεις, εἴτε δι' ἄλλο τι. [For the Athenians, you see, do not much care, I think, whenever they believe someone's clever, provided he's not a teacher of his wisdom, but they become indignant at anyone who they believe makes others like himself, whether out of envy, as you say, or for some other reason.]

Εὐθύφρων: τούτου οὖν πέρι ὅπως ποτὲ πρὸς ἐμὲ ἔχουσιν, οὐ πάνυ ἐπιθυμῶ πειραθῆναι. [Well, I don't want much to try them out on it, however they are disposed toward me.]

Σωκράτης: ἴσως γὰρ σὺ μὲν δοκεῖς σπάνιον σεαυτὸν παρέχειν καὶ διδάσκειν οὐκ ἐθέλειν τὴν σεαυτοῦ σοφίαν· ἐγὼ δὲ φοβοῦμαι μὴ ὑπὸ φιλανθρωπίας δοκῶ αὐτοῖς ὅτιπερ ἔχω ἐκκεχυμένως παντὶ ἀνδρὶ λέγειν, οὐ μόνον ἄνευ μισθοῦ, ἀλλὰ καὶ προστιθεὶς ἂν ἡδέως εἴ τίς μου ἐθέλει ἀκούειν. [Perhaps you're thought to offer yourself rarely and to be unwilling to teach your wisdom: but I'm afraid that they might think that out of my philanthropy I speak unreservedly to every man, and even that I would pay gladly in addition if anyone's willing to listen to me.] εἰ μὲν οὖν, ὃ νυνδὴ ἔλεγον, μέλλοιέν μου καταγελᾶν ὥσπερ [**3e**] σὺ φῂς σαυτοῦ, οὐδὲν ἂν εἴη ἀηδὲς παίζοντας καὶ γελῶντας ἐν τῷ δικαστηρίῳ διαγαγεῖν· εἰ δὲ σπουδάσονται, τοῦτ' ἤδη ὅπῃ ἀποβήσεται ἄδηλον πλὴν ὑμῖν τοῖς μάντεσιν. [Now if, as I was saying just now, they are going to laugh at me as you say they do at you, it wouldn't be unpleasant to spend the time in playing and laughing in the courtroom; but if they are in earnest, then it is unclear how it will turn out, except to you seers.]

Εὐθύφρων: ἀλλ' ἴσως οὐδὲν ἔσται, ὦ Σώκρατες, πρᾶγμα, ἀλλὰ σύ τε κατὰ νοῦν ἀγωνιῇ τὴν δίκην, οἶμαι δὲ καὶ ἐμὲ τὴν ἐμήν. [Perhaps it will be no trouble, Socrates, but you will manage the suit as you like it, just as I believe I'll manage mine.]

Σωκράτης: ἔστιν δὲ δὴ σοί, ὦ Εὐθύφρων, τίς ἡ δίκη; [What is your suit, Euthyphro?] φεύγεις αὐτὴν ἢ διώκεις; [Are you defendant or plaintiff?]

Εὐθύφρων: διώκω. [Plaintiff.]

Σωκράτης: Τίνα; [Against whom?]

[**4a**]

Εὐθύφρων: ὃν διώκων αὖ δοκῶ μαίνεσθαι. [Whom I'm thought mad to be plaintiff against.]

Σωκράτης: τί δέ; [What?] πετόμενόν τινα διώκεις; [You are not plaintiff against anyone who flies?]

Εὐθύφρων: πολλοῦ γε δεῖ πέτεσθαι, ὅς γε τυγχάνει ὢν εὖ μάλα πρεσβύτης. [Oh, he's far from flying, as he happens to be a very old man.]

Σωκράτης: τίς οὗτος; [Who is he?]

Εὐθύφρων: ὁ ἐμὸς πατήρ. [My father]

Σωκράτης: ὁ σός, ὦ βέλτιστε; [Yours, most excellent man?]

Εὐθύφρων: πάνυ μὲν οὖν. [Yes, of course.]

Σωκράτης: ἔστιν δὲ τί τὸ ἔγκλημα καὶ τίνος ἡ δίκη; [What is the charge, and the suit's about what?]

Εὐθύφρων: φόνου, ὦ Σώκρατες. [About murder, Socrates.]

Σωκράτης: Ἡράκλεις. [Heracles!] ἦ που, ὦ Εὐθύφρων, ἀγνοεῖται ὑπὸ τῶν πολλῶν ὅπῃ ποτὲ ὀρθῶς ἔχει· οὐ γὰρ οἶμαί γε τοῦ [**4b**] ἐπιτυχόντος [ὀρθῶς] αὐτὸ πρᾶξαι ἀλλὰ πόρρω που ἤδη σοφίας ἐλαύνοντος. [I suppose it's certain, Euthyphro, that the multitude are ignorant of what way is correct, for it's not for anyone at all, I believe, to do it correctly but only for someone who's already far advanced in wisdom.]

Εὐθύφρων: πόρρω μέντοι νὴ Δία, ὦ Σώκρατες. [Far advanced's the word, by Zeus, Socrates.]

Σωκράτης: ἔστιν δὲ δὴ τῶν οἰκείων τις ὁ τεθνεὼς ὑπὸ τοῦ σοῦ πατρός; [So it's one of your relatives, the dead man whom your father killed?] ἢ δῆλα δή; [No doubt that's obvious?] οὐ γὰρ ἄν που ὑπέρ γε ἀλλοτρίου ἐπεξῇσθα φόνου αὐτῷ. [You surely wouldn't prosecute him for murder on account of someone outside the family.]

Εὐθύφρων: γελοῖον, ὦ Σώκρατες, ὅτι οἴει τι διαφέρειν εἴτε ἀλλότριος εἴτε οἰκεῖος ὁ τεθνεώς, ἀλλ' οὐ τοῦτο μόνον δεῖν φυλάττειν, εἴτε ἐν δίκῃ ἔκτεινεν ὁ κτείνας εἴτε μή, καὶ εἰ μὲν ἐν δίκῃ, ἐᾶν, εἰ δὲ μή, ἐπεξιέναι, ἐάνπερ ὁ κτείνας συνέστιός [**4c**] σοι καὶ ὁμοτράπεζος ᾖ· ἴσον γὰρ τὸ μίασμα γίγνεται ἐὰν συνῇς τῷ τοιούτῳ συνειδὼς καὶ μὴ ἀφοσιοῖς σεαυτόν τε καὶ ἐκεῖνον τῇ δίκῃ ἐπεξιών. [It's ridiculous, Socrates, that you believe it makes any difference whether the murdered was related or not, but not that one must only guard this, whether the murderer killed in justice or not, and if in justice, to ignore it, but if not, to prosecute, whether or not the murderer's of your own hearth and table; for the pollution is the same if you knowingly consort with him and do not purify[2] both yourself and him by prosecuting in a suit.] ἐπεὶ ὅ γε ἀποθανὼν πελάτης τις ἦν ἐμός, καὶ ὡς ἐγεωργοῦμεν ἐν τῇ Νάξῳ, ἐθήτευεν ἐκεῖ παρ' ἡμῖν. [In this case, the man who died was a certain client of mine, and when we were farming in Naxos, he labored there for us.] παροινήσας οὖν καὶ ὀργισθεὶς τῶν οἰκετῶν τινι τῶν ἡμετέρων ἀποσφάττει αὐτόν. [Now he became quite drunk and in anger at one of our household slaves slew him.] ὁ οὖν πατὴρ συνδήσας τοὺς πόδας καὶ τὰς χεῖρας αὐτοῦ, καταβαλὼν εἰς τάφρον τινά, πέμπει δεῦρο ἄνδρα πευσόμενον τοῦ ἐξηγητοῦ ὅτι χρείη [**4d**] ποιεῖν. [My father then bound his hands and feet and threw him in a ditch, and sent a man here (to Athens) to learn from the exegete what he must do.] ἐν δὲ τούτῳ τῷ χρόνῳ τοῦ δεδεμένου ὠλιγώρει τε καὶ ἠμέλει ὡς ἀνδροφόνου καὶ οὐδὲν ὂν πρᾶγμα εἰ καὶ ἀποθάνοι, ὅπερ οὖν καὶ ἔπαθεν· ὑπὸ γὰρ λιμοῦ καὶ ῥίγους καὶ τῶν δεσμῶν ἀποθνήσκει πρὶν τὸν ἄγγελον παρὰ τοῦ ἐξηγητοῦ ἀφικέσθαι. [But in the meantime he paid no attention to the bound man but neglected him as a murderer, thinking it would be no matter even if he did die, which is exactly what happened: he died of hunger, cold, and the bonds before the messenger returned from the exegete.] ταῦτα δὴ οὖν καὶ ἀγανακτεῖ ὅ τε πατὴρ καὶ οἱ ἄλλοι οἰκεῖοι, ὅτι ἐγὼ ὑπὲρ τοῦ ἀνδροφόνου τῷ πατρὶ φόνου ἐπεξέρχομαι οὔτε ἀποκτείναντι, ὥς φασιν ἐκεῖνοι, οὔτ' εἰ ὅτι μάλιστα ἀπέκτεινεν, ἀνδροφόνου γε ὄντος τοῦ ἀποθανόντος, οὐ δεῖν φροντίζειν ὑπὲρ τοῦ τοιούτου—ἀνόσιον [**4e**] γὰρ εἶναι τὸ ὑὸν πατρὶ φόνου ἐπεξιέναι—κακῶς εἰδότες, ὦ Σώκρατες, τὸ θεῖον ὡς ἔχει τοῦ ὁσίου τε πέρι καὶ τοῦ ἀνοσίου. [So now my father and my other relations are indignant that I for the sake of the murderer prosecute my father for murder who, as they say, didn't kill him, and even if, to grant the point, he did kill, since the dead man was a murderer anyhow, I mustn't pay any attention to that sort—it's unholy for a son to prosecute his father for murder—ill knowing, Socrates, how the divine is disposed to the holy and the unholy.]

Σωκράτης: σὺ δὲ δὴ πρὸς Διός, ὦ Εὐθύφρων, οὑτωσὶ ἀκριβῶς οἴει ἐπίστασθαι περὶ τῶν θείων ὅπῃ ἔχει, καὶ τῶν ὁσίων τε καὶ ἀνοσίων, ὥστε τούτων οὕτω πραχθέντων ὡς σὺ λέγεις, οὐ φοβῇ δικαζόμενος τῷ πατρὶ ὅπως μὴ αὖ σὺ ἀνόσιον πρᾶγμα τυγχάνῃς πράττων; [Then do you, by Zeus, Euthyphro, believe you know so accurately about divine things how they are disposed, both the holy and unholy, that when this was done as you say, you're not afraid in indicting your father that you in turn might happen to be doing an unholy action?]

Εὐθύφρων: οὐδὲν γὰρ ἄν μου ὄφελος εἴη, ὦ Σώκρατες, οὐδέ [**5a**] τῳ ἂν διαφέροι Εὐθύφρων τῶν πολλῶν ἀνθρώπων, εἰ μὴ τὰ τοιαῦτα πάντα ἀκριβῶς εἰδείην. [No, Socrates, for otherwise I would be of no use at all, nor would Euthyphro differ from any of the multitude of men, unless I knew all matters like this accurately.]

Σωκράτης: ἆρ' οὖν μοι, ὦ θαυμάσιε Εὐθύφρων, κράτιστόν ἐστι μαθητῇ σῷ γενέσθαι, καὶ πρὸ τῆς γραφῆς τῆς πρὸς Μέλητον αὐτὰ ταῦτα προκαλεῖσθαι αὐτόν, λέγοντα ὅτι ἔγωγε καὶ ἐν τῷ ἔμπροσθεν χρόνῳ τὰ θεῖα περὶ πολλοῦ ἐποιούμην εἰδέναι, καὶ νῦν ἐπειδή με ἐκεῖνος αὐτοσχεδιάζοντά φησι καὶ καινοτομοῦντα περὶ τῶν θείων ἐξαμαρτάνειν, μαθητὴς δὴ γέγονα σός—"καὶ εἰ μέν, ὦ Μέλητε," φαίην ἄν, "Εὐθύφρονα ὁμολογεῖ [**5b**] σοφὸν εἶναι τὰ τοιαῦτα, [καὶ] ὀρθῶς νομίζειν καὶ ἐμὲ ἡγοῦ καὶ μὴ δικάζου· εἰ δὲ μή, ἐκείνῳ τῷ διδασκάλῳ λάχε δίκην πρότερον ἢ ἐμοί, ὡς τοὺς πρεσβυτέρους διαφθείροντι ἐμέ τε καὶ τὸν αὑτοῦ πατέρα, ἐμὲ μὲν διδάσκοντι, ἐκεῖνον δὲ νουθετοῦντί τε καὶ κολάζοντι"—καὶ ἂν μή μοι πείθηται μηδὲ ἀφίῃ τῆς δίκης ἢ ἀντ' ἐμοῦ γράφηται σέ, αὐτὰ ταῦτα λέγειν ἐν τῷ δικαστηρίῳ ἃ προυκαλούμην αὐτόν; [In that case, my wonderful Euthyphro, it's best for me to become your pupil, and before the indictment of Meletus comes to court to challenge him on this very point, saying that I had thought it very important to know about divine things even in the past, and now since he says in improvising and making innovations in divine things I'm at fault, I have become your pupil—"And if, Meletus," I should say, "you agree that Euthyphro is wise in these matters, then reckon that I too believe correctly and do not condemn me; but if you don't, let that teacher get the suit rather than me, since he corrupts the elders, me and his father, me by teaching, him by rebuking and punishing"—and then if he's not persuaded nor releases me from the suit and indicts you instead of me, then wouldn't it be best to make these very points on which I challenged him in the courtroom?]

Εὐθύφρων: ναὶ μὰ Δία, ὦ Σώκρατες, εἰ ἄρα ἐμὲ ἐπιχειρήσειε [**5c**] γράφεσθαι, εὕροιμ' ἄν, ὡς οἶμαι, ὅπῃ σαθρός ἐστιν, καὶ πολὺ ἂν ἡμῖν πρότερον περὶ ἐκείνου λόγος ἐγένετο ἐν τῷ δικαστηρίῳ ἢ περὶ ἐμοῦ. [Yes, by Zeus, Socrates, if he should ever try to indict me, I'd discover, I believe, where he's rotten, and our talk in court would far sooner be about him than about me.]

Σωκράτης: καὶ ἐγώ τοι, ὦ φίλε ἑταῖρε, ταῦτα γιγνώσκων μαθητὴς ἐπιθυμῶ γενέσθαι σός, εἰδὼς ὅτι καὶ ἄλλος πού τις καὶ ὁ Μέλητος οὗτος σὲ μὲν οὐδὲ δοκεῖ ὁρᾶν, ἐμὲ δὲ οὕτως ὀξέως [ἀτεχνῶς] καὶ ῥᾳδίως κατεῖδεν ὥστε ἀσεβείας ἐγράψατο. [So I, you see, being aware of this, my dear fellow, desire to become your pupil, knowing that apparently no one else nor this Meletus either seems to see you, but he so sharply (artlessly) and easily spied me out that he's indicted me for impiety.] νῦν οὖν πρὸς Διὸς λέγε μοι ὃ νυνδὴ σαφῶς εἰδέναι διισχυρίζου, ποῖόν τι τὸ εὐσεβὲς φῂς εἶναι καὶ τὸ ἀσεβὲς [**5d**] καὶ περὶ φόνου καὶ περὶ τῶν ἄλλων; [Now then, by Zeus, tell me what you were insisting just now you know so plainly, what sort of thing you say the pious and the impious are in regard to murder and other things?] ἢ οὐ ταὐτόν ἐστιν ἐν πάσῃ πράξει τὸ ὅσιον αὐτὸ αὑτῷ, καὶ τὸ ἀνόσιον αὖ τοῦ μὲν ὁσίου παντὸς ἐναντίον, αὐτὸ δὲ αὑτῷ ὅμοιον καὶ ἔχον μίαν τινὰ ἰδέαν κατὰ τὴν ἀνοσιότητα πᾶν ὅτιπερ ἂν μέλλῃ ἀνόσιον εἶναι; [Or isn't the holy taken alone by itself in every action the same, and, in turn, the unholy opposite to everything holy, similar to itself, and anything whatever that is unholy has some one look according to unholiness?

Εὐθύφρων: πάντως δήπου, ὦ Σώκρατες. [Wholly so, Socrates.]

Σωκράτης: λέγε δή, τί φῂς εἶναι τὸ ὅσιον καὶ τί τὸ ἀνόσιον; [Say then, what do you say the holy is, and what the unholy?]

Εὐθύφρων: λέγω τοίνυν ὅτι τὸ μὲν ὅσιόν ἐστιν ὅπερ ἐγὼ νῦν ποιῶ, τῷ ἀδικοῦντι ἢ περὶ φόνους ἢ περὶ ἱερῶν κλοπὰς ἤ τι ἄλλο τῶν τοιούτων ἐξαμαρτάνοντι ἐπεξιέναι, ἐάντε πατὴρ [**5e**] ὢν τυγχάνῃ ἐάντε μήτηρ ἐάντε ἄλλος ὁστισοῦν, τὸ δὲ μὴ ἐπεξιέναι ἀνόσιον· ἐπεί, ὦ Σώκρατες, θέασαι ὡς μέγα σοι ἐρῶ τεκμήριον τοῦ νόμου ὅτι οὕτως ἔχει—ὃ καὶ ἄλλοις ἤδη εἶπον, ὅτι ταῦτα ὀρθῶς ἂν εἴη οὕτω γιγνόμενα—μὴ ἐπιτρέπειν τῷ ἀσεβοῦντι μηδ' ἂν ὁστισοῦν τυγχάνῃ ὤν. [I say that the holy is just what I'm doing now, prosecuting him who is unjust in murder, robbery of sacred things, or being at fault in anything similar, whether he happens to be father, mother, or anyone whatsoever, and not to prosecute is unholy: and observe, Socrates, what a great sign I'll tell you that the law is so—I've already told it to others, that if things were done in this way they'd be correct—viz., not to yield to the impious no matter who he happens to be.] αὐτοὶ γὰρ οἱ ἄνθρωποι τυγχάνουσι νομίζοντες τὸν Δία τῶν θεῶν ἄριστον καὶ δικαιότατον, [**6a**] καὶ τοῦτον ὁμολογοῦσι τὸν αὑτοῦ πατέρα δῆσαι ὅτι τοὺς ὑεῖς κατέπινεν οὐκ ἐν δίκῃ, κἀκεῖνόν γε αὖ τὸν αὑτοῦ πατέρα ἐκτεμεῖν δι' ἕτερα τοιαῦτα· ἐμοὶ δὲ χαλεπαίνουσιν ὅτι τῷ πατρὶ ἐπεξέρχομαι ἀδικοῦντι, καὶ οὕτως αὐτοὶ αὑτοῖς τὰ ἐναντία λέγουσι περί τε τῶν θεῶν καὶ περὶ ἐμοῦ. [Men themselves really happen to believe Zeus is the best and most just of the gods, and they agree he bound his own father because he had swallowed his sons not in justice, and his father in turn had castrated his own father for similar reasons; but now they are angry at me because I prosecute my unjust father, and they contradict themselves in speaking about the gods and me.]

Σωκράτης: ἆρά γε, ὦ Εὐθύφρων, τοῦτ' ἔστιν [οὗ] οὕνεκα τὴν γραφὴν φεύγω, ὅτι τὰ τοιαῦτα ἐπειδάν τις περὶ τῶν θεῶν λέγῃ, δυσχερῶς πως ἀποδέχομαι; [Is this the reason, then, Euthyphro, why I am indicted, because whenever anyone says things like that about the gods, I hardly accept it?] διὸ δή, ὡς ἔοικε, φήσει τίς με ἐξαμαρτάνειν. [Hence someone, it seems, will say that I'm at fault.] νῦν οὖν εἰ καὶ σοὶ ταῦτα συνδοκεῖ τῷ [**6b**] εὖ εἰδότι περὶ τῶν τοιούτων, ἀνάγκη δή, ὡς ἔοικε, καὶ ἡμῖν συγχωρεῖν. [If, however, you too who know these matters so well believe the same, then we are compelled as well, it seems, to consent.] τί γὰρ καὶ φήσομεν, οἵ γε καὶ αὐτοὶ ὁμολογοῦμεν περὶ αὐτῶν μηδὲν εἰδέναι; [What else shall we assert since we ourselves agree to know nothing about them?] ἀλλά μοι εἰπὲ πρὸς Φιλίου, σὺ ὡς ἀληθῶς ἡγῇ ταῦτα οὕτως γεγονέναι; [But tell me, by Zeus of Friendship, do you truly believe these events happened so?]

Εὐθύφρων: καὶ ἔτι γε τούτων θαυμασιώτερα, ὦ Σώκρατες, ἃ οἱ πολλοὶ οὐκ ἴσασιν. [Yes, I do, Socrates, and things more wonderful than these, which the multitude does not know about.]

Σωκράτης: καὶ πόλεμον ἄρα ἡγῇ σὺ εἶναι τῷ ὄντι ἐν τοῖς θεοῖς πρὸς ἀλλήλους, καὶ ἔχθρας γε δεινὰς καὶ μάχας καὶ ἄλλα τοιαῦτα πολλά, οἷα λέγεταί τε ὑπὸ τῶν ποιητῶν, καὶ ὑπὸ τῶν [**6c**] ἀγαθῶν γραφέων τά τε ἄλλα ἱερὰ ἡμῖν καταπεποίκιλται, καὶ δὴ καὶ τοῖς μεγάλοις Παναθηναίοις ὁ πέπλος μεστὸς τῶν τοιούτων ποικιλμάτων ἀνάγεται εἰς τὴν ἀκρόπολιν; [So you believe there truly was a war among the gods against one another, and awful hatreds, battles, and much else like that, the sort that are spoken of by the poets, and with which the good painters have adorned the sacred things among us, both other things as well as the great peplus that's full of such adornments, which is brought up to the Acropolis in the great Panathenaea?] ταῦτα ἀληθῆ φῶμεν εἶναι, ὦ Εὐθύφρων; [Shall we say these things are true, Euthyphro?]

Εὐθύφρων: μὴ μόνον γε, ὦ Σώκρατες, ἀλλ' ὅπερ ἄρτι εἶπον, καὶ ἄλλα σοι ἐγὼ πολλά, ἐάνπερ βούλῃ, περὶ τῶν θείων διηγήσομαι, ἃ σὺ ἀκούων εὖ οἶδ' ὅτι ἐκπλαγήσῃ. [Not only those, Socrates, but as I was saying just now, I shall inform you of much else, if you wish, about divine things, which if you hear them I know quite well you will be flabbergasted.]

Σωκράτης: οὐκ ἂν θαυμάζοιμι. [I should not wonder if I were.] ἀλλὰ ταῦτα μέν μοι εἰς αὖθις ἐπὶ σχολῆς διηγήσῃ· νυνὶ δὲ ὅπερ ἄρτι σε ἠρόμην πειρῶ [**6d**] σαφέστερον εἰπεῖν. [But at another time at my leisure you'll tell me, but now, about what I just asked you, try to speak more plainly.] οὐ γάρ με, ὦ ἑταῖρε, τὸ πρότερον ἱκανῶς ἐδίδαξας ἐρωτήσαντα τὸ ὅσιον ὅτι ποτ' εἴη, ἀλλά μοι εἶπες ὅτι τοῦτο τυγχάνει ὅσιον ὂν ὃ σὺ νῦν ποιεῖς, φόνου ἐπεξιὼν τῷ πατρί. [You didn't instruct me adequately before, my fellow, when I asked you what the holy was, but you said that what you are now doing happens to be the holy, prosecuting your father for murder.]

Εὐθύφρων: καὶ ἀληθῆ γε ἔλεγον, ὦ Σώκρατες. [And I told the truth, Socrates.]

Σωκράτης: Ἴσως. [Perhaps.] ἀλλὰ γάρ, ὦ Εὐθύφρων, καὶ ἄλλα πολλὰ φῂς εἶναι ὅσια. [And yet, Euthyphro, you say much else is holy.]

Εὐθύφρων: καὶ γὰρ ἔστιν. [And indeed it is.]

Σωκράτης: μέμνησαι οὖν ὅτι οὐ τοῦτό σοι διεκελευόμην, ἕν τι ἢ δύο με διδάξαι τῶν πολλῶν ὁσίων, ἀλλ' ἐκεῖνο αὐτὸ τὸ εἶδος ᾧ πάντα τὰ ὅσια ὅσιά ἐστιν; [Do you remember, then, that I didn't ask you to teach me this, one or two of the many holy things, but only that very look by which all holy things are holy?] ἔφησθα γάρ που μιᾷ ἰδέᾳ [**6e**] τά τε ἀνόσια ἀνόσια εἶναι καὶ τὰ ὅσια ὅσια· ἢ οὐ μνημονεύεις; [You did say, didn't you, that unholy things are unholy by one look, and likewise holy things are holy: don't you remember?]

Εὐθύφρων: Ἔγωγε. [Yes, I do.]

Σωκράτης: ταύτην τοίνυν με αὐτὴν δίδαξον τὴν ἰδέαν τίς ποτέ ἐστιν, ἵνα εἰς ἐκείνην ἀποβλέπων καὶ χρώμενος αὐτῇ παραδείγματι, ὃ μὲν ἂν τοιοῦτον ᾖ ὧν ἂν ἢ σὺ ἢ ἄλλος τις πράττῃ φῶ ὅσιον εἶναι, ὃ δ' ἂν μὴ τοιοῦτον, μὴ φῶ. [Teach me, then, what this very look is, so that, in keeping my eye on it and using it as an example, I shall say it is holy whatever you or anyone else does that is of the same sort, and whatever is not of the same sort, I shall say is not holy.]

Εὐθύφρων: ἀλλ' εἰ οὕτω βούλει, ὦ Σώκρατες, καὶ οὕτω σοι φράσω. [Well, if that's what you want, Socrates, I'll inform you of that as well.]

Σωκράτης: ἀλλὰ μὴν βούλομαί γε. [That's what I want, be sure.]

Εὐθύφρων: ἔστι τοίνυν τὸ μὲν τοῖς θεοῖς προσφιλὲς ὅσιον, τὸ [**7a**] δὲ μὴ προσφιλὲς ἀνόσιον. [The holy, then, is what is dear to the gods, and what is not dear is unholy.]

Σωκράτης: παγκάλως, ὦ Εὐθύφρων, καὶ ὡς ἐγὼ ἐζήτουν ἀποκρίνασθαί σε, οὕτω νῦν ἀπεκρίνω. [Very fine, Euthyphro, you've answered in just the way I was asking you to answer.] εἰ μέντοι ἀληθῶς, τοῦτο οὔπω οἶδα, ἀλλὰ σὺ δῆλον ὅτι ἐπεκδιδάξεις ὡς ἔστιν ἀληθῆ ἃ λέγεις. [Whether you answered truly, however, I do not yet know about that, but you will obviously go on to teach that it's true what you say.]

Εὐθύφρων: πάνυ μὲν οὖν. [Of course I shall.]

Σωκράτης: φέρε δή, ἐπισκεψώμεθα τί λέγομεν. [Come then, let us examine what you mean.] τὸ μὲν θεοφιλές τε καὶ θεοφιλὴς ἄνθρωπος ὅσιος, τὸ δὲ θεομισὲς καὶ ὁ θεομισὴς ἀνόσιος· οὐ ταὐτὸν δ' ἐστίν, ἀλλὰ τὸ ἐναντιώτατον, τὸ ὅσιον τῷ ἀνοσίῳ· οὐχ οὕτως; [What is dear to the gods and a man dear to the gods is holy, and what is hateful to the gods and he who is hateful to the gods is unholy: they are not the same, but most contrary, aren't they, the holy to the unholy?]

Εὐθύφρων: οὕτω μὲν οὖν. [So they are.]

Σωκράτης: καὶ εὖ γε φαίνεται εἰρῆσθαι; [And it appears to be well said?]

[**7b**]

Εὐθύφρων: δοκῶ, ὦ Σώκρατες. εἴρηται γάρ. [I think so, Socrates. For that is what I said.]

Σωκράτης: οὐκοῦν καὶ ὅτι στασιάζουσιν οἱ θεοί, ὦ Εὐθύφρων, καὶ διαφέρονται ἀλλήλοις καὶ ἔχθρα ἐστὶν ἐν αὐτοῖς πρὸς ἀλλήλους, καὶ τοῦτο εἴρηται; [But wasn't this too said, Euthyphro, that the gods are at strife and differ with one another and there are hatreds in them with regard to one another?]

Εὐθύφρων: εἴρηται γάρ. [Yes, that was said.]

Σωκράτης: ἔχθραν δὲ καὶ ὀργάς, ὦ ἄριστε, ἡ περὶ τίνων διαφορὰ ποιεῖ; [And differences about what, best man, make for hatreds and wrath?] ὧδε δὲ σκοπῶμεν. [Let us examine it this way.] ἆρ' ἂν εἰ διαφεροίμεθα ἐγώ τε καὶ σὺ περὶ ἀριθμοῦ ὁπότερα πλείω, ἡ περὶ τούτων διαφορὰ ἐχθροὺς ἂν ἡμᾶς ποιοῖ καὶ ὀργίζεσθαι ἀλλήλοις, ἢ ἐπὶ λογισμὸν ἐλθόντες περί γε τῶν τοιούτων ταχὺ ἂν [**7c**] ἀπαλλαγεῖμεν;

[Should you and I differ about a number, which is more, would that difference make us enemies and angry at each other, or wouldn't we, in coming to a counting, soon be quit of things like that?]

Εὐθύφρων: πάνυ γε. [Just so.]

Σωκράτης: οὐκοῦν καὶ περὶ τοῦ μείζονος καὶ ἐλάττονος εἰ διαφεροίμεθα, ἐπὶ τὸ μετρεῖν ἐλθόντες ταχὺ παυσαίμεθ' ἂν τῆς διαφορᾶς; [And should we differ about the greater and the smaller, in coming to a measurement, we should soon cease from our differences?]

Εὐθύφρων: ἔστι ταῦτα. [That's so.]

Σωκράτης: καὶ ἐπί γε τὸ ἱστάναι ἐλθόντες, ὡς ἐγῷμαι, περὶ τοῦ βαρυτέρου τε καὶ κουφοτέρου διακριθεῖμεν ἄν; [And so in coming to a weighing, I believe, we should judge about the heavier and the lighter?]

Εὐθύφρων: πῶς γὰρ οὔ; [Yes, of course.]

Σωκράτης: περὶ τίνος δὲ δὴ διενεχθέντες καὶ ἐπὶ τίνα κρίσιν οὐ δυνάμενοι ἀφικέσθαι ἐχθροί γε ἂν ἀλλήλοις εἶμεν καὶ ὀργιζοίμεθα; [Then in differing about what and being unable to come to what kind of decision would we be mutual enemies and angry at one another?] ἴσως οὐ πρόχειρόν σοί ἐστιν, ἀλλ' ἐμοῦ λέγοντος [**7d**] σκόπει εἰ τάδε ἐστὶ τό τε δίκαιον καὶ τὸ ἄδικον καὶ καλὸν καὶ αἰσχρὸν καὶ ἀγαθὸν καὶ κακόν. [Perhaps you don't have a ready answer, but examine when I say that it's this, the just and the unjust, beautiful and ugly, good and bad.] ἆρα οὐ ταῦτά ἐστιν περὶ ὧν διενεχθέντες καὶ οὐ δυνάμενοι ἐπὶ ἱκανὴν κρίσιν αὐτῶν ἐλθεῖν ἐχθροὶ ἀλλήλοις γιγνόμεθα, ὅταν γιγνώμεθα, καὶ ἐγὼ καὶ σὺ καὶ οἱ ἄλλοι ἄνθρωποι πάντες; [Aren't these the matters about which, if we differ and are unable to come to an adequate decision, we become mutual enemies, whenever we do become so, both you and I and all other men?]

Εὐθύφρων: ἀλλ' ἔστιν αὕτη ἡ διαφορά, ὦ Σώκρατες, καὶ περὶ τούτων. [But that's the difference, Socrates, and about these matters.]

Σωκράτης: τί δὲ οἱ θεοί, ὦ Εὐθύφρων; [What about the gods, Euthyphro?] οὐκ εἴπερ τι διαφέρονται, δι' αὐτὰ ταῦτα διαφέροιντ' ἄν; [If they differ at all, wouldn't they differ on account of these very points?]

Εὐθύφρων: πολλὴ ἀνάγκη. [Necessarily so.]

[**7e**]

Σωκράτης: καὶ τῶν θεῶν ἄρα, ὦ γενναῖε Εὐθύφρων, ἄλλοι ἄλλα δίκαια ἡγοῦνται κατὰ τὸν σὸν λόγον, καὶ καλὰ καὶ αἰσχρὰ καὶ ἀγαθὰ καὶ κακά·

οὐ γὰρ ἄν που ἐστασίαζον ἀλλήλοις εἰ μὴ περὶ τούτων διεφέροντο· ἦ γάρ; [Then different gods, my noble Euthyphro, believe different things are just, according to your argument, and likewise different things are beautiful and ugly, good and bad, for they surely wouldn't be at strife unless they did differ about these, or would they not?]

Εὐθύφρων: ὀρθῶς λέγεις. [What you say is correct.]

Σωκράτης: οὐκοῦν ἅπερ καλὰ ἡγοῦνται ἕκαστοι καὶ ἀγαθὰ καὶ δίκαια, ταῦτα καὶ φιλοῦσιν, τὰ δὲ ἐναντία τούτων μισοῦσιν; [And isn't it true that what each god believes beautiful, good, and just, he loves, and the contraries, he hates?]

Εὐθύφρων: πάνυ γε. [Just so.]

Σωκράτης: ταὐτὰ δέ γε, ὡς σὺ φῄς, οἱ μὲν δίκαια ἡγοῦνται, [**8a**] οἱ δὲ ἄδικα, περὶ ἃ καὶ ἀμφισβητοῦντες στασιάζουσί τε καὶ πολεμοῦσιν ἀλλήλοις· ἆρα οὐχ οὕτω; [So the same things, as you say, some believe are just, and some unjust, about which they in fact dispute and are at strife and war with one another? Isn't that so?]

Εὐθύφρων: Οὕτω. [So.]

Σωκράτης: ταὔτ' ἄρα, ὡς ἔοικεν, μισεῖταί τε ὑπὸ τῶν θεῶν καὶ φιλεῖται, καὶ θεομισῆ τε καὶ θεοφιλῆ ταὔτ' ἂν εἴη. [Then the same things, as it seems, are hated and loved by the gods, and the same things would be hateful to the gods and dear to the gods.]

Εὐθύφρων: Ἔοικεν. [It seems so.]

Σωκράτης: καὶ ὅσια ἄρα καὶ ἀνόσια τὰ αὐτὰ ἂν εἴη, ὦ Εὐθύφρων, τούτῳ τῷ λόγῳ. [Then by this argument, Euthyphro, the same things would be both holy and unholy.]

Εὐθύφρων: Κινδυνεύει. [I am afraid so.]

Σωκράτης: οὐκ ἄρα ὃ ἠρόμην ἀπεκρίνω, ὦ θαυμάσιε. [Then you didn't reply to what I asked, my wonder.] οὐ γὰρ τοῦτό γε ἠρώτων, ὃ τυγχάνει ταὐτὸν ὂν ὅσιόν τε καὶ ἀνόσιον· ὃ δ' ἂν θεοφιλὲς ᾖ καὶ θεομισές ἐστιν, ὡς ἔοικεν. [For I didn't ask you that, what one thing happens to be both holy and unholy; and, as it seems whatever is dear to the gods is also hateful to the gods.] [**8b**] ὥστε, ὦ Εὐθύφρων, ὃ σὺ νῦν ποιεῖς τὸν πατέρα κολάζων, οὐδὲν θαυμαστὸν εἰ τοῦτο δρῶν τῷ μὲν Διὶ προσφιλὲς ποιεῖς, τῷ δὲ Κρόνῳ καὶ τῷ Οὐρανῷ ἐχθρόν, καὶ τῷ μὲν Ἡφαίστῳ φίλον, τῇ δὲ Ἥρᾳ ἐχθρόν, καὶ εἴ τις ἄλλος τῶν θεῶν ἕτερος ἑτέρῳ διαφέρεται περὶ αὐτοῦ, καὶ ἐκείνοις κατὰ τὰ αὐτά. [Hence, Euthyphro, the punishment you are now giving your father—it's nothing wonderful if in acting so you do what is dear to Zeus but hateful to Cronus and Uranus, and dear to Hephaestus but hateful to Hera, and if any god differs with any other about it, then also it is with them in the same way.]

Εὐθύφρων: ἀλλ' οἶμαι, ὦ Σώκρατες, περί γε τούτου τῶν θεῶν οὐδένα ἕτερον ἑτέρῳ διαφέρεσθαι, ὡς οὐ δεῖ δίκην διδόναι ἐκεῖνον ὃς ἂν ἀδίκως τινὰ ἀποκτείνῃ. [But I think, Socrates, about this none of the gods differ the one with the other, namely, that he must not pay a penalty who ever unjustly kills another.]

Σωκράτης: τί δέ; ἀνθρώπων, ὦ Εὐθύφρων, ἤδη τινὸς ἤκουσας [**8c**] ἀμφισβητοῦντος ὡς τὸν ἀδίκως ἀποκτείναντα ἢ ἄλλο ἀδίκως ποιοῦντα ὁτιοῦν οὐ δεῖ δίκην διδόναι; [So, Euthyphro, have you ever heard up to now even any man disputing that he who unjustly killed or does anything else unjustly must not pay a penalty?]

Εὐθύφρων: οὐδὲν μὲν οὖν παύονται ταῦτα ἀμφισβητοῦντες καὶ ἄλλοθι καὶ ἐν τοῖς δικαστηρίοις: ἀδικοῦντες γὰρ πάμπολλα, πάντα ποιοῦσι καὶ λέγουσι φεύγοντες τὴν δίκην. [Why, they don't cease disputing this both elsewhere and in court, for in committing very many injustices, they do and say anything to avoid a penalty.]

Σωκράτης: ἦ καὶ ὁμολογοῦσιν, ὦ Εὐθύφρων, ἀδικεῖν, καὶ ὁμολογοῦντες ὅμως οὐ δεῖν φασὶ σφᾶς διδόναι δίκην; [And do they really agree, Euthyphro, that they were unjust, and in spite of agreeing to that they deny they must pay a penalty?]

Εὐθύφρων: οὐδαμῶς τοῦτό γε. [That is not at all what happens.]

Σωκράτης: οὐκ ἄρα πᾶν γε ποιοῦσι καὶ λέγουσι· τοῦτο γὰρ οἶμαι οὐ τολμῶσι λέγειν οὐδ' ἀμφισβητεῖν, ὡς οὐχὶ εἴπερ [**8d**] ἀδικοῦσί γε δοτέον δίκην, ἀλλ' οἶμαι οὔ φασιν ἀδικεῖν· ἢ γάρ; [Therefore, they don't do and say anything whatsoever; for this I believe they do not dare bring themselves to say, that even if they were unjust they mustn't pay, but I believe they deny they were unjust: isn't that so?]

Εὐθύφρων: ἀληθῆ λέγεις. [You speak truly.]

Σωκράτης: οὐκ ἄρα ἐκεῖνό γε ἀμφισβητοῦσιν, ὡς οὐ τὸν ἀδικοῦντα δεῖ διδόναι δίκην, ἀλλ' ἐκεῖνο ἴσως ἀμφισβητοῦσιν, τὸ τίς ἐστιν ὁ ἀδικῶν καὶ τί δρῶν καὶ πότε. [Therefore, they don't dispute about that, that the unjust man must not pay a penalty, but perhaps they dispute this, who was unjust, what did he do, and when.]

Εὐθύφρων: ἀληθῆ λέγεις. [You speak truly.]

Σωκράτης: οὐκοῦν αὐτά γε ταῦτα καὶ οἱ θεοὶ πεπόνθασιν, εἴπερ στασιάζουσι περὶ τῶν δικαίων καὶ ἀδίκων ὡς ὁ σὸς λόγος, καὶ οἱ μέν φασιν ἀλλήλους ἀδικεῖν, οἱ δὲ οὔ φασιν; [Then don't the gods undergo the same, if they are at strife about things just and unjust, as your argument goes, and do some assert they wrong one another, while others deny it?] ἐπεὶ ἐκεῖνό γε δήπου, ὦ θαυμάσιε, οὐδεὶς οὔτε θεῶν οὔτε [**8e**] ἀνθρώπων τολμᾷ λέγειν, ὡς οὐ τῷ γε ἀδικοῦντι δοτέον δίκην. [Since it's surely certain, my wonder, that neither any god nor man dares bring himself to say, that the unjust must not pay a penalty.]

Εὐθύφρων: ναί, τοῦτο μὲν ἀληθὲς λέγεις, ὦ Σώκρατες, τό γε κεφάλαιον. [Yes, that's true what you say, Socrates, as a summing-up.]

Σωκράτης: ἀλλ' ἕκαστόν γε οἶμαι, ὦ Εὐθύφρων, τῶν πραχθέντων ἀμφισβητοῦσιν οἱ ἀμφισβητοῦντες, καὶ ἄνθρωποι καὶ θεοί, εἴπερ ἀμφισβητοῦσιν θεοί· πράξεώς τινος πέρι διαφερόμενοι οἱ μὲν δικαίως φασὶν αὐτὴν πεπρᾶχθαι, οἱ δὲ ἀδίκως· ἆρ' οὐχ οὕτω; [But it is about the particular, I believe, Euthyphro, that disputants do dispute, both men and gods, if gods dispute at all; in differing about a certain action, some say it was done justly, others unjustly: isn't that so?]

Εὐθύφρων: πάνυ γε. [Just so.]

[**9a**]

Σωκράτης: ἴθι νυν, ὦ φίλε Εὐθύφρων, δίδαξον καὶ ἐμέ, ἵνα σοφώτερος γένωμαι, τί σοι τεκμήριόν ἐστιν ὡς πάντες θεοὶ ἡγοῦνται ἐκεῖνον ἀδίκως τεθνάναι, ὃς ἂν θητεύων ἀνδροφόνος γενόμενος, συνδεθεὶς ὑπὸ τοῦ δεσπότου τοῦ ἀποθανόντος, φθάσῃ τελευτήσας διὰ τὰ δεσμὰ πρὶν τὸν συνδήσαντα παρὰ τῶν ἐξηγητῶν περὶ αὐτοῦ πυθέσθαι τί χρὴ ποιεῖν, καὶ ὑπὲρ τοῦ τοιούτου δὴ ὀρθῶς ἔχει ἐπεξιέναι καὶ ἐπισκήπτεσθαι φόνου τὸν ὑὸν τῷ πατρί; ἴθι, περὶ τούτων πειρῶ τί μοι [**9b**] σαφὲς ἐνδείξασθαι ὡς παντὸς μᾶλλον πάντες θεοὶ ἡγοῦνται ὀρθῶς ἔχειν ταύτην τὴν πρᾶξιν· κἄν μοι ἱκανῶς ἐνδείξῃ, ἐγκωμιάζων σε ἐπὶ σοφίᾳ οὐδέποτε παύσομαι. [Come then, my dear Euthyphro, teach me as well, that I might become wiser, what proof you have that all the gods believe him to have unjustly died, who while a hired hand became a murderer, then bound by the master of him who died, died because of the bonds before the binder could learn from the exegetes what he must do about him, and for an affair like this it is correct for a son to prosecute and charge him with murder; come, try and show something plain to me about this, that the gods completely believe this action is correct; and if you show me adequately, I shall never cease praising you for your wisdom.]

Εὐθύφρων: ἀλλ' ἴσως οὐκ ὀλίγον ἔργον ἐστίν, ὦ Σώκρατες, ἐπεὶ πάνυ γε σαφῶς ἔχοιμι ἂν ἐπιδεῖξαί σοι. [But perhaps it's not a slight task, Socrates, though I could completely exhibit it to you.]

Σωκράτης: μανθάνω· ὅτι σοι δοκῶ τῶν δικαστῶν δυσμαθέστερος εἶναι, ἐπεὶ ἐκείνοις γε ἐνδείξῃ δῆλον ὅτι ὡς ἄδικά τέ ἐστιν καὶ οἱ θεοὶ ἅπαντες τὰ τοιαῦτα μισοῦσιν. [I understand: it is because you think I'm harder to teach than the judge since you'll obviously have to show them that it's unjust, and that all the gods hate things like that.]

Εὐθύφρων: πάνυ γε σαφῶς, ὦ Σώκρατες, ἐάνπερ ἀκούωσί γέ μου λέγοντος. [Very plain it'll be, too, Socrates, provided they listen to what I say.]

[**9c**]

Σωκράτης: ἀλλ' ἀκούσονται. [But they will listen.] ἐάνπερ εὖ δοκῇς λέγειν. [Provided you are thought to speak well.] τόδε δέ σου ἐνενόησα ἅμα λέγοντος καὶ πρὸς ἐμαυτὸν σκοπῶ· "εἰ ὅτι μάλιστά με Εὐθύφρων διδάξειεν ὡς οἱ θεοὶ ἅπαντες τὸν τοιοῦτον θάνατον ἡγοῦνται ἄδικον εἶναι, τί μᾶλλον ἐγὼ μεμάθηκα παρ' Εὐθύφρονος τί ποτ' ἐστὶν τὸ ὅσιόν τε καὶ τὸ ἀνόσιον; θεομισὲς μὲν γὰρ τοῦτο τὸ ἔργον, ὡς ἔοικεν, εἴη ἄν. [But this occurred to me while you were speaking, and I'm thinking to myself, "If Euthyphro should after all teach me all the gods believe such a death unjust, how have I learnt from Euthyphro what the holy and the unholy are? This deed might be, as it seems, hateful to the gods."] ἀλλὰ γὰρ οὐ τούτῳ ἐφάνη ἄρτι ὡρισμένα τὸ ὅσιον καὶ μή·τὸ γὰρ θεομισὲς ὂν καὶ θεοφιλὲς ἐφάνη. [But it just now was evident that it wasn't by this that what was holy and what not are defined, for what was hateful to the gods had come to sight as what was dear to the gods as well.] ὥστε τούτου μὲν ἀφίημί σε, ὦ Εὐθύφρων: εἰ βούλει, πάντες αὐτὸ [**9d**] ἡγείσθων θεοὶ ἄδικον καὶ πάντες μισούντων. [So I release you from this charge, Euthyphro, and if you wish, let all the gods believe it unjust and let them all hate it.] ἀλλ' ἆρα τοῦτο ὃ νῦν ἐπανορθούμεθα ἐν τῷ λόγῳ—ὡς ὃ μὲν ἂν πάντες οἱ θεοὶ μισῶσιν ἀνόσιόν ἐστιν, ὃ δ' ἂν φιλῶσιν, ὅσιον· ὃ δ' ἂν οἱ μὲν φιλῶσιν οἱ δὲ μισῶσιν, οὐδέτερα ἢ ἀμφότερα—ἆρ' οὕτω βούλει ἡμῖν ὡρίσθαι νῦν περὶ τοῦ ὁσίου καὶ τοῦ ἀνοσίου; [But isn't this the point we are now going over for correction in the argument—that whatever all the gods hate is unholy, and whatever they love is holy;

and whatever some love and others hate, is neither the one nor the other but both—don't you wish it to be thus defined for us now about the holy and the unholy?]

Εὐθύφρων: τί γὰρ κωλύει, ὦ Σώκρατες; [And what prevents it, Socrates?]

Σωκράτης: οὐδὲν ἐμέ γε, ὦ Εὐθύφρων, ἀλλὰ σὺ δὴ τὸ σὸν σκόπει, εἰ τοῦτο ὑποθέμενος οὕτω ῥᾷστά με διδάξεις ὃ ὑπέσχου. [Nothing prevents me so far, Euthyphro, but you examine your own, (and consider) if in setting it up so, you will most easily teach me what you promised.]

**[9e]**

Εὐθύφρων: ἀλλ' ἔγωγε φαίην ἂν τοῦτο εἶναι τὸ ὅσιον ὃ ἂν πάντες οἱ θεοὶ φιλῶσιν, καὶ τὸ ἐναντίον, ὃ ἂν πάντες θεοὶ μισῶσιν, ἀνόσιον. [But I should say this to be the holy, whatever all the gods love, and the opposite, whatever else the gods hate, unholy.]

Σωκράτης: οὐκοῦν ἐπισκοπῶμεν αὖ τοῦτο, ὦ Εὐθύφρων, εἰ καλῶς λέγεται, ἢ ἐῶμεν καὶ οὕτω ἡμῶν τε αὐτῶν ἀποδεχώμεθα καὶ τῶν ἄλλων, ἐὰν μόνον φῇ τίς τι ἔχειν οὕτω συγχωροῦντες ἔχειν; ἢ σκεπτέον τί λέγει ὁ λέγων; [Shall we reexamine this, Euthyphro, to see whether or not it's finely said, or shall we let it go and thus accept from ourselves and others and agree that something is so, provided only one asserts it is? or must we examine what the speaker means?]

Εὐθύφρων: σκεπτέον· οἶμαι μέντοι ἔγωγε τοῦτο νυνὶ καλῶς λέγεσθαι. [We must examine: I believe, however, that this point is finely said.]

**[10a]**

Σωκράτης: τάχ,' ὠγαθέ, βέλτιον εἰσόμεθα. [Soon, my good man, we'll know better.] ἐννόησον γὰρ τὸ τοιόνδε· ἆρα τὸ ὅσιον ὅτι ὅσιόν ἐστιν φιλεῖται ὑπὸ τῶν θεῶν, ἢ ὅτι φιλεῖται ὅσιόν ἐστιν; [Consider the following: the holy, is it loved by the gods because it is holy, or because it is loved is it holy?]

Εὐθύφρων: οὐκ οἶδ' ὅτι λέγεις, ὦ Σώκρατες. [I do not know what you mean, Socrates.]

Σωκράτης: ἀλλ' ἐγὼ πειράσομαι σαφέστερον φράσαι. [I'll try to indicate it more clearly.] λέγομέν τι φερόμενον καὶ φέρον καὶ ἀγόμενον καὶ ἄγον καὶ ὁρώμενον καὶ ὁρῶν καὶ πάντα τὰ τοιαῦτα μανθάνεις ὅτι ἕτερα ἀλλήλων ἐστὶ καὶ ᾗ ἕτερα; [We speak of something being carried and of carrying, led and leading, seen and seeing, and all things like that, you do understand, are different from one another and in what they are different?]

Εὐθύφρων: ἔγωγέ μοι δοκῶ μανθάνειν. [Yes, I think I understand.]

Σωκράτης: οὐκοῦν καὶ φιλούμενόν τί ἐστιν καὶ τούτου ἕτερον τὸ φιλοῦν; [Then isn't it also true that being loved is one thing and loving is different from this?]

Εὐθύφρων: πῶς γὰρ οὔ; [Of course it is.]

**[10b]**

Σωκράτης: λέγε δή μοι, πότερον τὸ φερόμενον διότι φέρεται φερόμενόν ἐστιν, ἢ δι' ἄλλο τι; [Then tell me, what is carried, is it being carried because it is carried, or for some other reason?]

Εὐθύφρων: οὔκ, ἀλλὰ διὰ τοῦτο. [No, but for this.]

Σωκράτης: καὶ τὸ ἀγόμενον δὴ διότι ἄγεται, καὶ τὸ ὁρώμενον διότι ὁρᾶται; [And what is led, because it is led, and what is seen, because it is seen?]

Εὐθύφρων: πάνυ γε. [Just so.]

Σωκράτης: οὐκ ἄρα διότι ὁρώμενόν γέ ἐστιν, διὰ τοῦτο ὁρᾶται, ἀλλὰ τὸ ἐναντίον διότι ὁρᾶται, διὰ τοῦτο ὁρώμενον· οὐδὲ διότι ἀγόμενόν ἐστιν, διὰ τοῦτο ἄγεται, ἀλλὰ διότι ἄγεται, διὰ τοῦτο ἀγόμενον· οὐδὲ διότι φερόμενον φέρεται, ἀλλὰ διότι φέρεται φερόμενον. [Therefore it isn't because it is something to be seen that it is seen, but the opposite, because it is seen, for this reason is it something seen; not because it is something to be led that it is led, but because it is led, for this reason is it something led; nor because it is something to be carried is it carried, but because it is carried is it something carried.] ἆρα κατάδηλον, ὦ Εὐθύφρων, ὃ **[10c]** βούλομαι λέγειν; [Isn't it perfectly clear, Euthyphro, what I wish to say?] βούλομαι δὲ τόδε, ὅτι εἴ τι γίγνεται ἤ τι πάσχει, οὐχ ὅτι γιγνόμενόν ἐστι γίγνεται, ἀλλ' ὅτι γίγνεται γιγνόμενόν ἐστιν· οὐδ' ὅτι πάσχον ἐστὶ πάσχει, ἀλλ' ὅτι πάσχει πάσχον ἐστίν· ἢ οὐ συγχωρεῖς οὕτω; [I mean this, that if something comes into being or undergoes something, not because it is something that is to come into being does it come into being, but because it comes into being is it something that comes into being; nor because it is something that is to undergo does it undergo, but because it undergoes is it something that undergoes: do you agree with this?]

Εὐθύφρων: Ἔγωγε. [Yes, I do.]

Σωκράτης: οὐκοῦν καὶ τὸ φιλούμενον ἢ γιγνόμενόν τί ἐστιν ἢ πάσχον τι ὑπό του; [Isn't also the something that's loved either something that comes into being or undergoes something by something?]

Εὐθύφρων: πάνυ γε. [Just so.]

Σωκράτης: καὶ τοῦτο ἄρα οὕτως ἔχει ὥσπερ τὰ πρότερα· οὐχ ὅτι φιλούμενόν ἐστιν φιλεῖται ὑπὸ ὧν φιλεῖται, ἀλλ' ὅτι φιλεῖται φιλούμενον; [Then this is exactly like the previous cases: not because it is something to be loved is it loved by those who love it, but because it is loved is it a thing that is loved.]

Εὐθύφρων: ἀνάγκη. [Necessarily.]

**[10d]**

Σωκράτης: τί δὴ οὖν λέγομεν περὶ τοῦ ὁσίου, ὦ Εὐθύφρων; [What then are they saying about the holy, Euthyphro?] ἄλλο τι φιλεῖται ὑπὸ θεῶν πάντων, ὡς ὁ σὸς λόγος; [Isn't it something loved by all the gods, as your argument goes?]

Εὐθύφρων: ναί. [Yes.]

Σωκράτης: ἆρα διὰ τοῦτο, ὅτι ὅσιόν ἐστιν, ἢ δι' ἄλλο τι; [Is it because of this, that it is holy, or for something else?]

Εὐθύφρων: οὔκ, ἀλλὰ διὰ τοῦτο. [No, but for this.]

Σωκράτης: διότι ἄρα ὅσιόν ἐστιν φιλεῖται, ἀλλ' οὐχ ὅτι φιλεῖται, διὰ τοῦτο ὅσιόν ἐστιν; [Then because it is holy is it loved, and not because it is loved, is it for this reason holy?]

Εὐθύφρων: ἔοικεν. [It seems so.]

Σωκράτης: ἀλλὰ μὲν δὴ διότι γε φιλεῖται ὑπὸ θεῶν φιλούμενόν ἐστι καὶ θεοφιλές. [But because it is loved by the gods is something loved and dear to the gods?]

Εὐθύφρων: πῶς γὰρ οὔ; [Of course it is.]

Σωκράτης: οὐκ ἄρα τὸ θεοφιλὲς ὅσιόν ἐστιν, ὦ Εὐθύφρων, οὐδὲ τὸ ὅσιον θεοφιλές, ὡς σὺ λέγεις, ἀλλ' ἕτερον τοῦτο τούτου. [What is dear to the gods, then, is not the holy, nor is the holy dear to the gods, as you say, Euthyphro, but this is different from that.]

**[10e]**

Εὐθύφρων: πῶς δή, ὦ Σώκρατες; [How so, Socrates?]

Σωκράτης: ὅτι ὁμολογοῦμεν τὸ μὲν ὅσιον διὰ τοῦτο φιλεῖσθαι, ὅτι ὅσιόν ἐστιν, ἀλλ' οὐ διότι φιλεῖται ὅσιον εἶναι· ἢ γάρ; [Because we agree that the holy is loved for this reason, because it is holy, and not because it is loved is it holy. Isn't that so?]

Εὐθύφρων: ναί. [Yes.]

Σωκράτης: τὸ δέ γε θεοφιλὲς ὅτι φιλεῖται ὑπὸ θεῶν, αὐτῷ τούτῳ τῷ φιλεῖσθαι θεοφιλὲς εἶναι, ἀλλ' οὐχ ὅτι θεοφιλές, διὰ τοῦτο φιλεῖσθαι.

[While, on the other hand, what is dear to the gods because it is loved by gods, by the very fact of being loved is it dear to the gods, and not because it is dear to the gods, for this reason is it loved.]

Εὐθύφρων: ἀληθῆ λέγεις. [You speak truly.]

Σωκράτης: ἀλλ' εἴ γε ταὐτὸν ἦν, ὦ φίλε Εὐθύφρων, τὸ θεοφιλὲς καὶ τὸ ὅσιον, εἰ μὲν διὰ τὸ ὅσιον εἶναι ἐφιλεῖτο τὸ [**11a**] ὅσιον, καὶ διὰ τὸ θεοφιλὲς εἶναι ἐφιλεῖτο ἂν τὸ θεοφιλές, εἰ δὲ διὰ τὸ φιλεῖσθαι ὑπὸ θεῶν τὸ θεοφιλὲς θεοφιλὲς ἦν, καὶ τὸ ὅσιον ἂν διὰ τὸ φιλεῖσθαι ὅσιον ἦν· νῦν δὲ ὁρᾷς ὅτι ἐναντίως ἔχετον, ὡς παντάπασιν ἑτέρω ὄντε ἀλλήλων. τὸ μὲν γάρ, ὅτι φιλεῖται, ἐστὶν οἷον φιλεῖσθαι· τὸ δ' ὅτι ἐστὶν οἷον φιλεῖσθαι, διὰ τοῦτο φιλεῖται. καὶ κινδυνεύεις, ὦ Εὐθύφρων, ἐρωτώμενος τὸ ὅσιον ὅτι ποτ' ἐστίν, τὴν μὲν οὐσίαν μοι αὐτοῦ οὐ βούλεσθαι δηλῶσαι, πάθος δέ τι περὶ αὐτοῦ λέγειν, ὅτι πέπονθε τοῦτο τὸ ὅσιον, φιλεῖσθαι ὑπὸ πάντων [**11b**] θεῶν· ὅτι δὲ ὄν, οὔπω εἶπες. εἰ οὖν σοι φίλον, μή με ἀποκρύψῃ ἀλλὰ πάλιν εἰπὲ ἐξ ἀρχῆς τί ποτε ὂν τὸ ὅσιον εἴτε φιλεῖται ὑπὸ θεῶν εἴτε ὁτιδὴ πάσχει—οὐ γὰρ περὶ τούτου διοισόμεθα—ἀλλ' εἰπὲ προθύμως τί ἐστιν τό τε ὅσιον καὶ τὸ ἀνόσιον; [But if they were the same, my dear Euthyphro, what is dear to the gods and holy, then, on the one hand, if because being holy the holy was loved, then because being dear to the gods would what is dear to the gods be loved; and, on the other, if because being loved by the gods what is dear were dear to the gods, then the holy would be holy because it was loved; but as you see now, how they are contrarily disposed, and how utterly different they are from one another. One, because it is loved, is it the sort of thing to be loved; the other, because it is the sort to be loved, for this is it loved. And you seem, Euthyphro, in being asked what the holy is, to be unwilling to make clear to me its being, but to speak of some affect about it, viz. the holy has undergone this, to be loved by all gods; but what it is, you have not yet said. If then it is pleasing to you, don't hide it from me, but tell me once more from the beginning what the holy is, whether it is loved by gods or undergoes anything whatsoever—we shall not differ about that—, but speak out eagerly, what are the holy and the unholy?]

Εὐθύφρων: ἀλλ,' ὦ Σώκρατες, οὐκ ἔχω ἔγωγε ὅπως σοι εἴπω ὃ νοῶ· περιέρχεται γάρ πως ἡμῖν ἀεὶ ὃ ἂν προθώμεθα καὶ οὐκ ἐθέλει μένειν ὅπου ἂν ἱδρυσώμεθα αὐτό. [And yet, Socrates, I do not know how I can tell you what I think; somehow or other whatever we propose always begins to move about for us and is unwilling to stay wherever we set it up.]

Σωκράτης: τοῦ ἡμετέρου προγόνου, ὦ Εὐθύφρων, ἔοικεν εἶναι [**11c**] Δαιδάλου τὰ ὑπὸ σοῦ λεγόμενα. καὶ εἰ μὲν αὐτὰ ἐγὼ ἔλεγον καὶ ἐτιθέμην, ἴσως ἄν με ἐπέσκωπτες ὡς ἄρα καὶ ἐμοὶ κατὰ τὴν ἐκείνου συγγένειαν τὰ ἐν τοῖς λόγοις ἔργα ἀποδιδράσκει καὶ οὐκ ἐθέλει μένειν ὅπου ἄν τις αὐτὰ θῇ· νῦν δὲ σαὶ γὰρ αἱ ὑποθέσεις εἰσίν. ἄλλου δή τινος δεῖ σκώμματος· οὐ γὰρ ἐθέλουσι σοὶ μένειν, ὡς καὶ αὐτῷ σοι δοκεῖ. [What you say, Euthyphro, seems to be the work of our ancestor Daedalus. So if I had said them and set them up, perhaps you would scoff at me and say that by my relation to him the deeds in speeches run away and are unwilling to stay wherever one places them; but as it is, the settings up are yours. So you need another jest. They are unwilling to stay still for you, as you yourself think.]

Εὐθύφρων: ἐμοὶ δὲ δοκεῖ σχεδόν τι τοῦ αὐτοῦ σκώμματος, ὦ Σώκρατες, δεῖσθαι τὰ λεγόμενα· τὸ γὰρ περιιέναι αὐτοῖς τοῦτο καὶ μὴ μένειν ἐν τῷ αὐτῷ οὐκ ἐγώ εἰμι ὁ ἐντιθείς, [**11d**] ἀλλὰ σύ μοι δοκεῖς ὁ Δαίδαλος, ἐπεὶ ἐμοῦ γε ἕνεκα ἔμενεν ἂν ταῦτα οὕτως. [But I think, Socrates, that needs quite the same jest, for in their going about and not staying in the same place, I am not the one who sets them in motion, but I think you're the Daedalus, since as far as I'm concerned, they would stay where they were.]

Σωκράτης: κινδυνεύω ἄρα, ὦ ἑταῖρε, ἐκείνου τοῦ ἀνδρὸς δεινότερος γεγονέναι τὴν τέχνην τοσούτῳ, ὅσῳ ὁ μὲν τὰ αὑτοῦ μόνα ἐποίει οὐ μένοντα, ἐγὼ δὲ πρὸς τοῖς ἐμαυτοῦ, ὡς ἔοικε, καὶ τὰ ἀλλότρια. καὶ δῆτα τοῦτό μοι τῆς τέχνης ἐστὶ κομψότατον, ὅτι ἄκων εἰμὶ σοφός· ἐβουλόμην γὰρ ἄν μοι τοὺς λόγους μένειν καὶ ἀκινήτως ἱδρῦσθαι μᾶλλον ἢ πρὸς τῇ [**11e**] Δαιδάλου σοφίᾳ τὰ Ταντάλου χρήματα γενέσθαι. καὶ τούτων μὲν ἅδην· ἐπειδὴ δέ μοι δοκεῖς σὺ τρυφᾶν, αὐτός σοι συμπροθυμήσομαι [δεῖξαι] ὅπως ἄν με διδάξῃς περὶ τοῦ ὁσίου. καὶ μὴ προαποκάμῃς· ἰδὲ γὰρ εἰ οὐκ ἀναγκαῖόν σοι δοκεῖ δίκαιον εἶναι πᾶν τὸ ὅσιον. [Then I seem, my fellow, to have proved cleverer in his art than that man, by as much as he only made his own things not stay still, but I, in addition to my own, as it seems, make also others.' And surely this is the finest part of my art, that I am unwillingly wise; for I would have wished for myself that the speeches did stay still and be established immovably, and I would have wished this even more than to have the money of Tantalus besides Daedalus's wisdom. But enough of that. As I think you're sluggish, I myself shall eagerly join you, so that you might teach me about the holy. And don't weary beforehand; see here, don't you think it necessary that everything holy be just?]

Εὐθύφρων: ἔμοιγε. [Yes, I do.]

Σωκράτης: ἆρ' οὖν καὶ πᾶν τὸ δίκαιον ὅσιον; ἢ τὸ μὲν ὅσιον [**12a**] πᾶν δίκαιον, τὸ δὲ δίκαιον οὐ πᾶν ὅσιον, ἀλλὰ τὸ μὲν αὐτοῦ ὅσιον, τὸ δέ τι καὶ ἄλλο; [Then also everything just is holy? Or is the holy everything that's just, but the just not everything that's holy, but part of it is holy, and part something else?]

Εὐθύφρων: οὐχ ἕπομαι, ὦ Σώκρατες, τοῖς λεγομένοις. [I do not follow, Socrates, what is being said.]

Σωκράτης: καὶ μὴν νεώτερός γέ μου εἶ οὐκ ἔλαττον ἢ ὅσῳ σοφώτερος· ἀλλ,' ὃ λέγω, τρυφᾷς ὑπὸ πλούτου τῆς σοφίας. [And yet you're as much younger than I am as you are wiser; but, as I say, the richness of your wisdom has made you sluggish.] ἀλλ,' ὦ μακάριε, σύντεινε σαυτόν· καὶ γὰρ οὐδὲ χαλεπὸν κατανοῆσαι ὃ λέγω. [But, blessed one, exert yourself, it isn't difficult to comprehend what I mean.] λέγω γὰρ δὴ τὸ ἐναντίον ἢ ὁ ποιητὴς ἐποίησεν ὁ ποιήσας—"Ζῆνα δὲ τὸν [θ'] ἕρξαντα καὶ ὃς τάδε πάντ' ἐφύτευσεν [**12b**] οὐκ ἐθέλει νεικεῖν· ἵνα γὰρ δέος ἔνθα καὶ αἰδώς." [I am saying the opposite of the poet, the poet who wrote, "Zeus is the one who did so, and even he who planted all the things / Is unwilling to contend with him; for where there is fear, there is also shame." ἐγὼ οὖν τούτῳ διαφέρομαι τῷ ποιητῇ. [Now I differ with the poet.] εἴπω σοι ὅπῃ; [Shall I tell you where?]

Εὐθύφρων: πάνυ γε. [Yes, do.]

Σωκράτης: οὐ δοκεῖ μοι εἶναι "ἵνα δέος ἔνθα καὶ αἰδώς" πολλοὶ γάρ μοι δοκοῦσι καὶ νόσους καὶ πενίας καὶ ἄλλα πολλὰ τοιαῦτα δεδιότες δεδιέναι μέν, αἰδεῖσθαι δὲ μηδὲν ταῦτα ἃ δεδίασιν· οὐ καὶ σοὶ δοκεῖ; [I don't think that's right, "Where there is fear, there also is shame"; for I think that many in fearing illnesses, poverty, and much else of the same sort do fear, but they are not ashamed at all before what they fear. Don't you think so too?]

Εὐθύφρων: πάνυ γε. [Just so.]

Σωκράτης: ἀλλ' ἵνα γε αἰδὼς ἔνθα καὶ δέος εἶναι· ἐπεὶ ἔστιν ὅστις αἰδούμενός τι πρᾶγμα καὶ αἰσχυνόμενος οὐ πεφόβηταί [**12c**] τε καὶ δέδοικεν ἅμα δόξαν πονηρίας; [But where there is shame, there also is fear; since whoever is ashamed at some matter, in feeling shame doesn't he simultaneously fear and tremble at the reputation for wickedness?]

Εὐθύφρων: δέδοικε μὲν οὖν. [He's afraid, for sure.]

Σωκράτης: οὐκ ἄρ' ὀρθῶς ἔχει λέγειν· "ἵνα γὰρ δέος ἔνθα καὶ αἰδώς," ἀλλ' ἵνα μὲν αἰδὼς ἔνθα καὶ δέος, οὐ μέντοι ἵνα γε δέος πανταχοῦ αἰδώς· ἐπὶ πλέον γὰρ οἶμαι δέος αἰδοῦς. μόριον γὰρ αἰδὼς δέους ὥσπερ ἀριθμοῦ περιττόν, ὥστε οὐχ ἵναπερ ἀριθμὸς ἔνθα καὶ περιττόν, ἵνα δὲ περιττὸν ἔνθα καὶ ἀριθμός. ἕπῃ γάρ που νῦν γε; [Then it's incorrect to say, "For where there is fear, there also is shame," but where there is shame, there also is fear, not, however, where there is fear is there everywhere shame; for I believe fear has a greater range than shame. Shame is a part of fear as odd is of number, since not where there is number is there also odd, but where there is the odd there also is number. Now you surely follow?]

Εὐθύφρων: πάνυ γε. [Just so.]

Σωκράτης: τὸ τοιοῦτον τοίνυν καὶ ἐκεῖ λέγων ἠρώτων· ἆρα ἵνα [**12d**] δίκαιον ἔνθα καὶ ὅσιον; ἢ ἵνα μὲν ὅσιον ἔνθα καὶ δίκαιον, ἵνα δὲ δίκαιον οὐ πανταχοῦ ὅσιον· μόριον γὰρ τοῦ δικαίου τὸ ὅσιον; οὕτω φῶμεν ἢ ἄλλως σοι δοκεῖ; [So also in speaking before I asked something similar: Where there is justice, is there also the holy? Or where there is the holy, there also is the just, and not where there is the just, is there everywhere the holy; for the holy is part of the just. Shall we assert this or do you think differently?]

Εὐθύφρων: οὔκ, ἀλλ' οὕτω. φαίνῃ γάρ μοι ὀρθῶς λέγειν. [No, but in this way, and what you say appears to me correct.]

Σωκράτης: ὅρα δὴ τὸ μετὰ τοῦτο. εἰ γὰρ μέρος τὸ ὅσιον τοῦ δικαίου, δεῖ δὴ ἡμᾶς, ὡς ἔοικεν, ἐξευρεῖν τὸ ποῖον μέρος ἂν εἴη τοῦ δικαίου τὸ ὅσιον. εἰ μὲν οὖν σύ με ἠρώτας τι τῶν νυνδή, οἷον ποῖον μέρος ἐστὶν ἀριθμοῦ τὸ ἄρτιον καὶ τίς ὢν τυγχάνει οὗτος ὁ ἀριθμός, εἶπον ἂν ὅτι ὃς ἂν μὴ σκαληνὸς ᾖ ἀλλ' ἰσοσκελής· ἢ οὐ δοκεῖ σοι; [Look at the point that comes after this. If the holy is part of the just, we must, as it seems, find out what part of the just the holy would be. Now, if you asked me any of the things mentioned just now, e.g., what part is the even of number, and what happens to be this number, I should say that it is whatever is not scalene but isosceles. Don't you think the same?]

Εὐθύφρων: ἔμοιγε. [Yes, I do.]

[**12e**]

Σωκράτης: πειρῶ δὴ καὶ σὺ ἐμὲ οὕτω διδάξαι τὸ ποῖον μέρος τοῦ δικαίου ὅσιόν ἐστιν, ἵνα καὶ Μελήτῳ λέγωμεν μηκέθ' ἡμᾶς ἀδικεῖν μηδὲ ἀσεβείας γράφεσθαι, ὡς ἱκανῶς ἤδη παρὰ σοῦ μεμαθηκότας τά τε εὐσεβῆ καὶ ὅσια καὶ τὰ μή. [Then you also try to teach me what part of the just the holy is, so that we may tell Meletus that no longer are we unjust, nor should he indict me for impiety as I have already learned sufficiently from you what are pious and holy things and what not.]

Εὐθύφρων: τοῦτο τοίνυν ἔμοιγε δοκεῖ, ὦ Σώκρατες, τὸ μέρος τοῦ δικαίου εἶναι εὐσεβές τε καὶ ὅσιον, τὸ περὶ τὴν τῶν θεῶν θεραπείαν, τὸ δὲ περὶ τὴν τῶν ἀνθρώπων τὸ λοιπὸν εἶναι τοῦ δικαίου μέρος. [The pious and holy, Socrates, are, I think, this part of the just, that which concerns the care of the gods, while what concerns the care of human beings is the remaining part of the just.]

Σωκράτης: καὶ καλῶς γέ μοι, ὦ Εὐθύφρων, φαίνῃ λέγειν, ἀλλὰ [**13a**] σμικροῦ τινος ἔτι ἐνδεής εἰμι· τὴν γὰρ θεραπείαν οὔπω συνίημι ἥντινα ὀνομάζεις. οὐ γάρ που λέγεις γε, οἷαίπερ καὶ αἱ περὶ τὰ ἄλλα θεραπεῖαί εἰσιν, τοιαύτην καὶ περὶ θεούς—λέγομεν γάρ που—οἷόν φαμεν ἵππους οὐ πᾶς ἐπίσταται θεραπεύειν ἀλλὰ ὁ ἱππικός· ἢ γάρ; [That's fine, Euthyphro, how you appear to me to speak, but I am still in want of a rather small point; for I do not yet understand what you gave the name caring to. You surely don't mean that just as there are carings of other things, there is also one of the gods—for we surely speak so—e.g., we say that not everyone knows how to take care of horses but the horseman. Is that so?]

Εὐθύφρων: πάνυ γε. [Just so.]

Σωκράτης: ἡ γάρ που ἱππικὴ ἵππων θεραπεία. [For surely the art of horsemanship is the caring of horses?]

Εὐθύφρων: ναί. [Yes.]

Σωκράτης: οὐδέ γε κύνας πᾶς ἐπίσταται θεραπεύειν ἀλλὰ ὁ κυνηγετικός. [Nor does everyone know how to take care of dogs but the hunter?]

Εὐθύφρων: οὕτω. [That's so.]

Σωκράτης: ἡ γάρ που κυνηγετικὴ κυνῶν θεραπεία. [For surely hunting is the caring of dogs?]

[**13b**]

Εὐθύφρων: ναί. [Yes.]

Σωκράτης: ἡ δέ γε βοηλατικὴ βοῶν. [And the art of herding is of cattle?]

Εὐθύφρων: πάνυ γε. [Just so.]

Σωκράτης: ἡ δὲ δὴ ὁσιότης τε καὶ εὐσέβεια θεῶν, ὦ Εὐθύφρων; οὕτω λέγεις; [And holiness and piety are of gods, Euthyphro? Do you say that?]

Εὐθύφρων: ἔγωγε. [Yes, I do.]

Σωκράτης: οὐκοῦν θεραπεία γε πᾶσα ταὐτὸν διαπράττεται; οἷον τοιόνδε· ἐπ' ἀγαθῷ τινί ἐστι καὶ ὠφελίᾳ τοῦ θεραπευομένου, ὥσπερ ὁρᾷς δὴ ὅτι οἱ ἵπποι ὑπὸ τῆς ἱππικῆς θεραπευόμενοι ὠφελοῦνται καὶ βελτίους γίγνονται· ἢ οὐ δοκοῦσί σοι; [Doesn't any kind of caring accomplish the same? For example, for the sake of some good and benefit of what is cared for, just as you see that horses if cared for by the art of horsemanship are benefited and become better. Don't you think so?]

Εὐθύφρων: ἔμοιγε. [Yes, I do.]

Σωκράτης: καὶ οἱ κύνες γέ που ὑπὸ τῆς κυνηγετικῆς, καὶ οἱ [**13c**] βόες ὑπὸ τῆς βοηλατικῆς, καὶ τἆλλα πάντα ὡσαύτως· ἢ ἐπὶ βλάβῃ οἴει τοῦ θεραπευομένου τὴν θεραπείαν εἶναι; [And surely dogs by the art of hunting, and cattle by the art of herding, and all else likewise; or do you believe caring is for the harm of what is cared for?]

Εὐθύφρων: μὰ Δί' οὐκ ἔγωγε. [No, by Zeus, I do not.]

Σωκράτης: ἀλλ' ἐπ' ὠφελίᾳ; [But for benefit?]

Εὐθύφρων: πῶς δ' οὔ: [Of course.]

Σωκράτης: ἦ οὖν καὶ ἡ ὁσιότης θεραπεία οὖσα θεῶν ὠφελία τέ ἐστι θεῶν καὶ βελτίους τοὺς θεοὺς ποιεῖ; καὶ σὺ τοῦτο συγχωρήσαις ἄν, ὡς ἐπειδάν τι ὅσιον ποιῇς, βελτίω τινὰ τῶν θεῶν ἀπεργάζῃ; [Then holiness, since it is caring of the gods, is a benefit of the gods and makes the gods better? And would you agree with this, that whenever you do something holy, you make one of the gods better?]

Εὐθύφρων: μὰ Δί' οὐκ ἔγωγε. [No, by Zeus, I do not.]

Σωκράτης: οὐδὲ γὰρ ἐγώ, ὦ Εὐθύφρων, οἶμαί σε τοῦτο λέγειν—πολλοῦ καὶ δέω—ἀλλὰ τούτου δὴ ἕνεκα καὶ ἀνηρόμην [**13d**] τίνα ποτὲ λέγοις τὴν θεραπείαν τῶν θεῶν, οὐχ ἡγούμενός σε τοιαύτην λέγειν. [Nor do I, Euthyphro, believe you meant that—far from it—, but it's for this reason I asked what you mean by the caring of the gods, believing that you do not mean that kind of caring.]

Εὐθύφρων: καὶ ὀρθῶς γε, ὦ Σώκρατες· οὐ γὰρ τοιαύτην λέγω. [And correctly so, Socrates, for I don't mean that kind.]

Σωκράτης: εἶεν· ἀλλὰ τίς δὴ θεῶν θεραπεία εἴη ἂν ἡ ὁσιότης; [All right. Then what kind of caring of the gods would holiness be?]

Εὐθύφρων: ἥνπερ, ὦ Σώκρατες, οἱ δοῦλοι τοὺς δεσπότας θεραπεύουσιν. [The way in which, Socrates, slaves care for their masters.]

Σωκράτης: μανθάνω· ὑπηρετική τις ἄν, ὡς ἔοικεν, εἴη θεοῖς. [I understand. It would be some kind of serving the gods, it seems.]

Εὐθύφρων: πάνυ μὲν οὖν. [Yes, of course.]

Σωκράτης: ἔχοις ἂν οὖν εἰπεῖν ἡ ἰατροῖς ὑπηρετικὴ εἰς τίνος ἔργου ἀπεργασίαν τυγχάνει οὖσα ὑπηρετική; οὐκ εἰς ὑγιείας οἴει; [Could you say, then, the art serving doctors happens to be serving for the production of what work? Don't you believe it is for health?]

Εὐθύφρων: ἔγωγε. [Yes, I do.]

**[13e]**

Σωκράτης: τί δὲ ἡ ναυπηγοῖς ὑπηρετική; εἰς τίνος ἔργου ἀπεργασίαν ὑπηρετική ἐστιν; [And what about the art serving shipbuilders? It serves for the production of what work?]

Εὐθύφρων: δῆλον ὅτι, ὦ Σώκρατες, εἰς πλοίου. [Obviously, Socrates, for a ship.]

Σωκράτης: καὶ ἡ οἰκοδόμοις γέ που εἰς οἰκίας; [And likewise, what serves housebuilders is for the production of a house?]

Εὐθύφρων: ναί. [Yes.]

Σωκράτης: εἰπὲ δή, ὦ ἄριστε· ἡ δὲ θεοῖς ὑπηρετικὴ εἰς τίνος ἔργου ἀπεργασίαν ὑπηρετικὴ ἂν εἴη; δῆλον γὰρ ὅτι σὺ οἶσθα, ἐπειδήπερ τά γε θεῖα κάλλιστα φῂς εἰδέναι ἀνθρώπων. [Say, then, best man, the art that serves gods would serve for the production of what work? Obviously you know, since you say you know most finely of human beings the divine things.]

Εὐθύφρων: καὶ ἀληθῆ γε λέγω, ὦ Σώκρατες. [And I tell the truth, Socrates.]

Σωκράτης: εἰπὲ δὴ πρὸς Διὸς τί ποτέ ἐστιν ἐκεῖνο τὸ πάγκαλον ἔργον ὃ οἱ θεοὶ ἀπεργάζονται ἡμῖν ὑπηρέταις χρώμενοι; [Say, then, by Zeus, what is that most fine work which the gods produce in employing us as servants?]

Εὐθύφρων: πολλὰ καὶ καλά, ὦ Σώκρατες. [There are many fine things, Socrates.]

**[14a]**

Σωκράτης: καὶ γὰρ οἱ στρατηγοί, ὦ φίλε· ἀλλ' ὅμως τὸ κεφάλαιον αὐτῶν ῥᾳδίως ἂν εἴποις, ὅτι νίκην ἐν τῷ πολέμῳ ἀπεργάζονται· ἢ οὔ; [So do generals, my dear, yet you could easily say the sum of them, viz., they produce victory in war. Isn't that so?]

Εὐθύφρων: πῶς δ' οὔ; [Of course.]

Σωκράτης: πολλὰ δέ γ,' οἶμαι, καὶ καλὰ καὶ οἱ γεωργοί· ἀλλ' ὅμως τὸ κεφάλαιον αὐτῶν ἐστιν τῆς ἀπεργασίας ἡ ἐκ τῆς γῆς τροφή. [And many are the fine things farmers produce, yet the sum of their production is nurture from the earth.]

Εὐθύφρων: πάνυ γε. [Just so.]

Σωκράτης: τί δὲ δὴ τῶν πολλῶν καὶ καλῶν ἃ οἱ θεοὶ ἀπεργάζονται; τί τὸ κεφάλαιόν ἐστι τῆς ἐργασίας; [Then what about the many fine things the gods produce? What is the sum of their production?]

Εὐθύφρων: καὶ ὀλίγον σοι πρότερον εἶπον, ὦ Σώκρατες, ὅτι [**14b**] πλείονος ἔργου ἐστὶν ἀκριβῶς πάντα ταῦτα ὡς ἔχει μαθεῖν· τόδε μέντοι σοι ἁπλῶς λέγω, ὅτι ἐὰν μὲν κεχαρισμένα τις ἐπίστηται τοῖς θεοῖς λέγειν τε καὶ πράττειν εὐχόμενός τε καὶ θύων, ταῦτ' ἔστι τὰ ὅσια, καὶ σῴζει τὰ τοιαῦτα τούς τε ἰδίους οἴκους καὶ τὰ κοινὰ τῶν πόλεων· τὰ δ' ἐναντία τῶν κεχαρισμένων ἀσεβῆ, ἃ δὴ καὶ ἀνατρέπει ἅπαντα καὶ ἀπόλλυσιν. [I just told you a little while ago, Socrates, it's a rather long task to learn accurately about all these matters, in what they are. However, I'll simply tell you this, if anyone knows how to speak and do, in praying and sacrificing, things grateful to the gods, these are holy, and such sayings and doings save both private houses and the common good of cities; and things contrary to the grateful are impious, which subvert and ruin everything.]

Σωκράτης: ἦ πολύ μοι διὰ βραχυτέρων, ὦ Εὐθύφρων, εἰ ἐβούλου, εἶπες ἂν τὸ κεφάλαιον ὧν ἠρώτων· ἀλλὰ γὰρ οὐ [**14c**] πρόθυμός με εἶ διδάξαι—δῆλος εἶ. καὶ γὰρ νῦν ἐπειδὴ ἐπ' αὐτῷ ἦσθα ἀπετράπου, ὃ εἰ ἀπεκρίνω, ἱκανῶς ἂν ἤδη παρὰ σοῦ τὴν ὁσιότητα ἐμεμαθήκη. νῦν δὲ ἀνάγκη γὰρ τὸν ἐρῶντα τῷ ἐρωμένῳ ἀκολουθεῖν ὅπῃ ἂν ἐκεῖνος ὑπάγῃ, τί δὴ αὖ λέγεις τὸ ὅσιον εἶναι καὶ τὴν ὁσιότητα; οὐχὶ ἐπιστήμην τινὰ τοῦ θύειν τε καὶ εὔχεσθαι; [So, Euthyphro, had you wished, in far fewer words you could have told me the sum of what I asked, but in fact you're not eager to teach me—that's obvious—, for even just now, when you were about to, you turned away, which if you had answered, I should have adequately by now learned from you about holiness. As it is, the lover must follow the beloved wherever he leads him. What really do you say the holy and holiness are? Isn't it a certain kind of knowledge of sacrificing and praying?]

Εὐθύφρων: ἔγωγε. [Yes, I say so.]

Σωκράτης: οὐκοῦν τὸ θύειν δωρεῖσθαί ἐστι τοῖς θεοῖς, τὸ δ' εὔχεσθαι αἰτεῖν τοὺς θεούς; [Isn't sacrificing a giving of gifts to the gods, and praying an asking of the gods?]

Εὐθύφρων: καὶ μάλα, ὦ Σώκρατες. [Quite right, Socrates.]

**[14d]**

Σωκράτης: ἐπιστήμη ἄρα αἰτήσεως καὶ δόσεως θεοῖς ὁσιότης ἂν εἴη ἐκ τούτου τοῦ λόγου. [Then knowledge of asking and offering to gods must by this argument be holiness.]

Εὐθύφρων: πάνυ καλῶς, ὦ Σώκρατες, συνῆκας ὃ εἶπον. [It's very fine, Socrates, how you've understood what I said.]

Σωκράτης: ἐπιθυμητὴς γάρ εἰμι, ὦ φίλε, τῆς σῆς σοφίας καὶ προσέχω τὸν νοῦν αὐτῇ, ὥστε οὐ χαμαὶ πεσεῖται ὅτι ἂν εἴπῃς. ἀλλά μοι λέξον τίς αὕτη ἡ ὑπηρεσία ἐστὶ τοῖς θεοῖς; αἰτεῖν τε φῂς αὐτοὺς καὶ διδόναι ἐκείνοις; [It's because I am desirous, my dear, of your wisdom, and I apply my mind to it, so that nothing of what you say will fall to the ground. But tell me, what is this serving of the gods? Do you assert it is asking them and offering to them?]

Εὐθύφρων: ἔγωγε. [Yes, I do.]

Σωκράτης: ἆρ' οὖν οὐ τό γε ὀρθῶς αἰτεῖν ἂν εἴη ὧν δεόμεθα παρ' ἐκείνων, ταῦτα αὐτοὺς αἰτεῖν; [Wouldn't it be, then, the correct asking of what we need from them, to ask them for these?]

Εὐθύφρων: ἀλλὰ τί; [But of course.]

**[14e]**

Σωκράτης: καὶ αὖ τὸ διδόναι ὀρθῶς, ὧν ἐκεῖνοι τυγχάνουσιν δεόμενοι παρ' ἡμῶν, ταῦτα ἐκείνοις αὖ ἀντιδωρεῖσθαι; οὐ γάρ που τεχνικόν γ' ἂν εἴη δωροφορεῖν διδόντα τῳ ταῦτα ὧν οὐδὲν δεῖται. [And, in turn, the correct offering of what they happen to need from us, to bring these gifts to them? For it surely wouldn't be at all skillful to bring gifts and offer to someone things of which he had no need?]

Εὐθύφρων: ἀληθῆ λέγεις, ὦ Σώκρατες. [You speak truly, Socrates.]

Σωκράτης: ἐμπορικὴ ἄρα τις ἂν εἴη, ὦ Εὐθύφρων, τέχνη ἡ ὁσιότης θεοῖς καὶ ἀνθρώποις παρ' ἀλλήλων. [Then holiness, Euthyphro, must be a certain kind of commercial art between gods and human beings.]

Εὐθύφρων: ἐμπορική, εἰ οὕτως ἥδιόν σοι ὀνομάζειν. [Commercial it is, if you are pleased to call it so.]

Σωκράτης: ἀλλ' οὐδὲν ἥδιον ἔμοιγε, εἰ μὴ τυγχάνει ἀληθὲς ὄν. φράσον δέ μοι, τίς ἡ ὠφελία τοῖς θεοῖς τυγχάνει οὖσα ἀπὸ τῶν δώρων ὧν παρ' ἡμῶν λαμβάνουσιν; ἃ μὲν γὰρ διδόασι [**15a**] παντὶ δῆλον· οὐδὲν γὰρ ἡμῖν ἐστιν ἀγαθὸν ὅτι ἂν μὴ ἐκεῖνοι δῶσιν. ἃ δὲ παρ' ἡμῶν λαμβάνουσιν, τί ὠφελοῦνται; ἢ τοσοῦτον αὐτῶν πλεονεκτοῦμεν κατὰ τὴν ἐμπορίαν, ὥστε πάντα τὰ ἀγαθὰ παρ' αὐτῶν λαμβάνομεν, ἐκεῖνοι δὲ παρ' ἡμῶν οὐδέν; [But I'm not at all pleased, unless it happens to be true. But point out to me, what really is the benefit the gods have from the gifts they accept from us? For what they give is obvious to everyone: we have no good that they do not give; while what they take from us, how are they benefited? Or do we so much get the better of them in our commerce, that we get all goods from them, and they none from us?]

Εὐθύφρων: ἀλλ' οἴει, ὦ Σώκρατες, τοὺς θεοὺς ὠφελεῖσθαι ἀπὸ τούτων ἃ παρ' ἡμῶν λαμβάνουσιν; [Do you really believe, Socrates, the gods are benefited by those things they get from us?]

Σωκράτης: ἀλλὰ τί δήποτ' ἂν εἴη ταῦτα, ὦ Εὐθύφρων, τὰ παρ' ἡμῶν δῶρα τοῖς θεοῖς; [Then what else would these things be for, Euthyphro, our gifts to the gods?]

Εὐθύφρων: τί δ' οἴει ἄλλο ἢ τιμή τε καὶ γέρα καί, ὅπερ ἐγὼ ἄρτι ἔλεγον, χάρις; [What else do you believe they're for except honor and respect, and, as I said just now, gratitude?]

[**15b**]

Σωκράτης: κεχαρισμένον ἄρα ἐστίν, ὦ Εὐθύφρων, τὸ ὅσιον, ἀλλ' οὐχὶ ὠφέλιμον οὐδὲ φίλον τοῖς θεοῖς; [Then the holy, Euthyphro, is what is grateful, and neither beneficial nor dear to the gods?]

Εὐθύφρων: οἶμαι ἔγωγε πάντων γε μάλιστα φίλον. [But I believe it is most certainly dear.]

Σωκράτης: τοῦτο ἄρ' ἐστὶν αὖ, ὡς ἔοικε, τὸ ὅσιον, τὸ τοῖς θεοῖς φίλον. [Then this is again, it seems, the holy, what is dear to the gods.]

Εὐθύφρων: μάλιστά γε. [Certainly.]

Σωκράτης: θαυμάσῃ οὖν ταῦτα λέγων ἐάν σοι οἱ λόγοι φαίνωνται μὴ μένοντες ἀλλὰ βαδίζοντες, καὶ ἐμὲ αἰτιάσῃ τὸν Δαίδαλον βαδίζοντας αὐτοὺς ποιεῖν, αὐτὸς ὢν πολύ γε τεχνικώτερος τοῦ Δαιδάλου καὶ κύκλῳ περιιόντα ποιῶν; ἢ οὐκ αἰσθάνῃ ὅτι ὁ λόγος ἡμῖν περιελθὼν πάλιν εἰς ταὐτὸν [**15c**] ἥκει; μέμνησαι γάρ που ὅτι ἐν τῷ πρόσθεν τό τε ὅσιον καὶ τὸ θεοφιλὲς οὐ ταὐτὸν ἡμῖν ἐφάνη ἀλλ' ἕτερα ἀλλήλων· ἢ οὐ μέμνησαι; [Will you then wonder in saying so if your speeches evidently do not stay still but walk, and will you accuse me of being the Daedalus in making them go round in a circle? Or aren't you aware that our argument has turned round and returned to the same spot? Surely you remember that previously the holy and the dear to the gods appeared as not the same but different from one another? Don't you remember?]

Εὐθύφρων: ἔγωγε. [Yes, I do.]

Σωκράτης: νῦν οὖν οὐκ ἐννοεῖς ὅτι τὸ τοῖς θεοῖς φίλον φῂς ὅσιον εἶναι; τοῦτο δ' ἄλλο τι ἢ θεοφιλὲς γίγνεται; ἢ οὔ; [Don't you realize, then, that now you are asserting that what is dear to the gods is holy? And this proves to be nothing else than the dear to the gods, doesn't it?]

Εὐθύφρων: πάνυ γε. [Just so.]

Σωκράτης: οὐκοῦν ἢ ἄρτι οὐ καλῶς ὡμολογοῦμεν, ἢ εἰ τότε καλῶς, νῦν οὐκ ὀρθῶς τιθέμεθα. [Then isn't it true that either it wasn't fine as we agreed just before, or if then it was fine, it's incorrect how we place it now?]

Εὐθύφρων: ἔοικεν. [It seems so.]

Σωκράτης: ἐξ ἀρχῆς ἄρα ἡμῖν πάλιν σκεπτέον τί ἐστι τὸ ὅσιον, ὡς ἐγὼ πρὶν ἂν μάθω ἑκὼν εἶναι οὐκ ἀποδειλιάσω. [**15d**] ἀλλὰ μή με ἀτιμάσῃς ἀλλὰ παντὶ τρόπῳ προσσχὼν τὸν νοῦν ὅτι μάλιστα νῦν εἰπὲ τὴν ἀλήθειαν· οἶσθα γὰρ εἴπερ τις ἄλλος ἀνθρώπων, καὶ οὐκ ἀφετέος εἶ ὥσπερ ὁ Πρωτεὺς πρὶν ἂν εἴπῃς. εἰ γὰρ μὴ ᾔδησθα σαφῶς τό τε ὅσιον καὶ τὸ ἀνόσιον, οὐκ ἔστιν ὅπως ἄν ποτε ἐπεχείρησας ὑπὲρ ἀνδρὸς θητὸς ἄνδρα πρεσβύτην πατέρα διωκάθειν φόνου, ἀλλὰ καὶ τοὺς θεοὺς ἂν ἔδεισας παρακινδυνεύειν μὴ οὐκ ὀρθῶς αὐτὸ ποιήσοις, καὶ τοὺς ἀνθρώπους ᾐσχύνθης· νῦν δὲ εὖ οἶδα ὅτι [**15e**] σαφῶς οἴει εἰδέναι τό τε ὅσιον καὶ μή. εἰπὲ οὖν, ὦ βέλτιστε Εὐθύφρων, καὶ μὴ ἀποκρύψῃ ὅτι αὐτὸ ἡγῇ. [Then we must examine again from the beginning what the holy is, since I shall not willingly play the coward before I do learn. Then don't dishonor me, but now in every way apply your mind as best you may and tell the truth; for you know, if any human being does, and just like Proteus you mustn't be let go of before you speak. If you didn't plainly know the holy and the unholy, it's impossible that you would ever try to prosecute an aged father for murder on behalf of a hired hand, but rather you'd be afraid of the gods in running the risk of not acting correctly, and ashamed before men. But as it is, I am quite sure you believe you plainly know what is holy and what is not. Then tell, my most excellent Euthyphro, and don't hide what you believe it is.]

Εὐθύφρων: εἰς αὖθις τοίνυν, ὦ Σώκρατες· νῦν γὰρ σπεύδω ποι, καί μοι ὥρα ἀπιέναι. [At another time, Socrates, for now I have business elsewhere, and it is time for me to go.]

Σωκράτης: οἷα ποιεῖς, ὦ ἑταῖρε. [What you are doing, my fellow.] ἀπ' ἐλπίδος με καταβαλὼν μεγάλης ἀπέρχῃ ἣν εἶχον, ὡς παρὰ σοῦ μαθὼν τά τε ὅσια καὶ μὴ καὶ τῆς πρὸς Μέλητον γραφῆς ἀπαλλάξομαι, ἐνδειξάμενος [**16a**] ἐκείνῳ ὅτι σοφὸς ἤδη παρ' Εὐθύφρονος τὰ θεῖα γέγονα καὶ ὅτι οὐκέτι ὑπ' ἀγνοίας αὐτοσχεδιάζω οὐδὲ καινοτομῶ περὶ αὐτά, καὶ δὴ καὶ τὸν ἄλλον βίον ὅτι ἄμεινον βιωσοίμην. [You're going away and casting me down from my great hope I had that, in learning from you what are holy and what not, I should get rid of Meletus's indictment, showing him that I had become wise in divine things from Euthyphro, and no longer out of ignorance do I improvise and make innovations about them, and so I should have lived the rest of my life better.[3]

**Notes**

1. Strauss: "strange at first hearing."
2. The word translated as "purify," ἀφοσιόω, is related to the term translated as "holy" by Benardete and referred to as "pious" by Strauss: ὅσιος, a term Strauss seems to treat as synonymous with εὐσεβής. See introduction, p. 13n19.
3. Or: "the other life better?"

# SELECTED BIBLIOGRAPHY


Allen, Reginald. *Plato's "Euthyphro" and the Earlier Theory of Forms*. New York: Humanities Press, 1970.

Ambler, Wayne. "Plato's *Euthyphro* on Divine and Human Wisdom." In *Socrates in the Cave: On the Philosopher's Motive in Plato*, edited by Paul J. Diduch and Michael P. Harding, 233–50. New York: Palgrave Macmillan, 2019.

Anderson, Albert. "Socratic Reasoning in the *Euthyphro*." *Review of Metaphysics* 22, no. 3 (1969): 461–81.

Anderson, Daniel E. "Socrates' Concept of Piety." *Journal of the History of Philosophy* 5, no. 1 (1967): 1–13.

Anscombe, G. E. M. "On Piety, or: Plato's *Euthyphro*." *From Plato to Wittgenstein: Essays by G. E. M. Anscombe*. Exeter: Imprint Academic, 2011.

Bezzel, Chris. "Zur Struktur des platonischen Frühdialogs (*Euthyphron*)." *Zeitschrift für philosophische Forschung* 17, no. 1 (1963): 42–65.

Blits, Jan H. "The Holy and the Human: An Interpretation of Plato's *Euthyphro*." *Apeiron* 14, no. 1 (1980): 19–40.

Brickhouse, Thomas C., and Nicholas D. Smith. *The Philosophy of Socrates*. Boulder, CO: Westview Press, 2000.

———. *Plato's Socrates*. New York: Oxford University Press, 1996.

———. *Routledge Philosophy GuideBook to Plato and the Trial of Socrates*. New York: Routledge, 2004.

———. *Socrates on Trial*. Princeton: Princeton University Press, 1989.

Brouwer, James. "The Inverted Nature of the *Euthyphro* 10a–11b." *Dialogue: Canadian Philosophical Review* 41, no. 1 (2002): 45–70.

Brown, John. "The Logic of *Euthyphro* 10a–11b." *Philosophical Quarterly* 14, no. 1 (1964): 1–14.

Bruell, Christopher. *On the Socratic Education: An Introduction to the Shorter Platonic Dialogues*. Lanham, MD: Rowman and Littlefield, 1999.

Burger, Ronna. "Making New Gods." In *Plato and Platonism*, edited by Johannes M. van Ophuijsen, 39–59. Washington, DC: Catholic University Press, 1999.

———. *On Plato's "Euthyphro."* Munich: Carl Friedrich von Siemens Stiftung, 2015.

Burns, Steven A. M. "Doing Business with the Gods." *Canadian Journal of Philosophy* 15, no. 2 (1985): 311–25.

Calef, Scott Warren. "Piety and the Unity of Virtue in *Euthyphro* 11e–14c." *Oxford Studies in Ancient Philosophy* 13, no. 1 (1995): 1–26.

Candlish, Stewart. "*Euthyphro* 6d–9b and Its Misinterpretations." *Apeiron* 17, no. 1 (1983): 28–32.

Cobb, William S. "Plato on the Possibility of an Irreligious Morality." *International Journal for Philosophy of Religion* 25, no. 1 (1989): 3–12.

———. "The Religious and the Just in Plato's *Euthyphro*." *Ancient Philosophy* 5, no. 1 (1985): 41–6.

Cohen, S. Marc. "Socrates on the Definition of Piety: *Euthyphro* 10a–11b." *Journal of the History of Philosophy* 9, no. 1 (1971): 1–13.

Davis, Michael. "The Grammar of the Soul: On Plato's *Euthyphro*." *Logos and Eros: Essays Honoring Stanley Rosen*. South Bend, IN: St. Augustine's Press, 2006.

Dimas, Panos. "Euthyphro's Thesis Revisited." *Phronesis* 51, no. 1 (2006): 1–28.

Ebery, David. "Identity and Explanation in the *Euthyphro*." *Oxford Studies in Ancient Philosophy* 52, no. 1 (2017): 77–112.

Edwards, Mark. "In Defense of Euthyphro." *American Journal of Philology* 121 (2): 213–24.

Evans, Matthew. "Lessons from *Euthyphro* 10A–11B." *Oxford Studies in Ancient Philosophy* 42, no. 1 (2012): 1–38.

Fendt, Gene. "Five Readings of *Euthyphro*." *Philosophy and Literature* 38, no. 2 (2014): 495–509.

Fischer, Norman J. "Euthyphro's Choice." *Philosophy and Literature* 38, no. 2 (2014): 479–94.

Forschner, Maximilian. *Platon, "Euthyphron"* Göttingen: Vandenhoeck & Ruprecht, 2013.

Frede, Dorothea. "The Holy and the God-Loved: The Dilemma in Plato's *Euthyphro*." *The Monist* 105, no. 3 (2022): 293–308.

Furley, William D. "The Figure of Euthyphro in Plato's Dialogue." *Phronesis* 30, no. 2 (1985): 201–8.

Futter, Dylan Brian. "On Irony Interpretation: Socratic Method in Plato's *Euthyphro*." *British Journal of Philosophy*, 21, no. 6 (2013): 1030–51.

Gadamer, Hans-Georg. "Sokrates' Frömmigkeit des Nichtwissens." *Plato im Dialog: Gesammelte Werke* 7. Tübingen: Mohr Siebeck, 1991.

Garrett, Roland. "The Structure of Plato's *Euthyphro*." *Southern Journal of Philosophy* 12, no. 2 (1974): 165–83.

Garver, Eugene. "Euthyphro Prosecutes a Human Rights Violation." *Philosophy and Literature* 38, no. 2 (2014): 510–27.

Geach, P. T. "Plato's *Euthyphro*." *Monist* 50, no. 3 (1966): 369–82.

Gigon, Olof. "Platons *Euthyphron*." *Westöstliche Abhandlungen: Rudolf Tschudi zum 70. Geburtstag*. Wiesbaden: Harrassowitz, 1954.

Gottlieb, E. "Zum Problem des *Euthyphron*." *Archiv für die Geschichte der Philosophie* 37 (3/4): 270–9, 1926.

Hall, John C. "Plato: *Euthyphro* 10a1–11a10." *Philosophical Quarterly* 18, no. 1 (1968): 1–11.

Haslböck, Thomas. "Frömmigkeit als Tugend: Eine Interpretation von Platons *Euthyphron*." In *Platonisches Denken heute: Festschrift für Barbara Zehnpfennig*, edited by Bettina Fröhlich, Hendrik Hansen, Raul Heimann, 103–22. Baden-Baden: Nomos, 2021.

Heitsch, Ernst. "Frömmigkeit als Hilfe: Bemerkungen zum *Euthyphron*." In *Platon verstehen: Themen und Perspektiven*, edited by Marcel van Ackeren, 11–22. Darmstadt: Wissenschaftliche Buchgesellschaft, 2004.

Hoerber, Robert G. "Plato's 'Euthyphro.'" *Phronesis* 3, no. 2 (1958): 95–107.

Holland, Roy Fraser. "Euthyphro." *Proceedings of the Aristotelian Society* 82, no. 1 (1982): 1–16.

Irwin, Terence. "Socrates and Euthyphro: The Argument and its Revival." In *Remembering Socrates: Philosophical Essays*, edited by Lindsay Judson and Vassilis Karasmanis, 58–71. Oxford: Oxford University Press, 2006.

Judson, Lindsay. "Carried Away in the *Euthyphro*." In *Definition in Greek Philosophy*. Oxford: Oxford University Press, 2010.

Kidd, Ian Gray. "The Case of Homicide in Plato's *Euthyphro*," *"Owls to Athens": Essays on Classical Subjects Presented to Sir Kenneth Dover.* Oxford: Clarendon Press, 1990.

Kim, Alan. "A Chiastic Contradiction at *Euthyphro* 9e1–11b5." *Phronesis* 49, no. 3 (2004): 219–24.

Klonoski, Richard. "Exegetes and Seers in Plato's *Euthyphro*." *Classical Outlook* 64, no. 1 (1986): 7–8.

———. "The Portico of the Archon Basileus: On the Significance of the Setting of Plato's *Euthyphro*." *Classical Journal* 81, no. 2 (1985): 130–37.

———. "Setting and Characterization in Plato's *Euthyphro*." *Diálogos* 19, no. 44 (1984): 123–39.

Lewis, Marlo, Jr. "An Interpretation of Plato's *Euthyphro*." *Interpretation* 12 (1984): 225–60; 13 (1985): 33–65.

Mann, William E. "Piety: Lending a Hand to Euthyphro." *Philosophy and Phenomenological Research* 58, no. 1 (1998): 123–47.

McPherran, Mark L. "The Aporetic Interlude and Fifth Elenchus of Plato's *Euthyphro*." *Oxford Studies in Ancient Philosophy* 25, no. 1 (2002): 1–37.

———. "Justice and Pollution in the *Euthyphro*." *Apeiron* 35, no. 2 (2002): 105–29.

———. *The Religion of Socrates*. University Park: Pennsylvania State University Press, 1996.

———. "Socratic Piety in the *Euthyphro*." *Journal of the History of Philosophy* 23, no. 3 (1985): 283–309.

———. "Socratic Reason and Socratic Revelation." *Journal of the History of Philosophy* 29, no. 3 (1991): 345–73.

———. "Socratic Theology and Piety." In *The Bloomsbury Companion to Socrates*, edited by John Bussanich and Nicholas D. Smith, 257–75. London: Bloomsbury, 2013.

Morgan, Michael L. *Platonic Piety: Philosophy and Ritual in Fourth-Century Athens*. New Haven: Yale University Press.

Morris, T. F. "Plato's *Euthyphro*." *Heythrop Journal* 31, no. 3 (1990): 309–23.

Neumann, Harry. "On Plato's *Euthyphro* and Its Relation to the *Theaetetus* and the *Sophist*." PhD diss., Johns Hopkins University, 1962.

———. "The Problem of Piety in Plato's 'Euthyphro.'" *Modern Schoolman* 43, no. 3 (1966): 265–72.

Panagiotou, Spiro. "Plato's *Euthyphro* and the Attic Code on Homicide." *Hermes* 102 (1974): 419–37.

Patzig, Günther. "Logic in the *Euthyphro*." *Islamic Philosophy and Classical Tradition: Essays Presented by His Friends and Pupils to Richard Walzer on His Seventieth Birthday*. Columbia: University of South Carolina, 1972.

Priou, Alex. "Plato's *Minos* and the *Euthyphro*." *Polis* 35 (2018): 145–63.

Rabinowitz, W. Gerson. "Platonic Piety: An Essay Toward the Solution of an Enigma." *Phronesis* 3, no. 2 (1958): 108–20.

Ranasinghe, Nalin. *Socrates and the Gods: How to Read Plato's "Euthyphro," "Apology," and "Crito."* South Bend, IN: St. Augustine's Press, 2012.

Reynolds, Noel B. *Interpreting Plato's "Euthyphro" and "Meno."* Provo, UT: Brigham Young University, 1988.

Root, Erik S. "Quid Sit Deus: The *Clouds*, *Euthyphro*, and the Meaning of Political Philosophy." *Perspectives on Political Science* 37, no. 2 (2008): 153–62.

Rosen, Frederick. "Piety and Justice in Plato's 'Euthyphro.'" *Philosophy* 43, no. 164 (1968): 105–16.

Rosivach, Vincent J. "Euthyphron's Prosecution of His Father in the *Euthyphron*." *Classical Philology* 112, no. 2 (2017): 232–41.

Saxonhouse, Arlene. "The Philosophy of the Particular and the Universality of the City: Socrates' Education of Euthyphro." *Political Theory* 16, no. 2 (1988): 281–99.

Schnieder, Benjamin. "Das Meisterargument in Platons *Euthyphron*." *History of Philosophy and Logical Analysis* 18, no. 1 (2015): 227–57.

Sharpe, Matthew. "Uncovering Euthyphro's Treasure: Reading Plato's *Euthyphro* with Lacan." *Helios* 37, no. 1 (2010): 23–48.

Sharvy, Richard. "*Euthyphro* 9d–11b: Analysis and Definition Plato and Others." *Nous* 6, no. 2 (1972): 119–37.

Шичалин [Shichalin] Ю. А. Заметки о диалоге платоновского корпуса "Евтифрон" // Философия. 3, no. 1 (2019): 13–35.

Song, Euree. "Philanthropie und Frömmigkeit in Platons *Euthyphron*." *Archiv für Geschichte der Philosophie* 90, no. 1 (2008): 115–30.

Taylor, Christopher Charles Whiston. "The End of the *Euthyphro*." *Phronesis* 27 (1/2): 109–18.

Thayer, David. "Holiness, Piety, and Philosophy: A Study of Plato's *Euthyphro*." PhD diss., Pennsylvania State University, 1982.

Versenyi, L. *Holiness and Justice: An Interpretation of Plato's "Euthyphro."* Washington, DC: University Press of America, 1982.

Vlastos, Gregory. "Socratic Piety." *Socrates: Ironist and Moral Philosopher*. Ithaca: Cornell University Press, 1991.

Ward, Ann. "The Complexity of Divine Speech and the Quest for the Ideas in Plato's *Euthyphro*." In *Natural Right and Political Philosophy: Essays in Honor of Catherine Zuckert and Michael Zuckert*, edited by Ann Ward and Lee Ward, 36–49. South Bend: University of Notre Dame Press, 2013.

Weiss, Roslyn. "Virtue without Knowledge: Socrates' Conception of Holiness in Plato's *Euthyphro*." *Ancient Philosophy* 14, no. 2 (1982): 263–82, 1994.

Werner, Daniel. "Myth and the Structure of Plato's *Euthyphro*." *International Philosophical Quarterly* 52, no. 1 (2012): 41–62.

West, Thomas G., and Grace Starry West. *Four Texts on Socrates: Plato's "Euthyphro," "Apology," and "Crito," and Aristophanes' "Clouds."* Ithaca, NY: Cornell University Press, 1984.

Wildberg, Christian. "The Rise and Fall of the Socratic Notion of Piety." *Proceedings of the Boston Area Colloquium in Ancient Philosophy* 18, no. 1 (2003): 1–37.

Wolfsdorf, David. "*Euthyphro* 10a2–11b1: A Study in Platonic Metaphysics and its Reception since 1960." *Apeiron* 38, no. 1 (2005): 1–71.

Wolz, Henry G. "The Paradox of Piety in Plato's *Euthyphro* in Light of Heidegger's Conception of Authenticity." *Southern Journal of Philosophy* 12, no. 4 (1974): 493–511.

Woodruff, Paul. "Wrong Turns in the *Euthyphro*." *Apeiron* 52, no. 2 (2019): 117–36.

# CONTRIBUTORS

**Wayne Ambler** is Associate Professor Emeritus of the Herbst Program for Engineering, Ethics & Society at the University of Colorado Boulder. He has written on Aristotle, Xenophon, and Aristophanes and translated Xenophon's *Anabasis of Cyrus* and *Education of Cyrus* and several of Aristophanes's plays.

**Hannes Kerber** is a Postdoctoral Fellow of the Program on Constitutional Government and an Affiliate of the Center for American Political Studies at Harvard University. He is the Academic Program Manager of the Carl Friedrich von Siemens Stiftung in Munich, Germany, and teaches in the Department of Philosophy and Religious Studies at the University of Munich. He is the author of several studies on Leo Strauss, Hans-Georg Gadamer, and Gotthold Ephraim Lessing. In 2022, his book *Die Aufklärung der Aufklärung: Gotthold Ephraim Lessing und die Herausforderung des Christentums* received the the first Chodowiecki Prize by the Interdisziplinary Centre for European Enlightenment Studies.

**Svetozar Y. Minkov** is Professor in, and Director of, the Philosophy Program at Roosevelt University, where he has taught since 2005. He is the author or editor of, among others, *Enlightening Revolutions: Essays in Honor of Ralph Lerner*; *Francis Bacon's Inquiry "Touching Human Nature"*; *Hobbes's Critique of Religion*; *Leo Strauss on Science: Thoughts on the Relation Between Natural Science and Political Philosophy*; *Mastery of Nature: Promises and Prospects*; *Toward Natural Right and History: Essays and Lectures by Leo Strauss, 1936–1947*; and, with Ronna Burger, the forthcoming edition of the correspondence between Seth Benardete and Leo Strauss. He is the president of the Leo Strauss Foundation.

# INDEX OF GREEK TERMS

Includes references to forms and cognates of each entry

# INDEX OF NAMES